Mastering OpenStack

Design, deploy, and manage a scalable OpenStack infrastructure

Omar Khedher

[PACKT] open source *
PUBLISHING   community experience distilled

BIRMINGHAM - MUMBAI

Mastering OpenStack

First published: July 2015

Production reference: 1270715

Published by Packt Publishing Ltd.
Livery Place
35 Livery Street
Birmingham B3 2PB, UK.

ISBN 978-1-78439-564-3

www.packtpub.com

Credits

Author
Omar Khedher

Reviewers
Derek Chamorro
Ryan Hallisey
Dr. Benoit Hudzia
Bhargesh Patel

Commissioning Editor
Kartikey Pandey

Acquisition Editor
Usha Iyer

Content Development Editor
Merwyn D'souza

Technical Editors
Mrunal M. Chavan
Gaurav Suri

Copy Editors
Vedangi Narvekar
Vikrant Phadke
Stuti Srivastava

Project Coordinator
Neha Bhatnagar

Proofreader
Safis Editing

Indexer
Hemangini Bari

Production Coordinator
Shantanu N. Zagade

Cover Work
Shantanu N. Zagade

About the Author

Omar Khedher is a network engineer and cloud computing researcher. Based in the Netherlands, he has worked in a cloud computing solution project that turned into an OpenStack deployment and became integrated with it. Leveraging his skills as a system administrator in virtualization, storage, and networking, he is currently pursuing a PhD on performance research preparation in the cloud computing paradigm and architecture patterns in which OpenStack is taking an active part. He has recently authored a few academic publications based on new researches for the cloud performance improvement.

A big thanks goes out to my PhD supervisor, Dr. Mohamed, in KSA, my professional friend Belgacem in Tunisia for his guidance, critics, and my special colleagues at the company for sharing their knowledge at HiQInvest. I appreciate the encouragement provided by my new family in the Netherlands and the warmth they provided to make me feel at home. I would like to thank all the reviewers of this book for their accurate notes and precious remarks. I extend a special thank to Merwyn D'souza for his continued and great work on this book, which has been a big piece of work. I am grateful to William Sprakel, who has helped me dive into the cloud computing world and also Michiel Karnebeek and Rick Stokkingreef for sharing their knowledge. Of course, a big thank you to the OpenStack community for the wonderful work in making the cloud computing solution such a unique and wonderful experience.

About the Reviewers

Derek Chamorro is a network security engineer/architect with 15 years of experience in information technology. He first started his career with cable MSOs, working in a variety of roles ranging from technical support to network architecture. He has spent the last 3 years focused on abstracted computing and software-defined networking using a variety of new technologies to enhance security and automation within next-generation networks. Derek currently works at Cisco Systems as a technical engineering lead for Cisco Cloud services. He specializes in network virtualization and enjoys working with Open vSwitch development.

In his spare time, Derek enjoys distance running, Asian cooking, and microbrewing beer.

Ryan Hallisey is a software engineer at Red Hat. He has worked on OpenStack for 2 years. Primarily, his focus is on developing SELinux to function for enterprise OpenStack solutions as well as developing the Tripleo installer and containerizing OpenStack using Docker.

Dr. Benoit Hudzia is a cloud/system architect working on designing the next generation cloud technology as well as running the Irish operations for Stratoscale.

He previously worked as a senior researcher-architect for SAP on HANA Enterprise Cloud.

Benoit has authored more than 20 academic publications and is also the holder of numerous patents in the domains of virtualization, OS, cloud, distributed system, and so on. His code and ideas are included in various SAP commercial solutions as well as open source solutions such as the QEMU/KVM hypervisor, the Linux kernel, and OpenStack.

His research currently focuses on bringing together the flexibility of virtualization, cloud, and high-performance computing (also known as the "Lego cloud"). This framework aims to provide the memory, I/O, and CPU resource disaggregation of physical servers while enabling dynamic management and aggregation capabilities on Linux native applications as well as Linux/KVM VMs using commodity hardware.

Bhargesh Patel completed his MTech in computer engineering from Dharmsinh Desai University, Nadiad. He has more than 3 years of teaching experience in cloud computing security, big data mining, and networking. Currently, he is working with G H Patel College of Engineering and Technology, Vallabh Vidyanagar. His areas of interest are cloud computing, grid computing, data mining, operating systems, computer networks, and cyber security. Currently, he is working on cloud security and big data mining projects.

www.PacktPub.com

Support files, eBooks, discount offers, and more

For support files and downloads related to your book, please visit www.PacktPub.com.

Did you know that Packt offers eBook versions of every book published, with PDF and ePub files available? You can upgrade to the eBook version at www.PacktPub.com and as a print book customer, you are entitled to a discount on the eBook copy. Get in touch with us at service@packtpub.com for more details.

At www.PacktPub.com, you can also read a collection of free technical articles, sign up for a range of free newsletters and receive exclusive discounts and offers on Packt books and eBooks.

https://www2.packtpub.com/books/subscription/packtlib

Do you need instant solutions to your IT questions? PacktLib is Packt's online digital book library. Here, you can search, access, and read Packt's entire library of books.

Why subscribe?

- Fully searchable across every book published by Packt
- Copy and paste, print, and bookmark content
- On demand and accessible via a web browser

Free access for Packt account holders

If you have an account with Packt at www.PacktPub.com, you can use this to access PacktLib today and view 9 entirely free books. Simply use your login credentials for immediate access.

I would like to dedicate this book to my family, who supported me immensely throughout the writing of this book.

Table of Contents

Preface   **vii**

Chapter 1: Designing OpenStack Cloud Architecture   **1**

OpenStack – think again   **2**

Introducing the OpenStack logical architecture   **3**

  Keystone   4

  Swift   4

  Glance   5

  Cinder   6

  Nova   7

    nova-api   7

    nova-compute   8

    nova-volume   8

    nova-network   8

    nova-scheduler   9

  Queue   9

  Database   9

  Neutron   10

    The Neutron architecture   11

  Horizon   12

Gathering the pieces and building a picture   **13**

  Provisioning a flow under the hood   16

  Expanding the picture   19

A sample architecture setup   **21**

  Deployment   21

    The conceptual model design   22

    The logical model design   23

    The physical model design   31

Summary   **37**

Chapter 2: Deploying OpenStack – DevOps and OpenStack Dual Deal — 39

DevOps in a nutshell — 40
DevOps and cloud – everyone is coding — 41
DevOpsing OpenStack — 43
Breaking down the OpenStack pieces — 44
Making the infrastructure deployment professional — 45
Bringing OpenStack to the chain — 47
Continuous integration and delivery — 47
Eat the elephant — 49
Preparing the infrastructure code environment — 49
The Chef environment — 52
Prerequisites for settings — 53
Time to cook OpenStack — 58
Summary — 72

Chapter 3: Learning OpenStack Clustering – Cloud Controllers and Compute Nodes — 73

Understanding the art of clustering — 74
Asymmetric clustering — 75
Symmetric clustering — 75
Divide and conquer — 75
The cloud controller — 75
nova-conductor — 76
nova-scheduler — 77
X-api — 78
Image management — 79
Network outfit — 79
The Horizon decision — 80
Planning for the message queue — 80
Consolidating the database — 80
Cloud controller clustering — 81
Cooking the cloud controller — 83
The compute node — 86
Overcommitment considerations — 87
Deciding on the hypervisor — 89
Storing instances' alternatives — 96
Cooking the compute node — 97
Preparing for plan B — 99
Back up with backup-manager — 100
Simple recovery steps — 101
Summary — 102

Chapter 4: Learning OpenStack Storage – Deploying the Hybrid Storage Model — **103**

Understanding the storage types — **104**
  Ephemeral storage — 104
  Persistent storage — 104
    Object storage is not NAS/SAN — 104
  A spotlight on Swift — 105
    The Swift architecture — 105
    Physical design considerations — 108
    Swift hardware — 112
    The Swift network — 114
Cooking Swift — **115**
  Joining Cinder — 118
Choosing the storage — **120**
  CAP under scope — 121
  Stirring up the storage — 122
    Cinder can do more — 122
    Beyond Cinder – Ceph — 127
Summary — **140**

Chapter 5: Implementing OpenStack Networking and Security — **141**

The story of an API — **142**
Security groups — **143**
  Managing the security groups using Horizon — 145
  Managing the security groups using the Neutron CLI — 146
  Managing the security groups using the Nova CLI — 147
  An example of a web server DMZ — 150
Firewall as a Service — **152**
  Coupling a firewall with Neutron — 154
  The Neutron plugin — 157
    There can be more than one plugin — 158
    Empowering the traffic isolation — 158
  VPN as a Service – a case study — 160
    General settings — 160
    VPNaaS configuration — 164
Summary — **170**

Chapter 6: OpenStack HA and Failover — **171**

HA under the scope — **172**
  Do not mix them — 173
  HA levels in OpenStack — 173
  A strict service-level agreement — 174

Measuring HA   **175**
   The HA dictionary   177
   Hands on HA   178
     Understanding HAProxy   178
     OpenStack HA under the hood   181
Summary   **205**

Chapter 7: OpenStack Multinode Deployment – Bringing in Production   **207**
   Confirming the multinode setup   **208**
     Assigning physical nodes   208
     Preparing the OpenStack Initiator   210
   The network topology   **211**
     The OpenStack network mode   212
     The physical network topology   212
   The OpenStack deployment   **216**
     The MIN installation   216
     Chef server preinstallation   226
     Discover and cook   227
       Cooking time   228
       Testing the cloud   231
       Arming the deployment   232
   Summary   **244**

Chapter 8: Extending OpenStack – Advanced Networking Features and Deploying Multi-tier Applications   **245**
   Navigating through Neutron   **246**
     Neutron plugins   247
       Virtual switching infrastructure   247
     Load Balancer as a Service   261
       Work around LBaaS   262
       Integrate LBaaS in the cloud   263
       Stack in OpenStack   265
   Summary   **274**

Chapter 9: Monitoring OpenStack – Ceilometer and Zabbix   **275**
   Telemetry in OpenStack – Ceilometer   **276**
     Ceilometer definition   276
     Ceilometer glossary   277
     The Ceilometer architecture   278
     The Ceilometer installation   281

Ceilometer and heat   **287**
  Autoscaling   288
    Extending HOT for alarming   288
Arming OpenStack monitoring   **297**
  Zabbix in action   297
    Placing Zabbix   298
    Installing the Zabbix server   298
    Configuring the Zabbix agent on OpenStack nodes   300
Summary   **303**

**Chapter 10: Keeping Track for Logs – Centralizing Logs
with Logstash**   **305**
Tackling logging   **306**
  Demystifying logs in OpenStack   306
    The log's location   307
    Adjusting logs in OpenStack   308
Two eyes are better than one   **308**
  Logstash under the hood   309
    The Logstash workflow   310
  Placing the Logstash server   311
    Installing the Logstash server   312
    Configuring Logstash   316
Summary   **329**

**Chapter 11: Tuning OpenStack Performance – Advanced
Configuration**   **331**
Pushing the limits of the database   **332**
  Deciding the resources outfit   334
  Caching for OpenStack   334
    Memcached in OpenStack   336
Stressing RabbitMQ   **341**
Benchmarking OpenStack at scale   **344**
  Rally in a nutshell   344
  Meeting OpenStack SLA   345
  Installing Rally   346
  Rally in action   348
    Scenario example 1   350
    Scenario example 2   355
Summary   **362**
Index   **363**

Preface

Since its first official release in 2010, OpenStack has distinguished itself as the ultimate open source cloud operating system. Today, more than 200 companies worldwide have joined the development of the OpenStack project, which makes it an attractive cloud computing solution for thousands of organizations. The main reason behind the success of OpenStack is not the overwhelming number of features that it has implemented, but rather its good modularity. Thanks to its vast community around the world, OpenStack is growing very fast. Each release exposes new modules and administrative facilities that offer on-demand computing resources by provisioning a large set of networks of virtual machines. If you are looking for a cloud computing solution that scales out well, OpenStack is an ideal option. Nowadays, it is considered to be a mature cloud computing operating system. Several big, medium, and small enterprises have adopted it as a solution in their infrastructure. The nirvana of OpenStack comes from its architecture. Designing your cloud becomes much easier with more flexibility. It is an ideal solution if you intend either to design a start up cloud environment or to integrate it into your existing infrastructure. As you build your cloud using OpenStack, you will be able to integrate with legacy systems and third-party technologies by eliminating vendor lock-in as much as possible.

This book is designed to discuss what is new in OpenStack with regards to the new features and incubated projects. You will be guided through this book from design to deployment and implementation with the help of a set of best practices in every phase. Each topic is elaborated so that you can see the big and complete picture of a true production environment that runs OpenStack at scale. It will help you decide upon the ways of deploying OpenStack by determining the best outfit for your private cloud, such as the computer, storage, and network components.

If you are ready to start a real private cloud running OpenStack, master the OpenStack design, and deploy and manage a scalable OpenStack infrastructure, this book will prove to be a clear guide that exposes the latest features of the OpenStack technology and helps you leverage its power to design and manage any medium or large OpenStack infrastructure.

What this book covers

Chapter 1, Designing OpenStack Cloud Architecture, will focus on discussing the several components of the architecture of OpenStack. It will provide the basis that is needed to start with the first design of your OpenStack private cloud environment. The chapter will discuss the different models' designs, which will help you begin your first deployment of OpenStack from scratch. The chapter will contain practical examples and calculations that are framed in a theoretical approach to give you an idea about how you can choose the right hardware capacity for your first OpenStack environment and adapt such information to real-world deployments.

Chapter 2, Deploying OpenStack – DevOps and OpenStack Dual Deal, will introduce you to the first installation of the OpenStack environment using automation tools. You will learn how to get the entire infrastructure installed and customized using Chef. The chapter will highlight the adoption of the DevOps approach and cover several advantages of how you can conduct your first OpenStack deployment from a test to production environment with more flexibility. It will provide instructions on how to install and use the Chef cookbooks to install the first test environment and get ready for the production stage.

Chapter 3, Learning OpenStack Clustering – Cloud Controllers and Compute Nodes, will decompose the big parts of your deployment by further refining your design, which was elaborated on in the previous chapter. It will cover some best practices regarding the art of clustering. Next, you will learn how to distribute the main OpenStack services between the cloud controllers and the compute nodes and construct an efficient OpenStack cluster. It will put under the microscope the choice of the hypervisor and hardware specifications. A sample design of the Chef cookbooks will be implemented to help you learn how to automate a cloud controller and install the compute nodes. The chapter will also explore how to plan the backup of an OpenStack cluster.

Chapter 4, Learning OpenStack Storage – Deploying the Hybrid Storage Model, will cover the subject of storage in OpenStack. The chapter will start by focusing on the storage types and their use cases. You will learn about an object storage code named Swift and how it works in OpenStack. A real Swift deployment will be shown to help you calculate the hardware requirements. The chapter will also talk about the block storage code named Cinder in OpenStack. You will learn how to decide which storage type will fulfill your needs. It will also explore Ceph and its main architectural design. It will help you integrate it and install in your test OpenStack environment using Vagrant and Chef.

Chapter 5, Implementing OpenStack Networking and Security, will focus mainly on the networking security features in OpenStack. It will cover the concept of namespaces and security groups in OpenStack and how you can manage them using the Neutron and Nova APIs. In addition, it will explore the new networking security feature, Firewall as a Service. A case study will help you understand another networking feature in Neutron called VPN as a Service.

Chapter 6, OpenStack HA and Failover, will cover the topics of high availability and failover. For each component of the OpenStack infrastructure, this chapter will expose several HA options. The chapter will be replete with HA concepts and best practices, which will help you define the best HA OpenStack environment. It serves as a good complementary chapter for the previous chapters by bringing a geared, distributed, and fault-tolerant OpenStack architecture design. Numerous open source solutions, such as HAProxy, Keepalived, Pacemaker, and Corosync, will be discussed through a step-by-step instruction guide.

Chapter 7, OpenStack Multinode Deployment – Bringing in Production, will be your "first production day" guide. It will focus on how you can deploy a complete multinode OpenStack setup. A sample setup will be explained and described in detail by exposing the different nodes and their roles, the network topology, and the deployment approach. The chapter will contain a practical guide to OpenStack deployment using bare metal provision tools xCAT together with the Chef server. It will demonstrate the first run of a new OpenStack tenant.

Chapter 8, Extending OpenStack – Advanced Networking Features and Deploying Multi-tier Applications, will delve into the advanced OpenStack networking features. It will explain in depth the Neutron plugins such as Linux Bridge and Open vSwitch, how they differ from the architectural perspective, and how instances can be connected to networks with the Neutron plugins. The chapter will also cover Load Balancing as a Service, which is used to load balance the traffic between instances by exploring their fundamental components. In addition, an orchestration module named Heat will be introduced in this chapter and will be used to build a complete stack to show how a real load balancer is deployed in OpenStack.

Chapter 9, Monitoring OpenStack – Ceilometer and Zabbix, will explore another new incubated project called Ceilometer as a new telemetry module for OpenStack. The chapter will discuss briefly the architecture of Ceilometer and how you can install and integrate it into the existing OpenStack environment. The discussion on Heat will be resumed, and it will be used to expand a stack installation including Ceilometer. The purpose of this is to discover the capabilities of heat with regard to supporting the Ceilometer functions, such as alarms and notifications. This section will also make sure that the OpenStack environment is well-monitored using some external monitoring tools such as Zabbix for advanced triggering capabilities.

Chapter 10, Keeping Track for Logs – Centralizing Logs with Logstash, will talk about the problem of logging in OpenStack. The chapter will present a very sophisticated logging solution called Logstash. It will go beyond the tailing and grepping of single log lines to tackle complex log filtering. The chapter will provide instructions on how to install Logstash and forward the OpenStack log files to a central logging server. Furthermore, a few snippets will be be provided to demonstrate the transformation of the OpenStack data logs and events into elegant graphs that are easy to understand.

Chapter 11, Tuning OpenStack Performance – Advanced Configuration, will wrap things up by talking about how you can make the OpenStack infrastructure run better with respect to its performance. Different topics, such as the advanced configuration in the exiting OpenStack environment, will be discussed. The chapter will put under the microscope the performance enhancement of MySQL by means of hardware upgrade and software layering such as memcached. You will learn how to tune the OpenStack infrastructure component-by-component using a new incubated OpenStack project called Rally.

What you need for this book

This book assumes a moderate level of Linux system administration and cloud computing concepts' experience. Though this book will walk you through some snippets of real-life production environment running OpenStack, some rudimentary knowledge of the OpenStack components may be required. In addition to this, a basic knowledge and understanding of networking jargon and connectional design is required. If you possess some Ruby programming skills, this is a plus. The book does not specify any specific test environment. Feel free to use any lab environment that you feel more comfortable with, such as Oracle's VirtualBox, Vagrant, or the VMware workstation.

This book requires you to install and run OpenStack on physical hardware to support bare metal provisioning and, for this, a physical network infrastructure should be in place.

In this book, the following essential software is required:

- Operating System: CentOS 6.5
- The following software is required:
    - OpenStack — Havana or a later version
    - The Chef server
    - Vagrant
    - VirtualBox

Internet connectivity will be required to install the OpenStack packages and several other packages. Make sure that you use the most convenient hardware to perform tests of the snippets described in each chapter of this book.

Who this book is for

To speed up with the content of this book, prior knowledge of OpenStack is required. If you don't have experience in OpenStack, reading small snippets from the OpenStack community, `http://docs.openstack.org/admin-guide-cloud/content/ch_getting-started-with-openstack.html`, will bring you onto the same wavelength of this book. As the title of the book promises, you should not expect a long and detailed tutorial on the installation of OpenStack. Although some chapters provide specific details concerning the installation of the new components, you are expected to have some basic knowledge on how it works in general so that you can turn your focus to the advanced methods and tricks that treat the topic at hand. This book is essentially for the novice cloud and technical architects and the system administrators who are willing to deploy a cloud based on OpenStack in a medium to large IT infrastructure. The book is also meant for those who have already deployed an OpenStack environment and who are willing to discover new features and expand their knowledge of how this technology works and how you can integrate new incubated projects during the operational phase.

Conventions

In this book, you will find a number of text styles that distinguish between different kinds of information. Here are some examples of these styles and an explanation of their meaning.

Code words in text, database table names, folder names, filenames, file extensions, pathnames, dummy URLs, user input, and Twitter handles are shown as follows: "Create a new role named `packtpub-os-compute-worker.json`."

A block of code is set as follows:

```
heat_template_version:
description:
parameters:
  param1
    type:
    label:
    description:
    default:
  param2:
    ....
```

When we wish to draw your attention to a particular part of a code block, the relevant lines or items are set in bold:

```
input  {
. . .
   }
filter{
  if [type] == "openstack" {
    grok {
      patterns_dir => "/opt/logstash/patterns/"
      match=>[ "message","%{TIMESTAMP_ISO8601:timestamp}
  %{NUMBER:response} %{AUDITLOGLEVEL:level} %{NOTSPACE:module}
    \[%{GREEDYDATA:program}\] %{GREEDYDATA:content}"]
      }
```

Any command-line input or output is written as follows:

```
# yum clean all
# yum update -y
# yum install nginx redis -y
```

New terms and **important words** are shown in bold. Words that you see on the screen, for example, in menus or dialog boxes, appear in the text like this: "To install Ruby, you need to go from the Eclipse menu bar and navigate to **Help | Install New Software**."

 Warnings or important notes appear in a box like this.

 Tips and tricks appear like this.

Reader feedback

Feedback from our readers is always welcome. Let us know what you think about this book—what you liked or disliked. Reader feedback is important for us as it helps us develop titles that you will really get the most out of.

To send us general feedback, simply e-mail feedback@packtpub.com, and mention the book's title in the subject of your message.

If there is a topic that you have expertise in and you are interested in either writing or contributing to a book, see our author guide at www.packtpub.com/authors.

Customer support

Now that you are the proud owner of a Packt book, we have a number of things to help you to get the most from your purchase.

Downloading the example code

You can download the example code files from your account at http://www.packtpub.com for all the Packt Publishing books you have purchased. If you purchased this book elsewhere, you can visit http://www.packtpub.com/support and register to have the files e-mailed directly to you.

Downloading the color images of this book

We also provide you with a PDF file that has color images of the screenshots/diagrams used in this book. The color images will help you better understand the changes in the output. You can download this file from https://www.packtpub.com/sites/default/files/downloads/5643OS_ColoredImages.pdf.

Errata

Although we have taken every care to ensure the accuracy of our content, mistakes do happen. If you find a mistake in one of our books—maybe a mistake in the text or the code—we would be grateful if you could report this to us. By doing so, you can save other readers from frustration and help us improve subsequent versions of this book. If you find any errata, please report them by visiting http://www.packtpub.com/submit-errata, selecting your book, clicking on the **Errata Submission Form** link, and entering the details of your errata. Once your errata are verified, your submission will be accepted and the errata will be uploaded to our website or added to any list of existing errata under the Errata section of that title.

To view the previously submitted errata, go to https://www.packtpub.com/books/content/support and enter the name of the book in the search field. The required information will appear under the **Errata** section.

Piracy

Piracy of copyrighted material on the Internet is an ongoing problem across all media. At Packt, we take the protection of our copyright and licenses very seriously. If you come across any illegal copies of our works in any form on the Internet, please provide us with the location address or website name immediately so that we can pursue a remedy.

Please contact us at copyright@packtpub.com with a link to the suspected pirated material.

We appreciate your help in protecting our authors and our ability to bring you valuable content.

Questions

If you have a problem with any aspect of this book, you can contact us at questions@packtpub.com, and we will do our best to address the problem.

1
Designing OpenStack Cloud Architecture

Owing to the widespread use of OpenStack development around the globe, several enterprises have already started switching to a new and amazing way to gain infrastructural resources and reduce the investment costs of their respective IT environments. What makes this opportunity great is the open source experience that it offers. Well, you may claim that there are several other cloud solutions that are open source as well. What makes OpenStack unique is its exposure; it is *widely open* to other open source solutions along with being a shining example of a **multiport-integrated solution** with great flexibility. All that you really need is a good design to fulfill most of your requirements and the right decisions on how and what to deploy.

If you browse the pages of this book, you might wonder what makes a laminated cover entitled *Mastering*, such a great deal to you as a system administrator, cloud architect, DevOps engineer, or any technical personnel operating on the Linux platform. Basically, you may be working on a project, going on a vacation, building a house, or redesigning your fancy apartment. In each of these cases, you will always need a strategy. A Japanese military leader, Miyamoto Musashi, wrote the following — a very impressive thought on *perception and sight* — in *The Book of Five Rings, Start Publishing LLC*:

> *"In strategy, it is important to see distant things as if they were close and to take a distanced view of close things."*

Ultimately, based on what you learned from the OpenStack literature, and what you have deployed, or practiced, you will probably ask the famous key question: How does OpenStack work? Well, the OpenStack community is very rich in terms of topics and tutorials — some of which you may have already tried out. It is time to go ahead and raise the curtain on the OpenStack design and architecture.

Basically, the goal of this chapter is to get you from where you are today to the point where you can confidently build a private cloud based on OpenStack with your own design choice.

At the end of this chapter, you will have a good perspective on ways to design your project by putting the details under the microscope. You will also learn about how OpenStack services work together and be ready for the next stage of our adventure by starting the deployment of an OpenStack environment with best practices.

This chapter will cover the following points:

- Getting acquainted with the logical architecture of the OpenStack ecosystem and the way its different core components interact with each other
- Learning how to design an OpenStack environment by choosing the right core services for the right environment
- Designing the first OpenStack architecture for a large-scale environment while bearing in mind that OpenStack can be designed in numerous ways
- Learning some best practices and the process of capacity planning for a robust OpenStack environment

Let's start the mission by putting the spot light on the place where the core OpenStack components come in the first place.

OpenStack – think again

Today, cloud computing is about **Software as a Service (SaaS)**, **Platform as a Service (PaaS)**, and **Infrastructure as a Service (IaaS)**. The challenge that has been set by the public cloud is about agility, speed, and service efficiency. Most companies have expensive IT systems they have developed and deployed over the years, but they are siloed. In many cases, the IT systems are struggling to respond to the agility and speed of the public cloud services that are offered within their own private silos in their own private data center. The traditional data center model and siloed infrastructure might lead to unsustainability. In fact, today's enterprise data center focuses on what it takes to become a next-generation data center. The shift to the new data center generation has evolved the adoption of a model for the management and provision of software. This has been accompanied by a shift from workload isolation in the traditional model to a mixed model. With an increasing number of users utilizing cloud services, the next-generation data centers are able to handle multitenancy. The traditional one was limited to a single tenancy. Moreover, enterprises today look for scaling down next to scaling up. It is a huge step in the data center technology to shift the way of handling an entire infrastructure.

The big move to a software infrastructure has allowed administrators and operators to deliver a fully automated infrastructure within a minute. The next-generation data center reduces the infrastructure to a single, big, agile, scalable, and automated unit. The end result is that the administrators will have to program the infrastructure. This is where OpenStack comes into the picture—the next-generation data center operating system. The ubiquitous influence of OpenStack was felt by many big global cloud enterprises such as VMware, Cisco, Juniper, IBM, Red Hat, Rackspace, PayPal, and EBay, to name but a few. Today, many of them are running a very large scalable private cloud based on OpenStack in their production environment. If you intend to be a part of a winning, innovative cloud enterprise, you should jump to the next-generation data center and gain a valuable experience by adopting OpenStack in your IT infrastructure.

 To read more about the success stories of many companies, visit `https://www.openstack.org/user-stories`.

Introducing the OpenStack logical architecture

Before delving into the architecture of OpenStack, we need to refresh or fill gaps, if they do exist, to learn more about the basic concepts and usage of each core component.

In order to get a better understanding on *how it works*, it will be beneficial to first briefly parse *the things that make it work*. Assuming that you have already installed OpenStack or even deployed it in a small or medium-sized environment, let's put the essential core components under the microscope and go a bit further by taking the use cases and asking the question: What is the purpose of such a component?

Keystone

From an architectural perspective, Keystone presents the simplest service in the OpenStack composition. It is the core component that provides identity service and it integrates functions for authentication, catalog services, and policies to register and manage different tenants and users in the OpenStack projects. The API requests between OpenStack services are being processed by Keystone to ensure that the right user or service is able to utilize the requested OpenStack service. Keystone performs numerous authentication mechanisms such as username/password as well as a token-authentication-based system. Additionally, it is possible to integrate it with an existing backend directory such as **Lightweight Directory Access Protocol (LDAP)** and the **Pluggable Authentication Module (PAM)**.

A similar real-life example is a city game. You can purchase a gaming day card and profit by playing a certain number of games during a certain period of time. Before you start gaming, you have to ask for the card to get an access to the city at the main entrance of the city game. Every time you would like to try a new game, you must check in at the game stage machine. This will generate a request, which is mapped to a central authentication system to check the validity of the card and its warranty, to profit the requested game. By analogy, the token in Keystone can be compared to the gaming day card except that it does not diminish anything from your request. The identity service is being considered as a central and common authentication system that provides access to the users.

Swift

Although it was briefly claimed that Swift would be made available to the users along with the OpenStack components, it is interesting to see how Swift has empowered what is referred to as **cloud storage**. Most of the enterprises in the last decade did not hide their fears about a critical part of the IT infrastructure—the storage where the data is held. Thus, the purchasing of expensive hardware to be in the safe zone had become a habit. There are always certain challenges that are faced by storage engineers and no doubt, one of these challenges include the task of minimizing downtime while increasing the data availability. Despite the rise of many smart solutions for storage systems during the last few years, we still need to make changes to the traditional way. Make it cloudy! Swift was introduced to fulfill this mission.

We will leave the details pertaining to the Swift architecture for later, but you should keep in mind that Swift is an object storage software, which has a number of benefits:

- No central brain indicates no **Single Point Of Failure (SPOF)**
- Curative indicates autorecovery in case of failure

- Highly scalable for large petabytes store access by scaling horizontally
- Better performance, which is achieved by spreading the load over the storage nodes
- Inexpensive hardware can be used for redundant storage clusters

Glance

When I had my first presentation on the core components and architecture of OpenStack with my first cloud software company, I was surprised by a question raised by the CTO: What is the difference between Glance and Swift? Both handle storage. Well, despite my deployment of OpenStack (Cacti and Diablo were released at the time) and familiarity with the majority of the component's services, I found the question quite tough to answer! As a system architect or technical designer, you may come across the following questions: What is the difference between them? Why do I need to integrate such a solution? On one hand, it is important to distinguish the system interaction components so that it will be easier to troubleshoot and operate within the production environments. On the other hand, it is important to satisfy the needs and conditions that go beyond your IT infrastructure limits.

To alleviate any confusion, we keep it simple. Swift and Glance are storage systems. However, the difference between the two is in what they store. Swift is designed to be an object storage where you can keep data such as virtual disks, images, backup archiving, and so forth, while Glance stores metadata of images. Metadata can be information such as kernel, disk images, disk format, and so forth. Do not be surprised that Glance was originally designed to store images. Since the first release of OpenStack included only Nova and Swift (Austin code name October 21, 2010), Glance was integrated with the second release (Bexar code name February 23, 2011).

The mission of Glance is to be an image registry. From this point, we can conclude how OpenStack has paved the way to being more modular and loosely coupled core component model. Using Glance to store virtual disk images is a possibility. From an architectural level, including more advanced ways to query image information via the Image Service API provided by Glance through an independent image storage backend such as Swift brings more valuable performance and well-organized system core services. In this way, a client (can be a user or an external service) will be able to register a new virtual disk image, for example, to stream it from a highly scalable and redundant store. At this level, as a technical operator, you may face another challenge—performance. This will be discussed at the end of the book.

Cinder

You may wonder whether there is another way to have storage in OpenStack. Indeed, the management of the persistent block storage is being integrated into OpenStack by using Cinder. Its main capability to present block-level storage provides raw volumes that can be built into logical volumes in the filesystem and mounted in the virtual machine.

Some of the features that Cinder offers are as follows:

- **Volume management**: This allows the creation or deletion of a volume
- **Snapshot management**: This allows the creation or deletion of a snapshot of volumes
- You can attach or detach volumes from instances
- You can clone volumes
- Volume creation from snapshots is possible via Cinder
- You can copy images to volumes and vice versa

Several storage options have been proposed in the OpenStack core. Without a doubt, you may be asked this question: What kind of storage will be the best for you? With a decision-making process, a list of pros and cons should be made. The following is a very simplistic table that describes the difference between the storage types in OpenStack to avoid any confusion when choosing the storage management option for your future architecture design:

Specification	Storage Type	
	Object storage	Block storage
Performance	-	OK
Database storage	-	OK
Restoring backup data	OK	OK
Setup for volume providers	-	OK
Persistence	OK	OK
Access	Anywhere	Within VM
Image storage	OK	-

It is very important to keep in mind that unlike Glance and Keystone services, Cinder features are delivered by orchestrating volume providers through the configurable setup driver's architectures such as IBM, NetApp, Nexenta, and VMware.

Whatever choice you have made, it is always considered good advice since *nothing is perfect*. If Cinder is proven as an ideal solution or a replacement of the old **nova-volume** service that existed before the **Folsom** release on an architectural level, it is important to know that Cinder has organized and created a catalog of block-based storage devices with several differing characteristics. However, it is obvious if we consider the limitation of commodity storage redundancy and autoscaling. Eventually, the block storage service as the main core of OpenStack can be improved if a few gaps are filled, such as the addition of values:

- Quality of service
- Replication
- Tiering

The aforementioned Cinder specification reveals its *Non-vendor-lock-in* characteristic, where it is possible to change the backend easily or perform data migration between two different storage backends. Therefore, a better storage design architecture in a Cinder use case will bring a third party into the scalability game. More details will be covered in *Chapter 4*, *Learning OpenStack Storage – Deploying the Hybrid Storage Model*. For instance, you can keep in mind that Cinder is essential for our private cloud design, but it misses some capacity scaling features.

Nova

As you may already know, Nova is the most original core component of OpenStack. From an architectural level, it is considered one of the most complicated components of OpenStack.

In a nutshell, Nova runs a large number of requests, which are collaborated to respond to a user request into running VM. Let's break down the blob image of nova by assuming that its architecture as a distributed application needs orchestration to carry out tasks between different components.

nova-api

The nova-api component accepts and responds to the end user and computes the API calls. The end users or other components communicate with the OpenStack Nova API interface to create instances via OpenStack API or EC2 API.

 Nova-api initiates most of the orchestrating activities such as the running of an instance or the enforcement of some particular policies.

nova-compute

The nova-compute component is primarily a worker daemon that creates and terminates VM instances via the hypervisor's APIs (XenAPI for XenServer, Libvirt KVM, and the VMware API for VMware).

It is important to depict how such a process works. The following steps delineate this process:

1. Accept actions from the queue and perform system commands such as the launching of the KVM instances to take them out when updating the state in the database.

2. Working closely with nova-volume to override and provide iSCSI or Rados block devices in Ceph.

Ceph is an open source storage software platform for object, block, and file storage in a highly available storage environment. This will be further discussed in *Chapter 4, Learning OpenStack Storage – Deploying the Hybrid Storage Model.*

nova-volume

The nova-volume component manages the creation, attaching, and detaching of N volumes to compute instances (similar to Amazon's EBS).

Cinder is a replacement of the nova-volume service.

nova-network

The nova-network component accepts networking tasks from the queue and then performs these tasks to manipulate the network (such as setting up bridging interfaces or changing the IP table rules).

Neutron is a replacement of the nova-network service.

nova-scheduler

The nova-scheduler component takes a VM instance's request from the queue and determines where it should run (specifically which compute server host it should run on). At an application architecture level, the term *scheduling* or *scheduler* invokes a systematic search for the best outfit for a given infrastructure to improve its performance.

Nova also provides console services that allow end users to access the console of the virtual instance through a proxy such as nova-console, nova-novncproxy, and nova-consoleauth.

By zooming out the general components of OpenStack, we find that Nova interacts with several services such as Keystone for authentication, Glance for images, and Horizon for the web interface. For example, the Glance interaction is central; the API process can upload any query to Glance, while nova-compute will download images to launch instances.

Queue

Queue provides a central hub to pass messages between daemons. This is where information is shared between different Nova daemons by facilitating the communication between discrete processes in an asynchronous way.

Any service can easily communicate with any other service via the APIs and queue a service. One major advantage of the queuing system is that it can buffer a large buffer workload. Rather than using an RPC service, a queue system can queue a large workload and give an eventual consistency.

Database

A database stores most of the build-time and runtime state for the cloud infrastructure, including instance types that are available for use, instances in use, available networks, and projects. It is the second essential piece of sharing information in all OpenStack components.

Neutron

Neutron provides a real **Network as a Service (NaaS)** between interface devices that are managed by OpenStack services such as Nova. There are various characteristics that should be considered for Neutron:

- It allows users to create their own networks and then attach server interfaces to them
- Its pluggable backend architecture lets users take advantage of the commodity gear or vendor-supported equipment
- Extensions allow additional network services, software, or hardware to be integrated

Neutron has many core network features that are constantly growing and maturing. Some of these features are useful for routers, virtual switches, and the SDN networking controllers.

> Starting from the Folsom release, the **Quantum** network service has been replaced by a project named **Neutron**, which was incorporated into the mainline project in the subsequent releases. The examples elaborated in this book are based on the Havana release and later.

Neutron introduces new concepts, which includes the following:

- **Port**: Ports in Neutron refer to the virtual switch connections. These connections are where instances and network services attached to networks. When attached to the subnets, the defined MAC and IP addresses of the interfaces are plugged into them.
- **Networks**: Neutron defines networks as isolated Layer 2 network segments. Operators will see networks as logical switches that are implemented by the Linux bridging tools, Open vSwitch, or some other software. Unlike physical networks, this can be defined by either the operators or users in OpenStack.

> Subnets in Neutron represent a block of IP addresses associated with a network. They will be assigned to instances in an associated network.

- **Routers**: Routers provide gateways between various networks.
- **Private and floating IPs**: Private and floating IP addresses refer to the IP addresses that are assigned to instances. Private IP addresses are visible within the instance and are usually a part of a private network dedicated to a tenant. This network allows the tenant's instances to communicate when isolated from the other tenants.

○ Private IP addresses are not visible to the Internet.

○ Floating IPs are virtual IPs that Neutron maps instance to private IPs via **Network Access Translation (NAT)**. Floating IP addresses are assigned to an instance so that they can connect to external networks and access the Internet. They are exposed as public IPs, but the guest's operating system has completely no idea that it was assigned an IP address.

In Neutron's low-level orchestration of Layer 1 through Layer 3, components such as IP addressing, subnetting, and routing can also manage high-level services. For example, Neutron provides **Load Balancing as a Service (LBaaS)** utilizing HAProxy to distribute the traffic among multiple compute node instances.

 You can refer to the last updated documentation for more information on networking in OpenStack at `http://docs.openstack.org/networking-guide/intro_networking.html`.

The Neutron architecture

There are three main components of Neutron architecture that you ought to know in order to validate your decision later with regard to the use case for a component within the new releases of OpenStack:

- **Neutron-server**: It accepts the API requests and routes them to the appropriate neutron-plugin for its action
- **Neutron plugins and agents**: They perform the actual work such as the plugging in or unplugging of ports, creating networks and subnets, or IP addressing.

 Agents and plugins differ depending on the vendor technology of a particular cloud for the virtual and physical Cisco switches, NEC, OpenFlow, OpenSwitch, Linux bridging, and so on.

- **Queue**: This routes messages between the neutron-server and various agents as well as the database to store the plugin state for a particular queue

Neutron is a system that manages networks and IP addresses. OpenStack networking ensures that the network will not be turned into a bottleneck or limiting factor in a cloud deployment and gives users real self-service, even over their network configurations.

Another advantage of Neutron is its capability to provide a way for organizations to relieve stress within the network of cloud environments and to make it easier to deliver NaaS in the cloud. It is designed to provide a plugin mechanism that will provide an option for the network operators to enable different technologies via the Neutron API.

It also lets its tenants create multiple private networks and control the IP addressing on them.

As a result of the API extensions, organizations have additional control over security and compliance policies, quality of service, monitoring, and troubleshooting, in addition to paving the way to deploying advanced network services such as firewalls, intrusion detection systems, or VPNs. More details about this will be covered in *Chapter 5, Implementing OpenStack Networking and Security*, and *Chapter 8, Extending OpenStack – Advanced Networking Features and Deploying Multi-tier Applications*.

 Keep in mind that Neutron allows users to manage and create networks or connect servers and nodes to various networks.

The scalability advantage will be discussed in a later topic in the context of the **Software Defined Network (SDN)** technology, which is an attraction to many networks and administrators who seek a high-level network multitenancy.

Horizon

Horizon is the web dashboard that pools all the different pieces together from your OpenStack ecosystem.

Horizon provides a web frontend for OpenStack services. Currently, it includes all the OpenStack services as well as some incubated projects. It was designed as a stateless and data-less web application—it does nothing more than initiating actions in the OpenStack services via API calls and displaying information that OpenStack returns to the Horizon. It does not keep any data except the session information in its own data store. It is designed to be a reference implementation that can be customized and extended by operators for a particular cloud. It forms the basis for several public clouds—most notably the HP Public Cloud and at its heart, is its extensible modular approach to construction.

Horizon is based on a series of modules called **panels** that define the interaction of each service. Its modules can be enabled or disabled, depending on the service availability of the particular cloud. In addition to this functional flexibility, Horizon is easy to style with **Cascading Style Sheets (CSS)**.

Most cloud provider distributions provide a company's specific theme for their dashboard implementation.

Gathering the pieces and building a picture

Let's try to see how OpenStack works by chaining all the service cores covered in the previous sections in a series of steps:

1. A user accesses the OpenStack environment via a web interface (HTTP/REST).

2. Authentication is the first action performed. This is where Keystone comes into the picture.

3. A conversation is started with Keystone—"Hey, I would like to authenticate and here are my credentials".

4. Keystone responds "OK, then you may authenticate and give the token" once the credentials have been accepted

5. You may remember that the service catalog comes with the token as a piece of code, which will allow you to access resources. Now you have it!

6. The service catalog, during its turn, will incorporate the code by responding "Here are the resources available, so you can go through and get what you need from your accessible list".

 The service catalog is a JSON structure that exposes the resources available upon a token request.

You can use the following example on querying by tenant to get a list of servers:

```
$ curl -v -H "X-Auth-Token:token" http://192.168.27.47:8774/v2/
tenant_id/servers
```

A list of server details is returned on how to gain access to the servers:

```
{
    "server": {
        "adminPass": "verysecuredpassword",
        "id": "5aaee3c3-12ee-7633-b32b-635489236232fbfbf",
        "links": [
            {
```

```
                  "href": "http://myopenstack.com/v2/openstack/
     servers/5aaee3c3-12ee-7633-b32b-635489236232fbfbf",
                  "rel": "self"
            },
            {
                  "href": "http://myopenstack.com/v2/openstack/
     servers/5aaee3c3-12ee-7633-b32b-635489236232fbfbf",
                  "rel": "bookmark"
            }
        ]
     }
}
```

7. Typically, once authenticated, you can talk to an API node. There are different APIs in the OpenStack ecosystem (OpenStack API and EC2 API).

8. Once we authenticate and request access, we have the following services that will do the homework under the hood:

    ° Compute nodes that deal with hypervisor

    ° Volume services that deal with storage

    ° Network services that make all the connections between VLANs and virtual network interfaces that work and talk to each other

    The next figure resumes the first blob pieces on how OpenStack works:

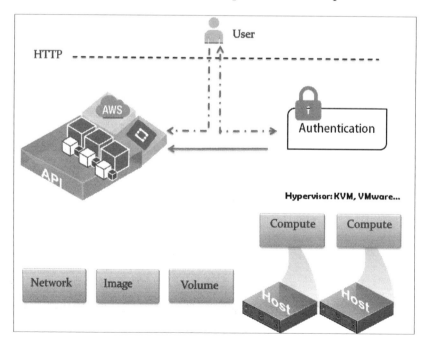

9. However, how do we get these services to talk? In such cases, you should think about the wondrous connector, the RabbitMQ queuing system.

For anyone who is non-familiar with the queuing system, we can consider an example of a central airport:

You have booked a flight and have been assigned a specific gateway that only you are interested in. This gateway gets you directly to your seat on the plane. A queuing system allows you to tune in to the server or service that you are interested in.

A queuing system takes care of issues such as; who wants to do the work? By analogy, since everybody listens to the airport assistance speaker channel, only one person (same passenger's destination) listens to that information and makes it work by joining the gateway.

Now, we have this information in the queue.

> If you have a look at the Python source tree, for any service, you will see a network directory for the network code, and there will be an `api.py` file for every one of these services.

Let's take an example. If you want to create an instance and implement it in the compute node, it might say "import the nova-compute node API and there is method/function there to create the instance". So, it will do all the jobs of getting over the wire and spinning up the server instances and doing the same for the appropriate node.

10. Another element of the picture is the schedule, which looks at the services and claims "this is what you have as memory, CPU, disk, network, and so on".

When a new request comes in, the scheduler might notify "you will get from these available resources available."

> The scheduling process in OpenStack can perform different algorithms such as simple, chance, and zone. An advanced way to do this is by deploying weight filtering by ranking the servers as its available resources.

Using this option, the node will spin up the server while you create your own rules. Here, you distribute your servers based on the number of processors and how much memory you may want in your spinning servers.

The last piece of this picture is that we need to get the information back. So, we have all these services that are doing something. Remember that they have a special airport gateway. Again, our queue performs some actions, and it sends notifications as these actions occur. They might be subscribed to find out certain things such as whether the network is up, the server is ready, or the server has crashed.

Provisioning a flow under the hood

It is important to understand how different services in OpenStack work together, leading to a running virtual machine. We have already seen how a request is processed in OpenStack via APIs. Now, we can go further and closely check how such services and subsystems, which includes authentication, computing, images, networks, queuing, and databases, work in tandem with performing a complete workflow to provide an instance in OpenStack. The next series of steps describes how service components work together once a submission of an instance provisioning request has been done:

1. A client enters the user credentials via Horizon, which makes the REST call to Keystone for authentication.

2. The authentication request will be handled by Keystone, which generates and sends back an authentication token. The token will be stored by Keystone, which will be used to authenticate against the rest of the OpenStack components by using APIs.

3. The action of **Launch Instance in the dashboard** will convert the creation of a new instance request into an API request, which will be sent to the nova-api service.

4. The nova-api service receives the authentication request and sends it for validation and access permission to Keystone.

5. Keystone checks the token and sends an authentication validation, which includes roles and permissions.

6. The nova-api service later creates an initial entry for an instance in the database and contacts the queuing system via an RPC call (`rpc.cast`). The call request will be sent to nova-scheduler to specify which host ID will run the instance.

7. The nova-scheduler contacts the queue and subscribes the new instance request.

8. The nova-scheduler performs the information gathering process from the database to find out the appropriate host based on its weighting and filtering algorithms.

9. Once a host has been chosen, the nova-scheduler sends back an RPC call (`rpc.cast`) to start launching an instance that remains in the queue.

10. The nova-compute contacts the queue and picks up the call issued by the nova-scheduler. Therefore, nova-compute proceeds with the subscription on the instance and sends an RPC call (`rpc.call`) in order to get instance-related information such as the instance characteristics (CPU, RAM, and disk) and the host ID. The RPC call remains in the queue.

11. The nova-conductor contacts the queue and picks up the call.

12. The nova-conductor contacts the queue and subscribes the new instance request. It interrogates the database to get instance information and publish its state in the queue.

13. The nova-compute picks the instance information from the queue and sends an authentication token in a REST call to the glance-api to get a specific image URI from a glance.

    The image URI will be obtained by the Image ID to find the requested one from the image repository.

14. The glance-api will verify the authentication token with Keystone.

15. Once validated, glance-api returns the image URI, including its metadata, which specifies the location details of the image that is being scrutinized.

> If the images are stored in a Swift cluster, the images will be requested as Swift objects via the REST calls. Keep in mind that it is not the job of nova-compute to fetch from the swift storage. Swift will interface via APIs to perform object requests. More details about this will be covered in *Chapter 4, Learning OpenStack Storage – Deploying the Hybrid Storage Model*.

16. The nova-compute sends the authentication token to a neutron-server via a REST call to configure the network for the instance.

17. The neutron-server checks the token with Keystone.

18. Once validated, the neutron-server contacts its agents, such as the neutron-l2-agent and neutron-dhcp-agent, by submitting the request in the queue.

19. Neutron agents pick the calls from the queue and reply by sending network information pertaining to the instance. For example, neutron-l2-agent gets the L2 configuration from Libvirt and publishes it in the queue. On the contrary, neutron-dhcp-agent contacts dnsmasq for the IP allocation and returns an IP reply in the queue.

Dnsmasq is a software that provides a network infrastructure such as the DNS forwarder and the DHCP server.

20. The neutron-server collects all the network settings from the queue and records it in the database. Therefore, it sends back an RPC call to the queue along with all the network details.

21. Nova-compute contacts the queue and grabs the instance network configuration.

22. Nova-compute sends the authentication token to cinder-api via a REST call to get the volume, which will be attached to the instance.

23. The cinder-api checks the token with Keystone.

24. Once validated, the cinder-api returns the volume information to the queue.

25. Nova-compute contacts the queue and grabs the block storage information.

26. At this stage, the nova-compute executes a request to the specified hypervisor via Libvirt to start the virtual machine.

27. In order to get the instance state, nova-compute sends an RPC call (rpc. call) to nova-conductor.

28. The nova-conductor picks the call from the queue and replies to the queue by mentioning the new instance state.

29. The polling instance state is always performed via nova-api, which consults the database to get the state information and sends it back to the client.

Let's figure out how things can be seen by referring to the following simple architecture diagram:

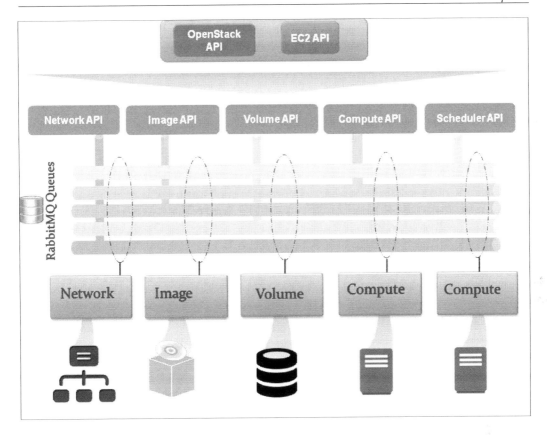

Expanding the picture

You may have certain limitations that are typically associated with network switches. Network switches create a lot of virtual LANs and virtual networks that specify whether there is a lot of input to data centers.

Let's imagine that we have 250 compute hosts scenario. You can conclude that a mesh of rack servers will be placed in the data center.

Now, you take the step to grow our data center, and to be geographically data-redundant in Europe and Africa: a data center in London, Amsterdam and Tunis.

We have a data center on each of these new locations and each of these locations are able to communicate with each other. At this point, a new terminology is introduced—cell concept.

To scale this out even further, we will take into consideration the entire system. We will take just the worker nodes and put them in other cells.

Another special scheduler works as a top-level cell and enforces the request into the child cell. Now, the child cells can do the work, and they can worry about VLAN and network issues.

The cells can share certain pieces of infrastructure, such as the database, authentication service Keystone, and some of the Glance image services. This is depicted in the following diagram:

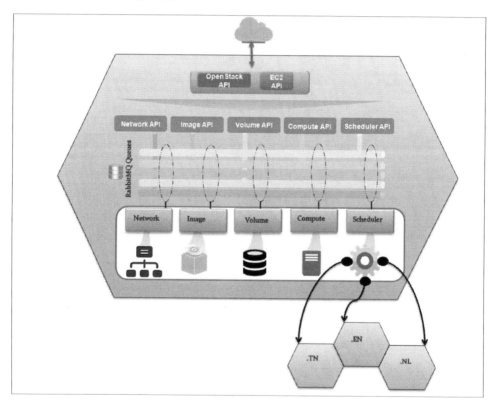

 More information about the concept of **cells** and configuration setup in OpenStack can be found for Havana release at the following reference: `http://docs.openstack.org/havana/config-reference/` `content/section_compute-cells.html`.

A sample architecture setup

Let us first go through the deployment process, which is explained in the following sections. Bear in mind that this is not a unique architecture that can be deployed.

Deployment

Deployment is a huge step in distinguishing all the OpenStack components that were covered previously. It confirms your understanding of how to start designing a complete OpenStack environment. Of course, assuming the versatility and flexibility of such a cloud management platform, OpenStack offers several possibilities that might be considered an advantage. However, on the other hand, you may face a challenge of taking the right design decision that suits your needs.

Basically, what you should consider in the first place is the responsibility in the Cloud. Depending on your cloud computing mission, it is essential to know what a coordinating IaaS is. The following are the use cases:

- **Cloud service brokerage**: This is a facilitating intermediary role of Cloud service consumptions for several providers, including maintenance
- **Cloud service provider**: This provides XaaS to private instances
- **Self cloud service**: This provides XaaS with its own IT for private usage

Apart from the knowledge of the aforementioned cloud service model providers, there are a few master keys that you should take into account in order to bring a well-defined architecture to a good basis that is ready to be deployed.

Though the system architecture design has evolved and is accompanied by the adoption of several methodology frameworks, many enterprises have successfully deployed OpenStack environments by going through a 3D process—a conceptual model design, logical model design, and physical model design.

It might be obvious that complexity increases from the conceptual to the logical design and from the logical to the physical design.

The conceptual model design

As the first conceptual phase, we will have a high-level reflection on what we will need from certain generic classes from the OpenStack architecture:

Class	Role
Compute	Stores virtual machine images Provides a user interface
Image	Stores disk files Provides a user interface
Object storage	Provides a user interface
Block storage	Provides volumes Provides a user interface
Network	Provides network connectivity Provides a user interface
Identity	Provides authentication
Dashboard	Graphical user interface

Let's map the generic basic classes in the following simplified diagram:

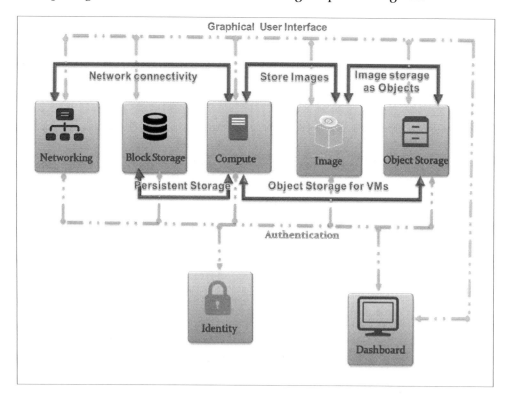

Keep in mind that the illustrated diagram will be refined over and over again since we will aim to integrate more services within our first basic design. In other words, we are following an *incremental* design approach within which we should exploit the flexibility of the OpenStack architecture.

At this level, we can have a vision and direction of the main goal without worrying about the details.

The logical model design

Based on the conceptual reflection phase, we are ready to construct the logical design. Most probably, you have a good idea about different OpenStack core components, which will be the basis of the formulation of the logical design that is done by laying down their logical representations.

Even though we have already taken the core of the OpenStack services component by component, you may need to map each of them to a logical solution within the complete design.

To do so, we will start by outlining the relations and dependencies between the services core of OpenStack. Most importantly, we aim to delve into the architectural level by keeping the details for the end. Thus, we will take into account the repartition of the OpenStack services between the new *package services*—the cloud controller and the compute node. You may wonder why such a consideration goes through a physical design classification. However, seeing the cloud controller and compute nodes as simple packages that encapsulate a bunch of OpenStack services, will help you refine your design at an early stage. Furthermore, this approach will plan in advance further high availability and scalability features, which allow you to introduce them later in more detail.

Chapter 3, Learning OpenStack Clustering – Cloud Controllers and Compute Nodes, describes in depth how to distribute the OpenStack services between cloud controllers and compute nodes.

Thus, the physical model design will be elaborated based on the previous theoretical phases by assigning parameters and values to our design. Let's start with our first logical iteration:

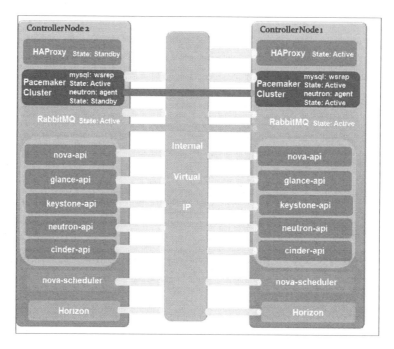

Obviously, in a highly available setup, we should achieve a degree of redundancy in each service within OpenStack. You may wonder about the critical OpenStack services claimed in the first part of this chapter—the database and message queue. Why can't they be separately clustered or *packaged* on their own? This is a pertinent question. Remember that we are still in the second logical phase where we try to dive *slowly and softly* into the infrastructure without getting into the details. Besides, we keep on going from general to specific models, where we focus more on the generic details. Decoupling RabbitMQ or MySQL from now on may lead to your design being overlooked. Alternatively, you may risk skipping other generic design topics. On the other hand, preparing a generic logical design will help you to not stick to just one possible combination, since the future physical designs will rely on it.

What about storage

The previous logical figure includes several essentials solutions for a high-scalable and redundant OpenStack environment such as **virtual IP** (**VIP**), HAProxy, and Pacemaker. The aforementioned technologies will be discussed in more detail in *Chapter 6, Openstack HA and Failover*.

Compute nodes are relatively simple as they are intended just to run the virtual machine's workload. In order to manage the VMs, the nova-compute service can be assigned for each compute node. Besides, we should not forget that the compute nodes will not be isolated; a Neutron agent and an optional Ceilometer compute agent may run this node.

What about storage?

You should now have a deeper understanding of the storage types within OpenStack—Swift and Cinder.

However, we did not cover a third-party software-defined storage called **Ceph**, which may combine or replace either or both of Swift and Cinder.

More details will be covered in *Chapter 4, Learning OpenStack Storage – Deploying the Hybrid Storage Model*. For now, we will design from a basic point where we have to decide how Cinder and/or Swift will be a part of our logical design.

Ultimately, a storage system becomes more complicated when it faces an exponential growth in the amount of data. Thus, the designing of your storage system is one of the critical steps that is required for a robust architecture.

Depending on your OpenStack business size environment, how much data do you need to store? Will your future PaaS construct a wide range of applications that run heavy-analysis data? What about the planned **Environment as a Service (EaaS)** model? Developers will need to incrementally back up their virtual machine's snapshots. *We need persistent storage.*

Don't put all your eggs in one basket. This is why we will include Cinder and Swift in the mission. Many thinkers will ask the following question: If one can be satisfied by ephemeral storage, why offer block storage? To answer this question, you may think about ephemeral storage as the place where the end user will not be able to access the virtual disk associated with its VM when it is terminated. Ephemeral storage should mainly be used in production that takes place in a high-scale environment, where users are actively concerned about their data, VM, or application. If you plan that your storage design should be 100 percent persistent, backing up everything *wisely* will make you feel better. This helps you figure out the best way to store data that grows exponentially by using specific techniques that allow them to be made available at any time. Remember that the current design applies for medium to large infrastructures. Ephemeral storage can also be a choice for certain users, for example, when they consider building a test environment. Considering the same case for Swift, we have claimed previously that the object storage might be used to store machine images, but when is this the case?

Simply, when you provide the extra hardware that fulfils certain Swift requirements: replication and redundancy.

Running a wide production environment while storing machine images on the local file system is not really good practice. First, the image can be accessed by different services and requested by thousands of users at a time. No wonder the controller is already exhausted by the forwarding and routing of the requests between the different APIs in addition to the computation of each resources through disk I/O, memory, and CPU. Each request will cause performance degradation, but it will not fail! Keeping an image in a filesystem under a heavy load will certainly bring the controller to a high latency and it may fail.

Henceforth, we might consider loosely coupled models, where the storage with a specific performance is considered a best fit for the production environment.

Thus, Swift will be used to store images, while Cinder will be used for persistent volumes for virtual machines (check the Swift controller node):

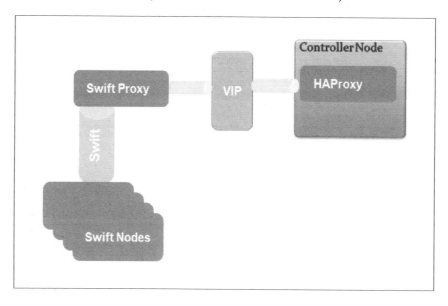

Obviously, Cinder LVM does not provide any redundancy capability between the Cinder LVM nodes. Losing the data in a Cinder LVM node is a disaster. You may want to perform a backup for each node. This can be helpful, but it will be a very tedious task! Let's design for resiliency. We have put what's necessary on the table. Now, what we need is a glue!

Networking

One of the most complicated system designing steps is the part concerning the network! Now, let's look under the hood to see how all the different services that were defined previously should be connected.

The logical networking design

OpenStack shows a wide range of networking configurations that vary between the basic and complicated. Terms such as Open vSwitch, Neutron coupled with the VLAN segmentation, and VMware NSX with Neutron are not intuitively obvious from their appearance to be able to be implemented without fetching their use case in our design. Thus, this important step implies that you may differ between different network topologies because of the reasons behind why every choice was made and why it may work for a given use case.

OpenStack has moved from simplistic network features to complicated features, but of course there is a reason—more flexibility! This is why OpenStack is here. It brings as much flexibility as it can! Without taking any random network-related decisions, let's see which network modes are available. We will keep on filtering until we hit the first correct target topology:

Network mode	Network specification	Implementation
Nova-network	Flat network design without VMs grouping or isolation	Nova-network FlatDHCP
	Multiple tenants and VMs Predefined fixed private IP space size	Nova-network VLANManager
Neutron	Multiple tenants and VMs Predefined switches and routers configuration	Neutron VLAN
	Increased tenants and VM groups Lower performance	Neutron GRE

The preceding table shows a simple differentiation between two different logical network designs for OpenStack. Every mode shows its own requirements, which is very important and should be taken into consideration before the deployment.

Arguing about our example choice, since we aim to deploy a very flexible large-scale environment, we will toggle the Neutron choice for networking management instead of the nova-network.

Note that it is also possible to keep on going with nova-network, but you have to worry about SPOF. Since the nova-network service can run on a single node (cloud controller) next to other network services such as DHCP and DNS, it is required in this case to implement your nova-network service in a multihost networking model, where cloning such a service in every compute node will save you from a bottleneck scenario. In addition, the choice was made for Neutron, since we started from a basic network deployment. We will cover more advanced features in the subsequent chapters of this book.

We would like to exploit a major advantage of Neutron compared to the nova-network, which is the virtualization of layers 2 and 3 of the OSI network model.

Remember that Neutron will enable us to support more subnets per private network segment. Based on Open vSwitch, you will discover that Neutron is becoming a vast network technology.

Let's see how we can expose our logical network design. For performance reasons, it is highly recommended to implement a topology that can handle different types of traffic by using separated logical networks.

In this way, as your network grows, it will still be manageable in case a sudden bottleneck or an unexpected failure affects a segment.

Network layout

Let us look at the different networks that are needed to operate the OpenStack environment.

The external network

The features of an external or a public network are as follows:

- Global connectivity
- It performs SNAT from the VM instances that run on the compute node to the Internet for floating IPs

SNAT refers to **Source Network Address Translation**. It allows traffic from a private network to go out to the Internet. OpenStack supports SNAT through its Neutron APIs for routers. More information can be found at http://en.wikipedia.org/wiki/Network_address_translation.

- It provides connection to the controller nodes in order to access the OpenStack interfaces

- It provides **virtual IPs (VIPs)** for public endpoints that are used to connect the OpenStack services APIs

> A VIP is an IP address that is shared among several servers. It involves a **one-to-many** mapping of the IP addresses. Its main purpose is to provide a redundancy for the attached servers and VIPs.

- It provides a connection to the external services that need to be public, such as an access to the Zabbix monitoring system

> While using VLANs, by tagging networks and combining multiple networks into one **Network Interface Card (NIC)**, you can optionally leave the public network untagged for that NIC to make the access to the OpenStack dashboard and the public OpenStack API endpoints simple.

The storage network

The main feature of a storage network is that it separates the storage traffic by means of a VLAN isolation.

The management network

An orchestrator node was not described previously since it is not a native OpenStack service. Different nodes need to get IP addresses, the DNS, and the DHCP service where the Orchestrator node comes into play. You should also keep in mind that in a large environment, you will need a node provisioning technique which your nodes will be configured to boot, by using PXE and TFTP.

Thus, the management network will act as an Orchestrator data network that provides the following:

- Administrative networking tasks
- OpenStack services communication
- Separate HA traffic

For a large-scale OpenStack environment, you can use a dedicated network for most of the critical internal OpenStack communication, such as the RabbitMQ messaging and the DB queries, by separating the messaging and database into separate cluster nodes.

The internal VM traffic

The features of the internal virtual machine network are as follows:

- Private network between virtual machines
- Nonroutable IPs
- Closed network between the virtual machines and the network L3 nodes, routing to the Internet, and the floating IPs backwards to the VMs

For the sake of simplicity, we will not go into the details of, for instance, the Neutron VLAN segmentation.

The next step is to validate our network design in a simple diagram:

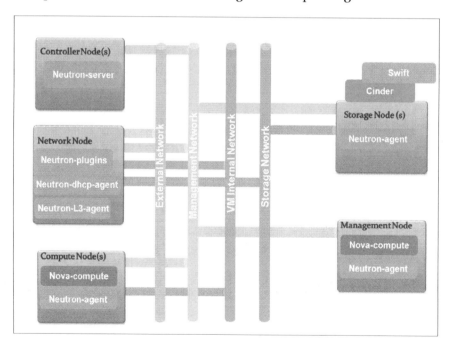

The physical model design

Finally, we will bring our logical design to life in the form of a physical design. At this stage, we need to assign parameters. The physical design encloses all the components that we dealt with previously in the logical design. Of course, you will appreciate how such an escalation in the design breaks down the complexity of the OpenStack environment and helps us distinguish between the types of hardware specifications that you will need.

We can start with a limited number of servers just to set the first deployment of our environment effectively. First, we will consider a small production environment that is highly scalable and extensible. This is what we have covered previously — expecting a sudden growth and being ready for an exponentially increasing number of requests to service instances.

You have to consider the fact that the hardware commodity selection will accomplish the mission of our *massive scalable architecture*.

Estimating your hardware capabilities

Since the architecture is being designed to scale horizontally, a commodity cost-effective hardware can be used.

In order to expect our infrastructure economy, it would be great to make some basic hardware calculations for the first estimation of our exact requirements.

Considering the possibility of experiencing contentions for resources such as CPU, RAM, network, and disk, you cannot wait for a particular physical component to fail before you take corrective action, which might be more complicated.

Let's inspect a real-life example of the impact of underestimating capacity planning. A Cloud-hosting company set up two medium servers, one for an e-mail server, and the other to host the official website. The company, which is one of our several clients, grew in a few months and eventually, we ran out of disk space. We expected such an issue to get resolved in a few hours, but it took days. The problem was that all the parties did not make proper use of the "cloud", which points to the "on demand" way. The issue had been serious for both the parties. The e-mail server, which is one of the most critical aspects of a company, had been overloaded and the **Mean Time To Repair (MTTR)** was increasing exponentially. The Cloud provider did not expect this!

Well, it might be ridiculous to write down your SLA report and describe in your incident management section the reason — we did not expect such growth! Later, after redeploying the virtual machine with more disk space, the e-mail server would irritate everyone in the company with a message saying, "We can authenticate but our e-mails are not being sent! They are queued!" The other guy claimed, "Finally, I have sent an e-mail 2 hours ago and I got a phone call that is received." Unfortunately, the cloud paradigm was designed to avoid such scenarios and bring more success factors that can be achieved by hosting providers. Capacity management is considered a day-to-day responsibility where you have to stay updated with regard to software or hardware upgrades.

Through a continuous monitoring process of service consumption, you will be able to reduce the IT risk and provide a quick response to the customer's needs.

From your first hardware deployment, keep running your capacity management processes by looping through tuning, monitoring, and analysis.

The next stop will take into account your tuned parameters and introduce within your hardware/software the right change, which involves a synergy of the change management process.

Let's make our first calculation based on certain requirements. We aim to run 200 VMs in our OpenStack environment.

CPU calculations

The following are the calculation-related assumptions:

- 200 virtual machines
- No CPU oversubscribing

 Processor oversubscription is defined as the total number of CPUs that are assigned to all the powered-on virtual machines multiplied by the hardware CPU core. If this number is greater than the GHz purchased, the environment is said to be oversubscribed.

- Number of GHz per core: 2.6 GHz
- Hyper-threading supported: use factor 2
- Number of GHz per VM (AVG compute units) = 2 GHz
- Number of GHz per VM (MAX compute units) = 16 GHz
- Intel Xeon E5-2648L v2 core CPU = 10
- CPU sockets per server = 2

- Number of CPU cores per virtual machine:

    *16 / (2.6 * 2) = 3.076*

We need to assign at least 3 CPU cores per VM.

The formula for its calculation will be as follows: *max GHz /(number of GHz per core x 1.3 for hyper-threading)*

 If your CPU does not support hyper-threading, you should multiply the number of GHz per core by 1.3 factors instead of 2.

- Total number of CPU cores:

    *(200 * 2) / 2.6 = 153.846*

We have 153 CPU cores for 200 VMs.

The formula for calculation will be as follows:

    (number of VMs x number of GHz per VM) / number of GHz per core

- Number of core CPU sockets:

    153 / 10 = 15.3

We will need 15 sockets.

The formula for calculation will be as follows:

    Total number of sockets / number of sockets per server

- Number of socket servers:

    15 / 2 = 7.5

You will need around 7 to 8 dual socket servers.

The formula for calculation will be as follows:

    Total number of sockets / Number of sockets per server

- The number of virtual machines per server with 8 dual socket servers will be calculated as follows:

    200 / 8 = 25

The formula for calculation will be as follows:

    Number of virtual machines / number of servers

We can deploy 25 virtual machines per server.

Memory calculations

Based on the previous example, 25 VMs can be deployed per compute node. Memory sizing is also important to avoid making unreasonable resource allocations.

Let's make an assumption list:

- 2 GB RAM per VM
- 8 GB RAM maximum dynamic allocation per VM
- Compute nodes supporting slots of: 2, 4, 8, and 16 GB sticks

  Keep in mind that it always depends on your budget and needs

- RAM available per compute node:

  8 * 25 = 200 GB

Considering the number of sticks supported by your server, you will need around 256 GB installed. Therefore, the total number of RAM sticks installed can be calculated in the following way:

256 / 16 = 16

The formula for calculation is as follows:

Total available RAM / MAX Available RAM-Stick size

The network calculations

To fulfill the plans that were drawn for the network previously, we need to achieve the best performance and networking experience. Let's have a look at our assumptions:

- 200 Mbits/second is needed per VM
- Minimum network latency

To do this, it might be possible to serve our VMs by using a 10 GB link for each server, which will give:

10000 Mbits/second / 25 VMs = 400 Mbits/second

This is a very satisfying value. We need to consider another factor—highly available network architecture. Thus, an alternative is using two data switches with a minimum of 24 ports for data.

Thinking about growth from now, two 48-port switches will be in place.

What about the growth of the rack size? In this case, you should think about the example of switch aggregation that uses the **Virtual Link Trunking (VLT)** technology between the switches in the aggregation. This feature allows each server rack to divide their links between the pair of switches to achieve a powerful active-active forwarding while using the full bandwidth capability with no requirement for a spanning tree.

 VLT is a layer 2 link aggregation protocol between the servers that are connected to the switches, offering a redundant, load-balancing connection to the core network and replacing the spanning-tree protocol.

Storage calculations

Considering the previous example, you need to plan for an initial storage capacity per server that will serve 25 VMs each.

Let's make the following assumptions:

- The usage of ephemeral storage for a local drive for the VM
- 100 GB for storage for each VM's drive
- The usage of persistent storage for remote attaching volumes to VMs

A simple calculation we provide for 200 VMs a space of $200*100 = 20\ TB$ of local storage.

You can assign 250 GB of persistent storage per VM to have $200*200 = 40\ TB$ of persistent storage.

Therefore, we can conclude how much storage should be installed by the server serving 20 VMs $150*25 = 3.5\ TB$ of storage on the server.

If you plan to include object storage as we mentioned earlier, we can assume that we will need 25 TB of object storage.

Most probably, you have an idea about the replication of object storage in OpenStack, which implies the usage of three times the required space for replication.

In other words, you should consider that the planning of X TB for object storage will be multiplied by three automatically based on our assumption; $25*3 = 75\ TB$.

Also, if you consider an object storage based on zoning, you will have to accommodate at least five times the needed space. This means; $25*5 = 125\ TB$.

Other considerations, such as the best storage performance using SSD, can be useful for a better throughput where you can invest more boxes to get an increased IOPS.

For example, working with SSD with 20K IOPS installed in a server with eight slot drives will bring you:

(20K * 8) / 25 = 6.4 K Read IOPS and 3.2K Write IOPS

That is not bad for a production starter!

Best practices

What about best practices? Is it just a theory? Does anyone adhere to such formulas? Well, let's bring some best practices under the microscope by exposing the OpenStack design flavor.

In a typical OpenStack production environment, the minimum requirement for disk space per compute node is 300 GB with a minimum RAM of 128 GB and a dual 8-core CPUs.

Let's imagine a scenario where, due to budget limitations, you start your first compute node with costly hardware that has a 600 GB disk space, 16-core CPUs, and 256 GB of RAM.

Assuming that your OpenStack environment continues to grow, you may decide to purchase more hardware—a big one at an incredible price! A second compute instance is placed to scale up.

Shortly after this, you may find out that the demand is increasing. You may start splitting requests into different compute nodes but keep on continuing scaling up with the hardware. At some point, you will be alerted to reaching your budget limit!

There are certainly times when the best practices aren't in fact the best for your design. The previous example illustrated a commonly overlooked requirement for the OpenStack deployment.

If the minimal hardware requirement is strictly followed, it may result in an exponential cost with regard to the hardware expenses, especially for new project starters.

Thus, you may choose what exactly works for you and consider the constraints that exist in your environment.

Keep in mind that the best practices are a *user manual* or a guideline; apply them when you find what you need to be deployed and how it should be set up.

On the other hand, do not stick to values, but stick to rules. Let's bring the previous example under the microscope again—scaling up shows more risk that may lead to failure than scaling out or horizontally. The reason behind such a design is to allow for a fast scale of transactions at the cost of a duplicated compute functionality and smaller systems at a lower cost.

Transactions and requests in the compute node may grow tremendously in a short time to a point that a single *big* compute node with 16 core CPUs starts failing performance wise, while a few *small* compute nodes with 4 core CPUs can proceed to complete the job successfully.

Summary

In this chapter, we learned about the design characteristics of OpenStack and the core components of such an ecosystem. We have also highlighted the design considerations around OpenStack and discussed the different possibilities of extending its functionalities. Now, we have a good starting point for the purpose of bringing the other incubated projects into production. You may notice that our first basic design covers most of the critical issues that one can face during the production. In addition, it is important to note that this first chapter might be considered as a main guideline for the next parts of this book. The next chapters will treat each concept and technology solution cited in this chapter in more detail by expanding the first basic design. Thus, the next chapter will take you from this generic architecture overview theory to a practical stage. Basically, you will learn how to deploy and expand what was designed by adopting an efficient infrastructure deployment approach—the *DevOps* style.

2
Deploying OpenStack – DevOps and OpenStack Dual Deal

"Besides black art, there is only automation and mechanization."

– Federico Garcia Lorca

Deploying an OpenStack environment based on the profiled design, as shown in the previous chapter, is not simple. Although we created our design by taking care of several aspects related to scalability and performance, we still have to make it real. If you are still looking at OpenStack as a single block system, you should take a step back and recheck what was explained in *Chapter 1, Designing OpenStack Cloud Architecture*.

Furthermore, in the introductory section of this book, we covered the role of OpenStack in the next generation of datacenters. The infrastructure has now become programmable through APIs. However, a large-scale infrastructure used by cloud providers needs a very different approach in order to set it up with a few thousand servers.

In our case, deploying and operating the OpenStack Cloud is not as simple as you might think. Thus, you need some *fun*. You need to make any operational task easier or, in other words, **automated**.

In this chapter, we will cover new topics about the ways to deploy OpenStack and start an excursion of the production day from which you will gain new best practices. The next part will cover the following points:

- Learning what the DevOps movement is and how it can be adopted in the cloud

- Knowing how to see your infrastructure as code and how to maintain it

- Getting closer to the DevOps way by including configuration management aspects in your cloud

- Making your OpenStack environment design deployable via automation

- Discovering and starting your first test deployment using Chef

DevOps in a nutshell

The term DevOps is a conjunction of development (software developers) and operations (manage and put software into production). Many IT organizations have started to adopt such a *concept*, but the question is how and what? Is it a job? Is it a process or a part of ITIL best practices?

DevOps is a *development and operations compound*, which basically defines a methodology of software development. It describes practices that streamline the software delivery process. This is not all. In fact, it is more about raising communication and integration between developments, operators (including administrators), and quality assurance. The essence of the DevOps movement is in the benefits of collaboration. Different disciplines can relate to DevOps and bring their experiences and skills together under the DevOps label to build a cover of **shared values**.

So, we agree that this is a methodology that puts several disciplines on the same wave length as shown in the following figure:

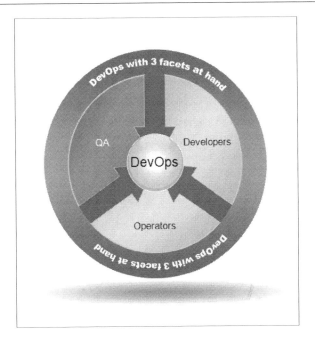

This new movement is intended to resolve the conflict between developers and operators. Delivering a new release affects the production systems that put different teams in a change conflict. DevOps fills the gap and optimizes each side focus.

 DevOps is neither a toolkit nor a job; it is the role of synergy.

Let's see how DevOps can incubate a cloud project.

DevOps and cloud – everyone is coding

Let's bring down the cloud architecture's layers under the scope and see what we have. Basically, we have **Software as a Service (SaaS)**, which operates at all layers of the IT stack. Then comes **Platform as a Service (PaaS)**, where databases and application containers are delivered on demand to reach the bottom, where we find **Infrastructure as a Service (IaaS)** delivering on-demand resources, such as virtual machines, networks, and storage. All these layers form complete, basic stacks of the cloud. You should think about how each layer of the cloud should be developed and implemented.

Obviously, layered dependency relies on the ability to create full stacks and deliver them under a request of simple steps. Remember that we are talking about a large scalable environment! The amazing switch to bigger environments nowadays is to simplify everything as much as possible. System architecture and software design are becoming more and more complicated. Every new release of software affords new functions and new configurations. Then, you are asked to integrate the new software in a particular platform where somehow, sufficient documentation about requirements or troubleshooting is missing! You may ask yourself questions such as: Did something change? What kind of change? To which person should we assign a ticket to fix it? What if it just does not work? According to your operational team, the software needs to be updated often in order to apply the new functions. The update might happen every time you get that e-mail asking you to update the software. You may start to wonder whether your operational team will be happy about this announcement, contrary to the software provider who sent the e-mail with the header; "we are happy to announce the release of the new version of our software; please push the button."

Let's take a serious example that crystallizes this situation. A company's operational team was extremely happy about purchasing a new storage appliance that worked well on redundancy. During the first few months, everyone was happy; nothing was broken! It worked like a charm!

When the day came to change the charm to a true headache, the storage system failed to fail over. Both nodes stopped working. No one could access any data! In spite of the existence of a backup somewhere else, the operational team did not like the "was that highly available?" part. After a long night of investigation, the error of causing the HA to fail was concluded from the log files: there was an appliance system update! The previous version was somehow automatically updated and broke the HA function in the active node. The update was propagated to the passive one. Unfortunately, the active version decided to fail over and tackle the cluster that was passive. However, that did not work. It was as if there was a bug somewhere in the code of the previous release!

What about if you are running similar solutions for other systems? Everything is running software to keep it running! In this case, it is wise to stop for a while and ask yourself questions such as this: What is missing? Shall I hire more people for system maintenance and troubleshooting? Obviously, if you take a look at the previous example, you will probably notice that the *owner* of the hardware does not really own it!

The simple reason is that being dependent on external parties will affect your infrastructure efficiency. Well, you may ask a pertinent question: Shall I rewrite the software appliance by myself? Let's reformulate the question: Shall I write the code? The answer, almost always, is yes! It is an ambiguous answer, right? Let's keep using examples in order to clear out this fogginess. We talked about DevOps, the synergetic point between developers and operational guys. Everything is communicated between them thanks to the magic of DevOps. Remember that it is our goal to simplify things as much as possible! Administrating and deploying a large infrastructure would not be possible without adopting a new philosophy: **Infrastructure as code**. At this point, we bring in another aspect of the DevOps style: we see our machines as pieces of code! In fact, we have now assigned the main tasks of DevOps.

Where everything will be seen as code, it might be possible to model a given infrastructure as modules of code. What you need to do is just abstract, design, implement, and deploy the infrastructure.

Furthermore, in such a paradigm, it will be essential to adhere to the same discipline as an infrastructure developer as compared to a software developer.

Without doubt, these terms are quite misty at the first glance. For this reason, you should ask this question related to our main topic about OpenStack: if infrastructure as code is so important for a well-organized infrastructure deployment, what is the case with OpenStack? The answer to this question is relatively simple: developers, network, and compute engineers and operators are working alongside each other to develop OpenStack Cloud that will run our next generation data center. This is the DevOps spirit.

DevOpsing OpenStack

OpenStack is an open source project, and its code is extended, modified, and fixed in every release. Of course, it is not your primary mission to check the code and dive into its different modules and functions. This is not our goal! What can we do with DevOps, then? Eventually, we will "DevOps" the code that makes the code run! As you might have noticed, a key measure of the success of a DevOps story is automation. Everything in a given infrastructure must be automated!

Breaking down the OpenStack pieces

Let's gather what we covered previously and signal a few steps towards our first OpenStack deployment:

- Break down the OpenStack infrastructure into independent and reusable services
- Integrate the services in such a way that you can provide the expected functionalities in the OpenStack environment.

It is obvious that OpenStack includes many services, as discussed in *Chapter 1, Designing OpenStack Cloud Architecture*. What we need to do is see these services as packages of code in our "infrastructure as code" experience. The next step will investigate how to integrate the services and deploy them via automation.

Starting to deploy the services that are seen as code is similar to writing a web application or some software. Here are important points you should not ignore during the entire deployment process:

- Simplify and modularize the OpenStack services
- Integrate OpenStack services to use other services
- Compose OpenStack services as building blocks by accomplishing a complete integration between systems
- Facilitate the modification and improvement of services when demanded
- Use the right tool to build the services
- Be sure that the services provide the same results with the same inputs
- Switch your service vision from how to do it to what we want to do
- Details comes later; focus on the function of the service first

As an infrastructure developer, you will start building and running the entire infrastructure on which all systems, either being tested or in production in a system management platform, are operating.

In fact, many system-management tools are intensely used nowadays due to their efficiency of deployment. In other words, there is need for automation!

You have probably used some of the automation tools, such as Chef, Puppet, Salt, Ansible, and many more. Before we go through them, we need to create a succinct, professional code-management step.

Making the infrastructure deployment professional

Ultimately, the code that abstracts, models, and builds the OpenStack infrastructure is committed to source code management. Most likely, we reach a point where we shift our OpenStack infrastructure from a code base to a redeployable one by following the latest software development best practices.

At this stage, you should be aware of the quality of your OpenStack infrastructure deployment, which roughly depends on the quality of the code that describes it.

Maintaining the code needs more attention in order to have a bug-free environment when it is delivered as a final release. We will consider the "bug" term in an infrastructure development context as harmful and functional to the system.

It is important to highlight a critical point that you should keep in mind during all deployment stages: automated systems are not able to understand human error when it is propagated to all pieces of your infrastructure. This is essential, and there is no way to ignore it. The same way is applicable to traditional software development discipline. You'll have to go through an ensemble of phases and cycles using agile methodologies to end up with a final release that is a *normally* bug-free software version in production.

Remember the example given previously? Surprises do happen! However, if an error occurs in a small corner of a specific system and needs to be fixed in that specific independent system, it might not be the same when considering the automation of a large infrastructure.

On the other hand, if mistakes cannot be totally eradicated at the first stage, you should think about introducing more flexibility into your systems by allowing wise changes without exaggeration. The code's life management is shown in the following figure:

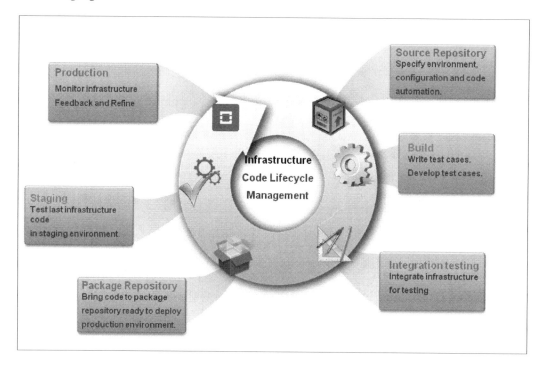

Changes can be scary — very scary indeed! To handle changes, it is recommended that you:

- Keep track and monitor the changes at every stage
- Flex the code and make it easy to change
- Refactor when it becomes difficult to change
- Test, test, and test

Keep checking every point that has been described previously till you start to get more confident that your OpenStack infrastructure is being conducted by code that won't break.

Bringing OpenStack to the chain

To keep the OpenStack environment working with a minimum rate of surprises, ensure that its infrastructure code delivers the functionalities that are required.

Beyond these considerations, we will put the OpenStack deployment in a toolchain, where it will inform you about how we will conduct the infrastructure development from the test stage to the production stage. Underpinning every tool selection must be the purpose of your testing endeavors, and it will also help you ensure that you build the right thing.

Continuous integration and delivery

Let's see how continuous integration can be applied to OpenStack. Whatever we use for system management tools or automation code will be kept as a standard and basic topology, as shown in the next model, where the following requirements are met:

- **SMTA** can be any **System Management Tool Artifact**, such as Chef cookbook, Puppet manifest, Ansible playbook, or juju charms.

- **VCS** or **Version Control System** stores the previous artifacts that are built continuously with a continuous integration server. **Git** can be a good outfit for our VCS. Alternatively, you can use other systems, such as CVS, Subversion, Bazaar, or any other system that you are most familiar with.

- **Jenkins** is a perfect tool that listens to changes in version control and makes the continuous integration testing automated in production clones for test purposes.

Take a look at the model:

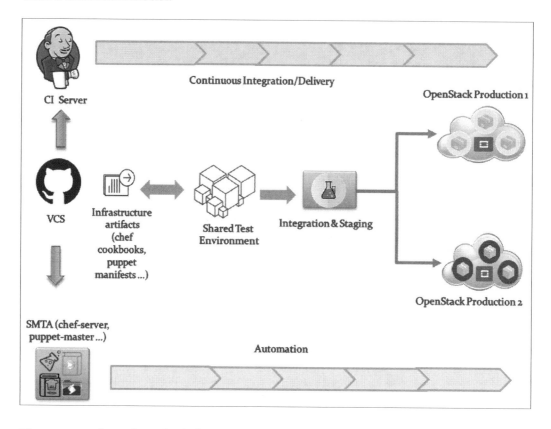

The proposed topology for infrastructure as code consists of infrastructure configuration files (Chef cookbooks, Puppet artifacts, and Vagrant files) that are recorded in a version control system and are built continuously by the means of a **continuous integration** (CI) server (Jenkins, in our case). Infrastructure configuration files can be used to set up a unit test environment (a virtual environment using Vagrant, for example) and makes use of any system-management tool to provision the infrastructure (Chef, Puppet, and so on). The CI server keeps listening to changes in version control and automatically propagates any new versions to be tested, and then it listens to target environments in production.

 Vagrant allows you to build a virtual environment very easily; it is based on Oracle VirtualBox (https://www.virtualbox.org/) to run virtual machines, so you will need these before moving on with the installation in your test environment.

Using such model designs could make our development and integration code infrastructure more valuable. Obviously, the previous OpenStack toolchain highlights the test environment before moving on to production, which is normal! However, you should give a lot of importance to, and care a good deal about, the testing stage, although this might be a very time-consuming task.

Especially in our case, with infrastructure code within OpenStack, things can be difficult for complicated and dependent systems. This makes it imperative to ensure an automated and consistent testing of the infrastructure code.

The best way to do this is to keep testing thoroughly in a repeated way till you gain confidence about your code. When you do, introducing changes to your code when it's needed shouldn't be an issue.

Let's keep on going, get the perfect tool running, and push the button.

Eat the elephant

At first sight, you may wonder what is the best automation tool that will be useful for our OpenStack "production day". We have already chosen Git and Jenkins to handle our continuous and delivery code infrastructure. It is time to choose the right tool for automation.

Eventually, it might be difficult to select the right tool. Most likely, you'll have to choose between several of them. Covering all the existing IT automation tools could fill an entire book or even books. Therefore, giving succinct hints on different tools might be helpful in order to distinguish the best outfit for certain particular setups. Of course, we are still talking about large infrastructures with heterogeneous systems, a lot of networking, and distributed services.

Giving the chance for one or more tools to be selected as system management parties can be effective and fast for our deployment. We will use Chef for the next deployment phase.

Preparing the infrastructure code environment

If you are not familiar with the Git command line, do not worry, because we will use an integrated development environment (such as Eclipse), which provides a great Git plugin.

Later, we will need to write and maintain code written in the Ruby programming language. Chef cookbooks are written in Ruby. Feel free to use your best development environment that supports and simplifies code branching and maintenance within your VCS. There are plenty of preferences for development environments and Ruby code editors, such as RubyMine (`https://www.jetbrains.com/ruby/`) and Komodo (`http://komodoide.com/`). The Netbeans IDE also comes up with a Ruby plugin (`http://plugins.netbeans.org/plugin/38549/ruby-and-rails`) and the Sublime text editor (`http://www.sublimetext.com/`) can be a good candidate for a lightweight text editor for code.

Feel free to use any Linux distribution. The next setup will use CentOS 6.5 64 bit as the standard operating system.

Ensure that Java and its dependencies are installed:

```
packtpub@dev$ sudo yum install java
packtpub@dev$ sudo yum install gcc-c++
```

You can download Eclipse for CentOS from here:

```
packtpub@dev$ wget http://mirror.netcologne.de/eclipse/technology/
epp/downloads/ release/juno/SR2/eclipse-automotive-juno-SR2-
incubation-linux-gtk-x86_64.tar.gz
```

Extract the Eclipse to the /opt directory:

```
packtpub@dev$ sudo tar -xvzf eclipse-automotive-juno-SR2-incubation-
linux-gtk-x86_64.tar.gz -C /opt/
```

Create a symlink:

```
packtpub@dev$ sudo ln -s /opt/eclipse/eclipse /usr/bin/eclipse
```

To install Ruby, you need to go from the Eclipse menu bar and navigate to **Help | Install New Software**. From the pending list, navigate to **Program Languages | Dynamic Languages Toolkit - Ruby Development Tools**:

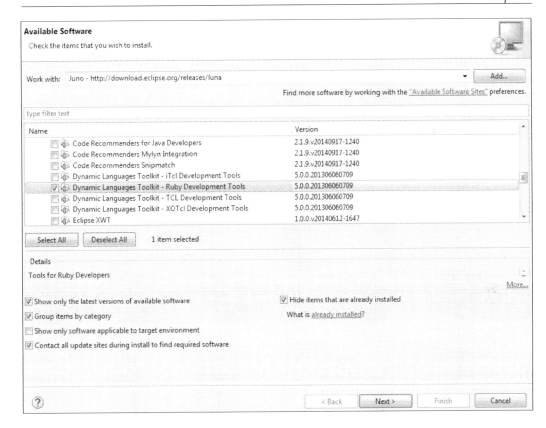

Install Git:

```
packtpub@dev$ sudo yum install git
```

Check the correctness of the Git installation:

```
packtpub@chef$ git --version
```

Bring the magic EGit plugin into the action link in order to develop with Git in Eclipse. We do this in the same way from the Eclipse update manager by navigating to the **Help | Install new Software** menu entry. You will need to add the following URL installation to EGit:

```
http://download.eclipse.org/egit/updates
```

You will then see the following screen:

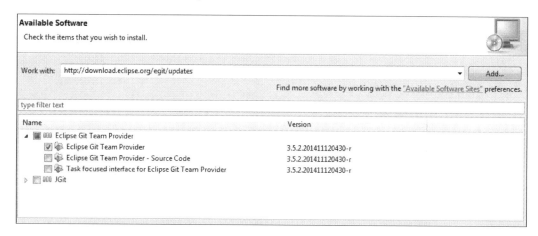

If you are not familiar with Chef, the following section will cover the basic setup and the most important parts of a Chef server, and you can see how it looks.

> If you do not have the Ruby plugin installed in your Eclipse environment by default, you can download and install it from SourceForge at
> `http://sourceforge.net/projects/rubyeclipse/files/`
> `rdt/0.8.0/org.rubypeople.rdt-0.8.0.604272100PRD.zip/`
> `download?use_mirror=freefr&download=.`

The Chef environment

When you think about a typical chef, you may think of cookbooks, recipes, and knives! These are what a chef needs in order to make awesome dishes. The taste of the food on a plate depends on the creativity of the chef. We do the same thing in terms of cooking: we use a basic cookbook, from which we derive the right recipes. We refine the recipes till we get what fulfills our needs.

Let's see how Chef defines its awesomeness:

- **Cookbook**: The grained unit of the configuration in Chef describes the kind of scenario that is there, and how it should be defined in order to deploy an application in a node.
- **Recipe**: This is the part of a cookbook that is authored in Ruby and defines the configuration of the nodes. Note that a recipe can use or be used by another recipe.

- **Node**: This is where we can apply the cookbook configurations.

- **Role**: This can be considered as a logical function for a node. It can be customized within a collection of recipes and cookbooks, in a particular order.

- **Attribute files**: The attributes are very important in order to change the settings of the nodes.

You should take into consideration the precedence level of the attributes that define what should be applied. Basically, the evaluation of such attributes against the node object will be done during each Chef run.

Keep the previous terms in your mind, but do not be surprised when you start to find much more than these terms during our deployment. We will cover them in a nutshell.

To read more about Chef, you can refer to the official Opscode website: https://docs.chef.io/.

Prerequisites for settings

Before installing the server, we need to set up the right hostname of our CentOS box, where we can define it as an FQDN with a domain suffix:

1. Open the /etc/sysconfig/network file and modify the HOSTNAME value to match your FQDN hostname:

   ```
   packtpub@chef$ sudo nano /etc/sysconfig/network
   HOSTNAME=chef.packtpub.com
   ```

2. Change the host that is associated to your IP address for your server found in the /etc/hosts file, as follows:

   ```
   packtpub@chef$ sudo nano /etc/hosts
   192.168.47.10    chef.packtpub.com    chef
   ```

3. Check your hostname via the following command:

   ```
   packtpub@chef$ hostname -f
   chef.packtpub.com
   ```

4. Make sure that your changes are persistent on reboot:

   ```
   packtpub@chef$ sudo /etc/init.d/network restart
   ```

You will need to adjust the settings, such as the hostname, FQDN, and IP address, to suit your needs.

5. As we are using CentOS, it will be much easier for a smooth installation process in order to modify iptables and SELinux. Note that it is not recommended that you entirely disable the `iptables` service in a production environment where you will have to create extra iptables rules and update your SELinux as well. We will need to allow access to the following ports:

   ° **TCP ports**: `80, 443` for the Chef server web user interface
   ° **TCP port**: `4000` for the Chef server Knife access

   The following commands will update the running iptables rules in your CentOS box:

```
packtpub@chef$ sudo iptables -A INPUT -p tcp --dport 80 -m state
--state NEW,ESTABLISHED -j ACCEPT
packtpub@chef$ sudo iptables -A INPUT -p tcp --dport 443 -m state
--state NEW,ESTABLISHED -j ACCEPT
packtpub@chef$ sudo iptables -A INPUT -p tcp --dport 4000 -m state
--state NEW,ESTABLISHED -j ACCEPT
```

6. Save the new policy update and restart the `iptables` service:

```
packtpub@chef$ sudo service iptables save
packtpub@chef$ sudo service iptables restart
```

7. Set SELinux to the permissive mode:

```
packtpub@chef$ sudo setenforce 0
```

The Chef server installation

The next setup describes some simple steps to install the Chef server:

1. In your local shell, run the following command to download the Chef server:

```
packtpub@chef$ sudo rpm -ivh https://opscode-omnibus
packages.s3.amazonaws.com/el/6/x86_64/chef-server-11.0.8-
1.el6.x86_64.rpm
```

2. Configure the Chef server:

```
packtpub@chef$ sudo chef-server-ctl reconfigure
```

3. Check whether the installation was successful or not:

```
packtpub@chef$ sudo chef-server-ctl test
Finished in 0.11742 seconds
0 examples, 0 failures
```

4. The server should be up and running. You can access the web interface via `https://chef.packtpub.com:443`:

 The Chef server user interface can be accessed using the FQDN edited previously: `https://FQDN:443`. You can use `https://CHEF_IP_ADDR:443`, where `CHEF_IP_ADDR` is the local IP address of your Chef server.

Enter admin as the username and p@ssw0d1 as the default password.

Workstation installation

We will need additionally one or more Chef workstation(s) as a development toolkit. This node's role is as follows:

- The Chef client is installed and Knife is configured
- It holds the local repository for the Chef server
- It installs Chef on the nodes via the knife bootstrap operation
- It dictates nodes, roles, and infrastructure environments to be uploaded to the Chef server

Our Chef workstation will hold the local repo, and then we can install it on our VCS node, where all the development will be performed and then uploaded to the Chef server.

 Knife in Chef refers to a tool which provides a **Command-Line Interface (CLI)** between a Chef server and the Chef repository. It can be installed in a Chef workstation and used to manage nodes, roles, cookbooks, and environments with the Chef server. To read more about Knife in Chef, refer to this link https://docs.chef.io/knife.html.

Let's install our Chef workstation:

1. Get the Chef client installed:

    ```
    packtpub@workstation$ curl -L https://www.opscode.com/chef/
    install.sh | bash
    ```

2. Verify the installation:

    ```
    packtpub@workstation$ chef-client -v
    ```

3. Create your chef-repos for a proper format of the Chef repository from GitHub by cloning the structure in /home/packtpub/:

    ```
    packtpub@workstation$ git clone https://github.com/ opscode/chef-
    repo.git
    ```

    ```
    packtpub@workstation$ cd /home/packtpub
    ```

    ```
    packtpub@workstation$ mkdir -p /chef-repo/.chef
    ```

    In order to authenticate against the Chef server, we will need to add some inputs for the key files from the Chef server web interface. Go to the **Clients** tab and click on **Edit** with the **chef-validator** client.

4. Copy the value of the **Private key** field. In your workstation, create a new file for the validator key:

```
packtpub@workstation$ vi /home/packtpub/chef-repo/.chef/chef-
validator.pem
```

5. Paste the content of the copied key and save and close the file.

We perform the same procedure to generate the admin user's key file. In the **Users** tab, click on **Edit**, which is associated with the admin user, and check **Regenerate Private Key** followed by **Save User**.

After copying the private key, create a new file `admin.pem` in `/home/packtpub/ chef-repo/.chef/` again and paste the content of the admin's private key:

1. Create the Knife configuration file:

```
packtpub@workstation$ knife configure -i


Overwrite /root/.chef/knife.rb? (Y/N) y

Please enter the chef server URL: [https://test.example.com:443]

https://chef-server.packtpub.com:443/

Please enter a name for the new user: [root] packtpub

Please enter the existing admin name: [admin]   Enter

Please enter the location of the existing admin's private key: [/
etc/chefserver/admin.pem] /home/packtpub/chef-repo/.chef/admin.pem

Please enter the validation clientname: [chef-validator]

Please enter the location of the validation key: [/etc/chef-
server/chef-validator.pem] /home/packtpub/chef-repo/.chef/chef-
validator.pem

Please enter the path to a chef repository (or leave blank):

Creating initial API user...

Please enter a password for the new user

Created user [pack-knife]

Configuration file written to /home/packtpub/chef-repo/.chef/
knife.rb
```

At the end, you should have the following list of files:

```
packtpub@workstation$  ls  /home/packtpub/chef-repo/.chef/

admin.pem chef-validator.pem knife.rb pack-knife.pem
```

2. Initialize our Git name and e-mail:

```
packtpub@workstation$ git config --global user.email
"masteropenstack@packtpub.com"

packtpub@workstation$ git config --global user.name
"masteropenstack"
```

3. Clean up the repository by adding the .chef line to .gitignore:

```
packtpub@workstation$ nano /home/packtpub/chef repo/.chef/.
gitignore
```

```
.rake_test_cache
.chef/*.pem
.chef/encrypted_data_bag_secret
.chef
```

4. Add and commit the current repository:

```
packtpub@workstation$ git add .

packtpub@workstation$ git commit -m 'Finish setting up'
```

5. Make sure that you are using the right Ruby version:

```
packtpub@workstation$ vi .bash_profile

packtpub@workstation$ echo 'export
PATH="/opt/chef/embedded/bin:$PATH"' >> ~/.bash_profile
```

6. Populate the bash profile settings:

```
packtpub@workstation$ source ~/.bash_profile
```

7. Test our workstation's Chef server connection:

```
packtpub@workstation$ knife user list
admin
packt-knife
```

Time to cook OpenStack

At this stage, we have a complete Chef environment where the OpenStack code infrastructure will be developed, refined, and released to production.

Let's take a look at the environment topology again. We need nodes and instances to test how our cookbooks will be applied and tested.

For this purpose, we will use a great tool for testing purposes: **Vagrant**.

Vagrant is open source software used to build virtualized development environments. Vagrant requires virtual machines to test Chef Cookbooks before going to production. VirtualBox is a good candidate which works together with Vagrant to provide a complete test environment. For more information on Vagrant, refer to the following link `https://docs.vagrantup.com/v2/getting-started/`.

Vagrant can be integrated with Chef. Then, from a Vagrant file, we push the button to make Chef run and get instances up, which makes it the cat's meow.

Where is my kitchen?

Be aware that Vagrant will be used for test purposes. This amazing tool will help you make sure you know how your OpenStack Chef cookbooks work.

This is a suitable test for the virtual machine manager candidate to achieve a clean state from your nodes. Furthermore, it might be possible to reproduce a whole test environment in each Chef run, which creates an initial state that mimics a production environment.

You can manage VMs by means of Vagrant using VirtualBox while using a Chef client as a provisioner. Then, we have our test development environment: **the OpenStack kitchen**. We will describe the use case of Vagrant later in this chapter.

OpenStack cookbooks

There are always challenges facing DevOps, and no doubt, they will occur after you have conducted your design to be deployed in a real environment. Meeting these challenges will drive you to acquire new skills related to creating a large complicated OpenStack infrastructure with simple code that you never thought you could master.

Several organizations and big companies have been involved in writing cookbooks for OpenStack in different ways. You might be tempted to think how you can use the existing cookbooks in the cookbook market as well as which ones to choose and how to develop them for your own needs.

Let's discuss what we need with the help of a simple, generic overview:

- Controller nodes
- Compute nodes
- Neutron nodes
- Swift as a single cluster

You may note that the controller node, as described in our first design, handles and runs the majority of native OpenStack services. You can derive many recipes from OpenStack cookbooks in GitHub. The Opscode community is also an option. We will base our first cookbooks on StackForge cookbooks. However, before that, we should take care of the cookbook dependencies for a clean setup.

StackForge aims to facilitate the usage of the OpenStack infrastructure by other projects, including continuous integration (Jenkins) and repository mirroring (GitHub). More information on the StackForge project can be found at `http://ci.openstack.org/stackforge.html`.

Individual cookbooks for each OpenStack service have been created in the StackForge GitHub repository, which can be found at `https://github.com/stackforge`. The cookbooks used by Chef from the StackForge repository are listed and described at `https://docs.chef.io/openstack_cookbooks.html`.

Resolving OpenStack cookbook dependencies

Without any doubt, the world of dependency is a world of pain! This is when you plan to install a cookbook that another one depends on it. Manual downloading for each one might depend on other cookbooks.

A trick for manual downloading can be to use the `knife cookbook site install` command, which is somehow great as it installs all the dependencies. However, the dependencies will be installed in your local repository, and you might not like to see them flapping in your directory. You will be delighted when you find out that there is a tool that can do this for you: **Berkshelf**.

This amazing cookbook manager downloads all dependencies recursively while keeping your local repository clean. Dependencies will be stored in a different location.

Berkshelf uses **Berksfile**, in which we commit our dependencies to our repository.

The first successful step to make this tool do the magic, is to ensure a proper installation. Somehow, Ruby versioning can be confusing if you have already installed Chef server or Chef workstation within Ruby version 1.8.7. It is recommended that you upgrade or switch to 1.9.1 or higher. Note that Berkshelf requires Ruby version 1.9.1 or higher.

If you already have 1.8.7, no worries; we will perform a trick without diving into Ruby setup errors.

We can use **Ruby Version Manager** (**rvm**) to switch between Ruby versions.

 Ruby is a very popular programming language that is used by Chef to write cookbooks. Different versions of Ruby may be necessary for different projects. Installing and running other Ruby gems (RubyGems) might require different Ruby versions. Using the rvm will allow you to easily install multiple, contained versions of Ruby and switch between them. For more information on rvm, refer to this link: `https://rvm.io/rvm/basics`.

1. Install rvm:

    ```
    packtpub@workstation$ curl -L get.rvm.io | bash -s stable fails
    ```

 If you get an error issued you will need to specify the gpg2 key. You will need to run a similar command line from the output shown in the curl command as follows: `gpg2 --keyserver hkp://keys.gnupg.net --recv-keys D39DC0E3`.

2. Source the rvm variables:

    ```
    packtpub@workstation$ source /etc/profile.d/rvm.sh
    ```

3. Install Ruby 1.9.2:

    ```
    packtpub@workstation$  rvm install 1.9.2
    ```

4. Set it as the default Ruby interpreter:

    ```
    packtpub@workstation$  rvm --default use 1.9.2
    ```

5. Install gem dependencies:

    ```
    packtpub@workstation$  sudo yum install rubygems
    ```

6. Install Berkshelf dependencies:

    ```
    packtpub@workstation$  sudo yum install gecode-devel gcc-c++  -y
    ```

7. Install Berkshelf :

    ```
    packtpub@workstation$  gem install berkshelf
    Fetching: nio4r-1.0.1.gem (100%)
    Building native extensions.  This could take a while...
    ```

Knife's command line will start to complain about the Ruby version when you fire it in your shell. Thus, you can always reset your default Ruby version 1.8.7 using this:

```
packtpub@workstation$  rvm system
```

Uploading cookbooks using Berkshelf

Let's create our main Berkshelf file, which will define all the cookbooks needed for our first deployment. We will tell Berkshelf to clone the cookbooks and their dependencies mainly from `supermarket.getchef.com`:

```
packtpub@workstation$ nano  /home/packtpub/chef-repo/Berksfile
source "https://supermarket.getchef.com"


cookbook 'apache2', '1.9.6'

cookbook 'apt', '2.3.8'

cookbook 'aws', '2.1.1'

cookbook 'build-essential', '1.4.2'

cookbook 'database', '2.2.0'

cookbook 'erlang', '1.4.2'

cookbook 'memcached', '1.7.2'

cookbook 'mysql', '5.4.4'

cookbook 'mysql-chef_gem', '0.0.4'

cookbook 'openssl', '1.1.0'

cookbook 'postgresql', '3.3.4'

cookbook 'python', '1.4.6'

cookbook 'rabbitmq', '3.0.4'

cookbook 'xfs', '1.1.0'

cookbook 'yum', '3.1.4'

cookbook 'selinux', '0.7.2'

cookbook 'yum-epel', '0.3.4'

cookbook 'galera', '0.4.1'

cookbook 'haproxy', '1.6.6'

cookbook 'keepalived', '1.2.0'

cookbook 'statsd', github: 'att-cloud/cookbook-statsd'

cookbook 'openstack-block-storage', github: 'stackforge/cookbook-
openstack-block-storage'

cookbook 'openstack-common', github: 'stackforge/cookbook-openstack-
common'

cookbook 'openstack-compute', github: 'stackforge/cookbook-openstack-
compute'

cookbook 'openstack-dashboard', github: 'stackforge/cookbook-openstack-
dashboard'
```

```
cookbook 'openstack-identity', github: 'stackforge/cookbook-openstack-
identity'

cookbook 'openstack-image', github: 'stackforge/cookbook-openstack-image'

cookbook 'openstack-network', github: 'stackforge/cookbook-openstack-
network'

cookbook 'openstack-object-storage', github: 'stackforge/cookbook-
openstack-object-storage'

cookbook 'openstack-ops-database', github: 'stackforge/cookbook-
openstack-ops-database'

cookbook 'openstack-ops-messaging', github: 'stackforge/cookbook-
openstack-ops-messaging'
```

Then, you need to just upload cookbooks as the following:

```
packtpub@workstation/home/packtpub/chef-repo $ berks install

Resolving cookbook dependencies...

packtpub@workstation/home/packtpub/chef-repo $ berks upload --no-ssl-
verify
```

Defining roles

Chef defines roles as a manner to group nodes, seeking simplicity deployment.
From run lists in all nodes, you will just need to assign the node that should be run.
Optionally, you will be able to customize them by overriding attribute values within
your roles. On the other hand, recipes define roles. Thus, you may notice the running
of a list of a bunch of recipes within a role. Besides, it can also include roles from
other run lists.

Let's cover a basic example using only recipes in the role run list within OpenStack.
In your `chef-repo` directory, create a new directory named `roles`.

Create the role:

```
$ nano roles/packtpub-os-base.json
```

Eventually, the `packtpub-os-base` role defines the base role of OpenStack nodes
that will be assigned to the majority of servers in our deployment. It provides
common attributes and recipes that define the OpenStack deployment, such as
setting network interfaces of hosts within the existing endpoints:

```
{
    "name": "packtpub-os-base.json",
    "description": "PacktPub OpenStack Base Role",
    "json_class": "Chef::Role",
    "default_attributes": {
    },
```

```
    "override_attributes": {
    },
    "chef_type": "role",
    "run_list": [
      "recipe[openstack-common]",
      "recipe[openstack-common::logging]",
      "recipe[openstack-common::set_endpoints_by_interface]",
      "recipe[openstack-common::sysctl]"
    ],
    "env_run_lists": {
    }
}
```

Let's carry on with the second role using the previous one.

Create a new role named packtpub-os-compute-worker.json. This role will define our OpenStack compute node:

```
{
    "name": "packtpub-os-compute-worker",
    "description": "PacktPub OpenStack Compute Role",
    "json_class": "Chef::Role",
    "default_attributes": {
    },
    "override_attributes": {
    },
    "chef_type": "role",
    "run_list": [
      "role[packtpub-os-base]",
      "recipe[openstack-compute::compute]"
    ],
    "env_run_lists": {
    }
}
```

You might notice that we have used the base role, packtpub-os-base, within the compute recipe that we have uploaded in our Chef.

At this point, feel free to add any role that will fit your design from our basic cookbooks added from supermarket.getchef.com. Distributing roles will depend on your choice and the number of nodes you plan to deploy for a certain service. We can assume that any change to a certain node deployment will be made from the Chef code.

In our custom design, we will need a controller node, which will run a bunch of services. A good practical design of cookbooks is to *wisely* break down your infrastructure into reusable roles and recipes. For example, our controller node will include networking, imaging, messaging, identity, and database services; going on making a one blob role which includes all the associated recipes might limit your attention and make you think about scaling out the nodes later. Remember that we are expanding and not rolling up the infrastructure.

Before creating our custom controller role, we will proceed by creating a basic one:

packtpub-os-base-controller

```
{
  "name": "packtpub-os-base-controller",
  "description": "PacktPub OpenStack Controller Role",
  "json_class": "Chef::Role",
  "default_attributes": {
  },
  "override_attributes": {
  },
  "chef_type": "role",
  "run_list": [
    "role[packtpub-os-base]",
    "role[packtpub-os-ops-database]",
    "recipe[openstack-ops-database::openstack-db]",
    "role[packtpub-os-ops-messaging]",
    "role[packtpub-os-identity]",
    "role[packtpub-os-image]",
    "role[packtpub-os-compute-setup]",
    "role[packtpub-os-compute-conductor]",
    "role[packtpub-os-compute-scheduler]",
    "role[packtpub-os-compute-api]",
    "role[packtpub-os-block-storage]",
    "role[packtpub-os-compute-cert]",
    "role[packtpub-os-compute-vncproxy]",
    "role[packtpub-os-dashboard]"
  ],
  "env_run_lists": {
  }
}
```

To upload all your created roles, you can use the following command:

```
packtpub@workstation$ knife role from file /home/packtpub/chef-
cookbooks/roles/*.rb
```

The basic cookbooks for OpenStack have been downloaded from `https://github.com/stackforge`. It is recommended that before starting your Chef deployment, you have to verify the roles and their names, the number of environments and their names. A good practice while customizing a cookbook or defining an OpenStack environment in Chef is to add as many thin roles as possible. If you face any error-naming convention while running Chef, try to adjust the role names in attribute files to reflect the same names within the defined roles.

Configuring the environment

Now we have a set of cookbooks uploaded to the Chef server and ready to be deployed. An extra step is needed to make them useful: Defining your environments. Note that we define the *playground* environment using Vagrant, where we will provision our test infrastructure, and the *cooking* environment, where we define our infrastructure details from one file and let Chef do the rest:

- **Playground environment**: Until now, we have our basic cookbooks ready to be uploaded within defined roles. They need customization and more development to adjust our infrastructure needs.

  Vagrant might be a very cost-effective and the simplest solution to make a full test environment work together with Chef.

  We can use a provider for Vagrant as a VirtualBox, where it can be installed as a virtual machine while our provisioner will be Chef.

Provisioning with Vagrant can also be performed using Puppet, and the providers can be VMware and Amazon AWS.

You can download and install Vagrant from `http://downloads.vagrantup.com`:

```
packtpub@workstation$ wget https://dl.bintray.com/mitchellh/
vagrant/vagrant_1.7.2_x86_64.rpm

packtpub@workstation$ rpm –ivh vagrant_1.7.2_x86_64.rpm

packtpub@workstation$ vagrant  --version

Vagrant version 1.7.2
```

VirtualBox needs to be installed as a Vagrant provider. VMware is
also a second alternative to run Vagrant boxes.

- **Vagrantfile**: The vagrant file will define all our OpenStack nodes and the
  general configuration, such as networking:

```
packtpub@workstation$  nano /home/packtpub/chef-repo/Vagrantfile
```

The contents of the Vagrant file are:

```
Vagrant.require_version ">= 1.1"

Vagrant.configure("2") do |config|
  # Omnibus plugin configuration
  config.omnibus.chef_version = :latest

  # OpenStack settings
  chef_environment = "vagrant-packtpub"

    controller_run_list = [
      "role[packtpub-os-base-controller]",
      "recipe[openstack-network::identity_registration]",
      "role[packtpub-os-network-openvswitch]",
      "role[packtpub-os-network-dhcp-agent]",
      "role[packtpub-os-network-metadata-agent]",
      "role[packtpub-os-network-server]"
    ]

  # virtualbox provider settings
  config.vm.provider "virtualbox" do |vb|
    vb.customize ["modifyvm", :id, "--cpus", 2]
    vb.customize ["modifyvm", :id, "--memory", 2048]
    vb.customize ["modifyvm", :id, "--nicpromisc2", "allow-all"]
    vb.customize ["modifyvm", :id, "--nicpromisc3", "allow-all"]
  end

  # OpenStack Controller

  config.vm.define :controller1 do |controller1|
    controller1.vm.hostname = "controller1"
    controller1.vm.box = "opscode-centos-6.5"
```

```
        controller1.vm.box_url = "http://opscode-vm-bento.
s3.amazonaws.com/vagrant/virtualbox/opscode_centos-6.5_chef-
provisionerless.box"

        controller1.vm.network "forwarded_port", guest: 443, host:
9443     # forward to dashboard using ssl : dashboard-ssl
        controller1.vm.network "forwarded_port", guest: 8773, host:
9773     # forward to EC2 api : compute-ec2-api
        controller1.vm.network "forwarded_port", guest: 8774, host:
9774     # forward to Compute API : compute-api
        controller1.vm.network "private_network", ip: "192.168.47.10"
        controller1.vm.network "private_network", ip: "172.16.11.10"

        controller1.vm.provision :chef_client do |chef|
          chef.run_list = controller_run_list
          chef.environment = chef_environment
          # Where to find our Chef Server by providing the
authorization key
          chef.chef_server_url = "https://chef.packtpub.com:443"
          chef.validation_key_path = "/home/packtpub/chef repo/.chef/
chef-validator.pem"
        end
      end

  # OpenStack Compute

    config.vm.define :compute1 do |compute1|
      compute1.vm.hostname = "compute1"
      compute1.vm.box = "opscode-centos-6.5"
      compute1.vm.box_url = "http://opscode-vm-bento.s3.amazonaws.
com/vagrant/virtualbox/opscode_centos-6.5_chef-provisionerless.
box"
      compute1.vm.network "private_network", ip: "192.168.47.11"
      compute1.vm.network "private_network", ip: "172.16.11.11"

      compute1.vm.provision :chef_client do |chef|
        chef.run_list = [ "role[packtpub-os-compute-worker]" ]
        chef.environment = chef_environment
        # Where to find our Chef Server by providing the
authorization key
        chef.chef_server_url = "https://chef.packtpub.com:443"
        chef.validation_key_path = "/home/packtpub/chef-repo/.chef/
chef-validator.pem"
      end
    end
end
```

- **Cooking environment**: We need to define our Chef environment to accomplish the environment setup within Vagrant.

 Use different environments for development and production to maintain cookbook changes in isolation.

You can create a development environment in many ways; from the Chef server GUI or via the Knife command line, as follows:

```
# knife environment create vagrant-packtpub -d "PacktPub Testing
Environment"
```

Our Chef environment file looks like the following:

```
{
  "name": "vagrant-packtpub",
  "description": "PacktPub Testing Environment",

  "cookbook_versions": {
  },
  "json_class": "Chef::Environment",
  "chef_type": "environment",
  "default_attributes": {
  },
  "override_attributes": {
    "mysql": {
      "allow_remote_root": true,
      "root_network_acl": "%"
    },
    "openstack": {
      "identity": {
        "bind_interface": "eth1"
      },
      "endpoints": {
        "host": "192.168.47.10",
        "mq": {
          "host": "192.168.47.10"
        },
        "db": {
          "host": "192.168.47.10"
        },
        "developer_mode": true,
        "network": {
          "debug": "True",
```

```
      "dhcp": {
        "enable_isolated_metadata": "True"
      },
      "metadata": {
        "nova_metadata_ip": "192.168.47.10"
      },
      "openvswitch": {
        "network_vlan_ranges": "physnet1:1000:2999",
        "tenant_network_type": "vlan",
        "external_network_bridge_interface": "eth2"
      },
      "api": {
        "bind_interface": "eth1"
      }
    },
    "image": {
      "api": {
        "bind_interface": "eth1"
      },
      "registry": {
        "bind_interface": "eth1"
      },
      "image_upload": true,
      "upload_images": [
        "centos",
        "cirros"
      ],
      "upload_image": {
          "centos": "http://cloud.centos.org/centos/7/devel/
CentOS-7-Atomic-CloudDockerHost-20140820_05.qcow2",
          "cirros": "https://launchpad.net/cirros/trunk/0.3.0/
+download/cirros-0.3.0-x86_64-disk.img"
      }
    },
    "compute": {
      "xvpvnc_proxy": {
        "bind_interface": "eth1"
      },
      "novnc_proxy": {
        "bind_interface": "eth1"
      },
      "libvirt": {
        "virt_type": "qemu"
      },
```

```
        "network": {
          "public_interface": "eth1",
          "service_type": "neutron"
        },
        "config": {
          "ram_allocation_ratio": 5.0
        }
      }
    }
  }
}
```

As we are using version control, it might be more convenient to create a new directory under chef-repo named; environments, which will hold our environments.

Additionally, this will help us test cookbooks in different versions with several specific attributes and bring them from development to staging, finishing with promoting them into production. Under chef-repo, create an environments directory, where the vagrant-packtpub.rb file will be placed:

```
packtpub@workstation:/chef repo$ git add environments/vagrant-
packtpub.rb
```

```
packtpub@workstation:/chef repo$ git commit -a -m "First OpenStack
Environment"
```

```
packtpub@workstation:/chef repo$ git push
```

Now, you can create the environment on the Chef server from our vagrant-packtpub.rb file by the means of the Knife command line:

```
packtpub@workstation:/chef repo$ knife environment from file
vagrant-packtpub.rb
```

- **Push the button**: At this point, we've done a lot of preparation and configuration to test and deploy OpenStack. Vagrant and Chef work in tandem with each other to bring a test environment with less pain and more simplicity. Everything is in place; what we need to do is to just push the button.

Set an environment file to specify which Vagrantfile to use:

```
packtpub@workstation $ export VAGRANT_VAGRANTFILE=vagrant-packtpub
```

Start the nodes:

```
packtpub@workstation $ vagrant up controller1
packtpub@workstation $ vagrant up compute1
```

Summary

In this chapter, we covered several topics and terminologies on how to develop and maintain a code infrastructure using the DevOps style.

Bringing your OpenStack infrastructure deployment to code will not only simplify node configuration, but also improve the automation process.

You should keep in mind that DevOps is neither a project nor a goal to attend to, but it is a methodology that will make your deployment successfully empowered by the team synergy with different departments.

Despite the existence of numerous system-management tools to bring our OpenStack up and running in an automated way, we have chosen the Chef server.

Puppet, Ansible, Salt, and others can do the job but in different ways. You should know that there is no one way to perform automation.

Chef is highly flexible and rich with tools that make life easier. In a similar manner, with Vagrant and Chef plugins, we were able to bring in a test environment in a wink.

Although we deployed a basic multinode setup of OpenStack in this chapter, the next chapter will take you to a third stage, where you can use strong approaches on towards extending our previous design by clustering, defining the cloud controller, and compute node distributions.

We will keep on going with what we learned from deployment automation using Chef under the umbrella of the DevOps style.

3
Learning OpenStack Clustering – Cloud Controllers and Compute Nodes

"If you want to go quickly, go alone. If you want to go far, go together."

–African proverb

Now that you have good knowledge of the approaches taken to deploy a large OpenStack infrastructure in an automated way, it is time to dive deeper and cover more specific conceptual designs within OpenStack.

In a large infrastructure, especially if you are looking to keep all your services up and running, it is essential that you ensure the OpenStack infrastructure is reliable and guarantees business continuity.

We already discussed several design aspects and highlighted some best practices of scalable architecture models within OpenStack in *Chapter 1, Designing OpenStack Cloud Architecture.*

We adopted a sample architecture based on the cloud controller and compute nodes, and on each of these, we divided and set up OpenStack services. This is a simplified way to design a scalable OpenStack environment.

Soon after, we discovered the magic of automation, where we resumed a basic setup of one cloud controller together with one compute node using the Chef server.

This chapter begins by covering some clustering aspects. It soon guides you to discover more OpenStack design patterns based on cloud controllers' and compute nodes' clustering. Bear in mind that this chapter will not treat high availability in detail and will not touch all OpenStack services layers. Instead, it will target covering a generic overview of several possibilities of the OpenStack clustering design. The art of clustering is the key to providing a solution that fits into a methodology that stresses standardized, consistent IT build-out OpenStack operations.

In this chapter, we will cover the following topics:

- Understanding the art of clustering
- Defining the use case of cloud controllers and compute nodes in an OpenStack environment
- Covering other OpenStack clustering models based on cloud controller and compute node distribution
- Understanding backup techniques of cloud controller and compute nodes for disaster recovery best practices
- Learning how to refine your infrastructure code based on the Chef server for a fast and automatic deployment

Understanding the art of clustering

Do not be afraid to claim that clustering actually provides high availability in a given infrastructure. The aggregation of the capacity of two or more servers is meant to be a server cluster. This aggregation will be performed by means of the accumulation of several machines.

 Do not get confused between **scaling up**, which is also called **vertical scaling**, and **scaling down**, which is also known as **horizontal scaling**. The horizontal scaling option refers to adding more commodity servers, unlike the vertical scaling option, which refers to adding more expensive and robust servers with more CPU and RAM.

This makes it imperative to differ between the terminologies of high availability, load balancing, and failing over, which will be detailed in depth in *Chapter 6, OpenStack HA and Failover*.

Keep this in mind for any of the previously mentioned terms: their configuration results always start from the clustering concept. You will discover how to differentiate between them in the next section.

Asymmetric clustering

Asymmetric clustering is mostly used for high availability purposes as well as for the scalability of read/write operations in databases, messaging systems, or files.

In such cases, a standby server is involved to take over only if the other server is facing an event of failure. We may call the passive server the *sleepy watcher*, where it can include the configuration of a failover.

Symmetric clustering

This is where all nodes are active and a participator handles the process of requests. This setup might be cost-effective by serving active applications and users.

A failed node can be discarded from the cluster, while others take over its workload and continue to handle transactions.

Symmetric clustering can be thought to be similar to a load-balancing cluster situation where all nodes share the workload by increasing the performance and scalability of services running in the cloud infrastructure.

Divide and conquer

OpenStack was designed to be horizontally scalable; we have already seen how its services have been widely distributed in two concepts: cloud controllers and compute nodes.

The cloud controller

The concept of cloud controllers aims to provide one or many kinds of central management and control over your OpenStack deployments. We can, for example, assume that all authentication and messaging transactions are being managed by the cloud controller by means of our magic hub: the message queue.

Considering a medium- or large-scale infrastructure, we will need, with no doubt, more than a single node. For an OpenStack cloud operator, controllers can be thought of as a service aggregator where the majority of running management services are needed for OpenStack to operate.

Let's see what a cloud controller cloud mainly handles:

- It presents a main gateway for access to cloud management and services consumption

- It provides the API services in order to bring different OpenStack components to talk to each other

- It concentrates on a set of highly available mechanisms for integrated services by the means of Pacemaker, Corosync, or HAProxy to expose a VIP for load-balancing utilities

- It provides critical infrastructure services, such as database and queue messaging

- It exposes the persistent storage, which might be backed onto separate storage nodes

Most probably, you have already noticed the main services of the cloud controller in *Chapter 1, Designing OpenStack Cloud Architecture,* but we did not take a deep look at why such services should run in the controller node in the first place. We will now suggest a second alternative.

We bring, for instance, the cloud controller as a node under the scope. This aggregates the most critical services for OpenStack. Thus, we can start by covering them in a nutshell.

nova-conductor

If you have tried to install OpenStack starting from the Grizzly release, while checking Nova services running in your OpenStack node, you may have noticed a new service called nova-conductor. Do not panic! This amazing new service has changed the way the nova-compute service accesses the database. Eventually, it was added for security reasons as compute nodes running the nova-compute service may conduct some vulnerability issues. You can imagine how attacking a virtual machine can bring the compute node under the control of the attacker. Even worse, it can compromise the database. Then, you can guess the rest: your entire OpenStack cluster is under attack! Keep in mind that nova-scheduler is intended to carry out database operations on behalf of compute nodes.

So, you can assume that nova-conductor compiles a new layer on top of nova-compute. Furthermore, instead of resolving the complexity of the database requests bottleneck, nova-conductor parallelizes the requests from compute nodes.

If you are using nova-network and multihost networking in your OpenStack environment, nova-compute will still require direct access to the database.

nova-scheduler

Several workflow scheduling studies and implementations have been recently conducted in cloud computing, generally in order to define the best placement of a resource provisioning.

In our case, we will decide which compute node will host the virtual machine. It's important to note that there are bunches of scheduling algorithms in OpenStack.

Such internal request information is received from the magic radio station in the OpenStack core: the message queue.

Nova-scheduler may also influence the performance of the hosts running virtual machines. Therefore, OpenStack supports a set of filters that implement the available nodes and give you the choice to configure its options based on a certain number of metrics and policy considerations. Additionally, nova-scheduler can be thought of as the *decision-maker box* in a cloud controller node by applying a few complicated algorithms for the efficient usage and placement of virtual machines.

On the other hand, you should understand that nova-scheduler assumes a given OpenStack cluster as a single host within aggregated resources of all hosts present in the cluster. This happens when you deal with different hypervisors running each of them and their specific scheduling resource's management, such as vCenter within **Distributed Resource Scheduler (DRS)**.

 DRS is a VMware load-balancing utility, which assigns computing workloads to available hardware resources.

Eventually, the scheduler in OpenStack, as you may understand at this stage, will be running in the cloud controller node. A very good point here needs to be investigated: what about different schedulers in a high availability environment? In this case, we exploit the openness of the OpenStack architecture by running multiple instances of each scheduler, as all of them are listening to the same queue.

It is important to know that cinder-scheduler is considered a scheduling service in OpenStack, which might be running in the cloud controller node for block storage management.

> The scheduler can be configured in a variety of options. Different scheduler settings can be found in /etc/nova/nova.conf. To read more about scheduling in OpenStack, refer to the following link: http://docs.openstack.org/icehouse/config-reference/content/section_compute-scheduler.html.

X-api

In a nutshell, we have already covered the nova-api service in *Chapter 1, Designing OpenStack Cloud Architecture*. It might be important to step forward and learn that nova-api is considered the *orchestrator engine* component in cloud controller specifications. Without any doubt, nova-api is assembled in the controller node after considering its main role by accepting all the incoming API requests from all components.

The nova-api service may also fulfill more complicated requests by passing messages within other daemons by means of writing to the databases and queuing messages. As this service is based on the endpoint concept where all API queries are initiated, nova-api provides two different APIs using either the OpenStack API or EC2 API. This makes it imperative to decide which API will be used before deploying a cloud controller node that may conduct to a real issue as you may decide to take over both APIs. The reason behind this is the *heterogeneity* of the information presentation used by each API; for example, OpenStack uses names and numbers to refer to instance, whereas the EC2 API uses identifiers based on hexadecimal values.

Additionally, we have brought compute, identity, image, network, and storage APIs to be placed in the controller node, which can also be chosen to run other API services.

For instance, we satisfy our deployment by gathering the majority of X-api services to run in the cloud controller node.

> An **Application Programming Interface** (**API**) enables public access to the OpenStack services and offers a way to interact with them. The API access can be performed either through a command line or through the Web. To read more about APIs in OpenStack, refer to the following link: http://developer.openstack.org/#api.

Image management

The cloud controller will also be responsible for the delivery and serving of images using glance-api and glance-registry, where a decision can be made about which backend will be used to launch the controller in the cloud.

 The glance-api supports several backend options to store images. Swift is a good alternative that allows storing images as objects and provides a scalable placement for image storage. Other alternatives are also possible such as filesystem backend, Amazon S3, and HTTP. *Chapter 4, Learning OpenStack Storage – Deploying the Hybrid Storage Model*, covers different storage models in OpenStack in more detail.

Network outfit

Just like OpenStack's Nova service provides an API for dynamic requests to compute resources, we adopt the same concept for the network by allowing its API to reside in the cloud controller, which supports extensions to provide advanced network capabilities, such as access lists and network monitoring using Neutron. As was assumed in our first model, separating most of the network workers is highly recommended. Therefore, the cloud controller will include only the Neutron server in the second iteration. On the other hand, you are tempted to think about the huge amount of traffic that hits a cloud controller with regard to its multirunning services; therefore, you should bear in mind the performance challenges that you may face. In this case, clustering best practices come in to help your deployment be more scalable and increase its performance. The previously mentioned techniques are essential but not sufficient. They need basic hardware support with at least 10 GB of **bonded** NICs, for example.

 The NIC bonding technique is used to increase the available bandwidth. Two or more bonded NICs appear to be the same physical device.

You can always refer to *Chapter 1, Designing OpenStack Cloud Architecture*, to use some calculation in order to make your cloud controller capable of responding to all requests smoothly without a bottleneck.

Complicating your performance metrics at such an early stage will not help to satisfy your topology resiliency. To do so, scalability features are always there to refine your deployment. Remember that we tend to scale horizontally when required.

The Horizon decision

As the OpenStack dashboard runs in the Apache web server based on the Python web application, providing a separate node that is able to reach the API servers in the second step might be an option if you later decide to decrease the load on your cloud controller node. Several OpenStack deployments in production run Horizon in the controller node but still leave it up to you to monitor it and take separate decisions.

Planning for the message queue

Definitely, your queuing message system should be clustered. This is another critical subsystem where your node may be in a halt status when the message queue fails.

We have chosen RabbitMQ to handle our queuing system as it has its native clustering support. However, it might be painful in a large-scale OpenStack environment.

A good practice is to keep in mind such complexity challenges that have to be undertaken when we start a simple cloud controller holding a RabbitMQ service.

It is a good thing that our design is very elastic and we can cluster by controller nodes; therefore, we bring in RabbitMQ clustered. With fewer controller nodes, which need more hardware specs, separating the RabbitMQ node cluster will be relatively easy.

Consolidating the database

The majority of disasters that could happen in any IT infrastructure indicate loss not only of data in production, but also historical data. Such critical points may lead to nonoperational and even nonrecoverable OpenStack environments. Thus, we have started working with MySQL clustering and high availability solutions at an early stage.

Physically, we started adopting MySQL using Galera running in the cloud controller. This held true until we got a basic environment running, for which you only need to provide a new node for the MySQL cluster pointing at the right controller. More details will be covered in *Chapter 6, OpenStack HA and Failover*. For the moment, we need a running setup that is easy to deploy and redeploy using Chef.

Cloud controller clustering

Being a proponent of the physical cloud controller, a machine's clustering effort is considered a step in the right direction: high availability. Several HA topologies will be discussed in *Chapter 6, OpenStack HA and Failover*.

As we have seen the use cases of several services at this point, which can be separated and clustered, we will extend our logical design of the cloud controller described in *Chapter 1, Designing OpenStack Cloud Architecture*. Keep in mind that OpenStack is a highly configurable platform and the rest of the description is an example that suits a certain requirement and specific conditions.

The next step is to confirm the first logical design. Questions such as this come up: does it satisfy certain requirements? Are all services in the safe HA zone?

Well, note that we include the MySQL Galera cluster to ensure HA for the database. Eventually, this means we are missing something! Depending on the quorum-based system of Galera, at least a third cloud controller has to join the cloud controller team.

Immediately, you may raise a question: should I add an extra cloud controller to make the replication and database HA achieved? What about a fourth or fifth controller?

Great! Keep this mindset for later. At this level, you assume that logically, your design is on the right path and you already know that some changes have to be made to fulfill some physical constraints.

Then, we extend our cluster setup with a third cloud controller:

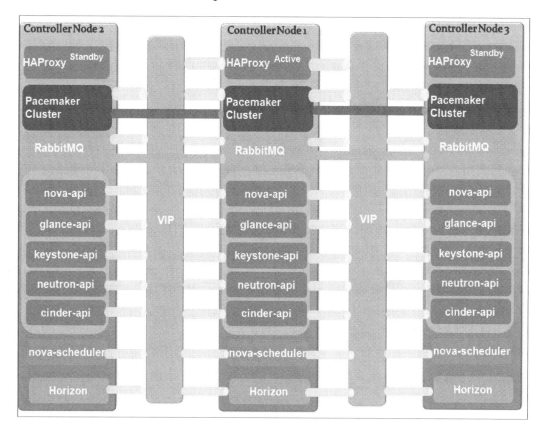

At this point, we ensure that our design is deployed in HA at an early stage. Remember, there should be **no** Single Point Of Failure in any layer!

> Redundancy is implemented by means of virtual IP and Pacemaker. Then, HAProxy will ensure load balancing. Databases and messaging queue servers have been implemented in active/active HA mode when MySQL uses Galera for replication, while RabbitMQ is built in a cluster capable mode. Other choices can be made for our current design by integrating, for example, with Corosync, Heartbeat, or Keepalived instead. Aspects of load balancing, high availability, and failover with relative solutions will be explained in detail in *Chapter 6, OpenStack HA and Failover*.

It is important to prepare how the cloud controllers should be clustered in advance. The previous diagram is an example design that scales as well and takes into account more advanced aspects, such as HA failover and load balancing. You can refer to *Chapter 6, OpenStack HA and Failover*, to check out more details and practical examples. For instance, the overall OpenStack cloud should expand easily by joining new nodes running several services that require more care. We continue later by adumbrating an automated approach to facilitating the horizontal expansion of the cloud.

Cooking the cloud controller

Once we have identified which service will be deployed in the cloud controller, we jump to the next step by bringing our Chef into action. We have already covered a general overview of the OpenStack cookbooks, which we have based on the Chef community website.

As we are aiming for a large-scale infrastructure, we would rather prepare the roles and recipes and make them more decoupled for service nodes to reach a level of high availability in the second stage. The cookbook design of the cloud controller seems quite complicated, which implies that its implementation might not be intuitively obvious at first glance, but a brief overview of the cookbooks' *relationships* will make it easier for you to highlight the flexibility of this model. Thus, you may intend to choose on your own how to distribute roles and recipes by maintaining the logic of dependency.

As you may notice in the next figure, we have gathered the majority of services in the cloud controller, except object storage and compute workers. On the other hand, assigned roles and recipes can be detached and reassigned to other nodes. We bring in the cloud controller for it to be deployed first in order to check our cookbooks' consistency.

Keeping in our mindset and whatever system management tools we might choose, underpinning every service component on our OpenStack cloud platform must be a flexible mantra, as much as possible, for the purpose of our first cloud controller deployment. Based on *Chapter 2, Deploying OpenStack – DevOps and OpenStack Dual Deal*, we have covered how to turn the code of our infrastructure into pieces by means of recipes, while gathering the pieces for a more customized design will form the roles.

This is described in the following cookbook diagram:

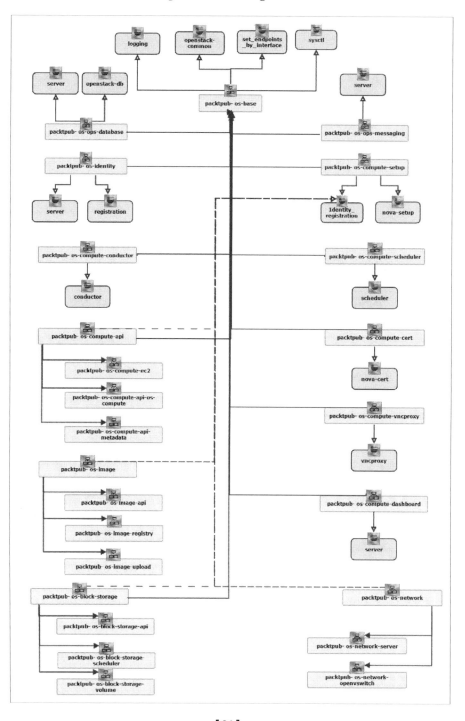

You may notice that roles can include not only recipes, but also other roles.

We can go through each role and describe how it is composed in a nutshell by taking a look at the following table:

Role name	Default recipe	Description
packtpub-os-base	• openstack-common • openstack-common::logging • openstack-common::set_endpoints_by_interface • openstack-common::sysctl	• openstack-common is a set of recipes and attributes describing general OpenStack deployment • openstack-common::logging installs and configures common logging attributes • openstack-common::set_endpoints_by_interface iterates over the endpoints per node hash and finds any occurrence of bind_interface to set the IP address • openstack-common::sysctl iterates over a node hash and updates its entries to /etc/sysctl.d/60-openstack.conf
packtpub-os-ops-database	• openstack-ops-database::server • openstack-ops-database::openstack-db	• openstack-ops-database::server selects the database server configuration using attributes • openstack-ops-database::openstack-db defines the required tables and users for OpenStack
packtpub-os-identity	• openstack-identity::server • openstack-identity::registration	• openstack-identity::server installs and configures Keystone services • openstack-identity::registration registers identity endpoint and service
packtpub-os-ops-messaging	openstack-ops-messaging::server	This installs a single RabbitMQ server instance
packtpub-os-compute-scheduler	openstack-compute::scheduler	This installs and configures a single instance of nova-scheduler
packtpub-os-compute-conductor	openstack-compute::conductor	This installs and configures a single instance of nova-conductor
packtpub-os-compute-cert	openstack-compute::nova-cert	This installs and configures a single instance of nova-cert
packtpub-os-compute-api	openstack-compute::identity-registration	This registers the identity endpoint for the Nova service
packtpub-os-compute-vncproxy	openstack-compute::vncproxy	This installs and configures a single instance of the Nova VNC service
packtpub-os-image	openstack-image::identity_registration	This registers the identity endpoint for the Glance service

Role name	Default recipe	Description
packtpub-os-compute-dashboard	openstack-dashboard::server	This installs and configures a single instance of Horizon
packtpub-os-block-storage	openstack-block-storage::identity_registration	This registers the identity endpoint for the Swift service
packtpub-os-network	openstack-network::identity_registration	This registers the identity endpoint for the Neutron service

> It is possible to customize the automation of the cloud controller based on roles and recipes defined in the default cookbooks provided by StackForge, covered in *Chapter 2, Deploying OpenStack – DevOps and OpenStack Dual Deal*. The main StackForge Chef repository can be found on GitHub at https://github.com/stackforge/openstack-chef-repo.

The compute node

Once the orchestrator has evaluated the instruments that should be integrated on the stage, we still need the *players* to accomplish the song. All we need are *worker horses* where our virtual machines' *brains* will live. Notice that the brain of this instance refers to where all the thinking processes are done.

The compute node should be separately deployed in the cluster mode as it forms the resources part of the OpenStack infrastructure. Even in another cloud deployment architecture, you may find that the computing part is mostly built in separate farms. It is imperative to give attention to the fact that compute node resources should not be overlooked in processing, memory, network, and storage resources.

From a deployment perspective, an OpenStack compute node might not be complicated to install as it will basically run nova-compute and the network agent for Neutron. However, its hardware and specification choice might not be obvious. The cloud controller presents a wide range of services, but we have agreed that using HA and a separate deployment will crystallize the cloud controller deployment. This way, we suffer less from the issue of service downtime. On the other hand, a compute node will be the *space* where the virtual machine will run, in other words, the space on which the end user will focus on. They only want to push the button and get the application running on the top of your IaaS layer. It is your mission to guarantee a satisfactory amount of resources.

A good design of cloud controller is needed but is not enough; we need to take care over compute nodes as well: compute resources.

Overcommitment considerations

We have already taken into consideration the need for CPU-supporting virtualization in *Chapter 1, Designing OpenStack Cloud Architecture*. What we need to understand now is the number of cores needed, which might affect the CPU power. Remember, for example, that hyper-threading is a highly recommended option for your CPU per compute node in order to double the number of existing cores.

It will be great if you could afford such powerful technology, which is common nowadays. On the other hand, in many cases, the physical compute nodes you purchase might be more powerful than are needed. To avoid such loss, you should keep in mind that sizing your compute nodes is important.

However, this magical catch-all formula that is applicable in all cases won't be easy to find. You will need to work through three main steps:

1. Estimate a sample calculation for the CPU and RAM size.
2. Use OpenStack resources' overcommitment without overlooking.
3. As much as possible, gather resources' usage statistics periodically.

In *Chapter 1, Designing OpenStack Cloud Architecture*, we covered how to estimate such resources. The next step is to extend your assumption by introducing the power of overcommitment in OpenStack.

The art of memory or CPU overcommitment is an enabled hypervisor feature, allowing the usage of more resource power by the virtual machine than the compute host has.

For example, it allows a host server with 4 GB of physical memory to run eight virtual machines, each with 1 GB of memory space allocated.

Well, there is no secrecy in this case! You should think about the hypervisor; just calculate the portion of physical memory not used per virtual machine and assign it to one that may need more RAM at certain moments. This is a technique based on the dynamic relocation of unused resources that are being held in an idle status. On the other hand, it might be a nice feature but without exaggeration!

It might be dangerous if resources are exhausted and lead to a server crash. Therefore, we need to dive into overcommitment use cases.

In OpenStack, you will be able to overcommit CPU and RAM resources by changing the default limit by their local configuration. Compute nodes use the *ratio* to determine how many VMs you can run per hardware thread or core and how much memory can be associated with the instance. By default, OpenStack uses 16:1 for CPU allocation and 1.5:1 for RAM allocation ratios.

The CPU allocation ratio

The default 16:1 CPU allocation ratio means that you can run a maximum of 16 virtual CPU cores for every physical CPU core within all running virtual machines. If you choose a physical node that has 24 cores, scheduling CPU resources will consider 24*16 available virtual cores. Thus, defining 4 virtual cores per instance, for example, will provide 96 instances on each compute node. Ensure that overcommitting the CPU only makes sense when running workloads are not extremely CPU-intensive. In the other case, you should limit its ratio value.

Some values of the CPU ratio commitment can be misused by changing it to 1:1, and then you will not be able to overcommit CPU anymore. Therefore, you will be limited to running no more vCPUs than there are physical CPU cores in your hardware. On the other hand, one virtual machine cannot have more virtual CPUs than the existing physical CPUs, whereas it is still possible to run more virtual machines than the number of existing physical CPU cores in the compute node.

Additionally, the new ratio value exposes a new way to refine resources' estimation. Let's add a new formula that might accomplish the resources cited in *Chapter 1, Designing OpenStack Cloud Architecture*.

The calculation formula to determine how many virtual instances can run on a compute node is as follows:

*(CPU overcommitment ratio * Number of physical cores)/Number of virtual cores per instance)*

The RAM allocation ratio

The default 1.5:1 memory allocation ratio means that allocating instances to compute nodes is still possible if the total instance memory usage is less than 1.5 times the amount of physical memory available. For example, a compute node with 96 GB of memory can run a number of instances that reach the value of the sum of RAM associated with 144 GB. In this case, this refers to a total of 36 virtual machines with 4 GB of RAM each.

Use the `cpu_allocation_ratio` and `ram_allocation_ratio` directives in `/etc/nova/nova.conf` to change the default settings.

What about surprises? You have done the required resource computation for your compute nodes and already estimated how many virtual machines within specific flavors can run for each.

Flavors in OpenStack are a set of hardware templates that define the amount of RAM, disk space, and the number of cores per CPU.

Remember that we only use overcommitment when it is needed. To make it more valuable, you should keep an eye on your servers. Bear in mind that collecting resource utilization statistics is essential and will eventually conduct a better ratio update when needed. Overcommitting is the starting point for performance improvement of your compute nodes; when you think about adjusting such a value, you will need to know exactly what you need! To answer this question, you will need active monitoring of the hardware usage at certain periods. For example, you might miss a sudden huge increase in resources' utilization requirements during the first or the last days of the month for certain user machines, whereas you were satisfied by their performance in the middle part of the month.

We are talking about peak times, which can differ from one physical machine to another. Users who use virtual instances cannot hold the same requirements all the time, for example, accounting systems. You may face a trade-off between big resource assignments to fulfill peak times and performance issues when committing resources. Remember that it is important to have a strong understanding of what your system is virtualizing. Furthermore, the more information you gather, the better prepared and the more ready you will be to face surprises. Besides, it becomes your mission to find the best optimized way of handling those requirements dynamically. Then, you will need to pick the right hypervisor(s).

Deciding on the hypervisor

The hypervisor is the heart engine of your OpenStack compute node. This is called the **virtual machine monitor** (**VMM**), which provides a set of manageability functions for virtual machines to access the hardware layer. The amazing part about hypervisors in OpenStack is the wide range of VMMs that it can offer, including KVM, VMware ESXi, QEMU, UML, Xen, Hyper-V, LXC, bare metal, and lately, Docker.

If you already have some experience with one or more of these, it will be better to take a look at how they differ at an architectural level. Currently, the last OpenStack release at the time of writing this book was **Juno**, which has many hypervisor features added or extended. Keep in mind that not all of these support the same features. The Hypervisor Support Matrix (`https://wiki.openstack.org/wiki/HypervisorSupportMatrix`) is a good reference that can help you to choose what fits your needs.

Obviously, the former hypervisors are not the same, based on their nature and use cases. For example, **Quick EMUlator** (**QEMU**) and **User Mode Linux** (**UML**) might be used for general development purposes, while Xen requires a nova-compute installation on a paravirtualized platform.

Paravirtualization is an improvement of virtualization technology in which the guest operating system is compiled prior to installation in a virtual machine. Xen and IBM have adopted this technology keeping in mind the high-performance deliverance that it can provide. The operating system and the hypervisor work efficiently in tandem, which helps avoid the overheads imposed by the native system resource emulation.

Most probably, you have heard about most of these previously mentioned hypervisors, but what do you think Docker could be?

It is interesting to discover another attractive point about OpenStack, which has steadily grown and can include any virtual technology in its ecosystem, such as the Docker driver for OpenStack nova-compute.

Out of the box, Docker helps enterprises deploy their applications in highly portable and self-sufficient containers, independent of the hardware and hosting provider. It brings the software deployment in to a secure, automated, and repeatable environment. What makes Docker special is its usage of the terms of several containers, which can be managed on a single machine. Additionally, it becomes more powerful when it is used alongside Nova. Therefore, it would be possible to manage hundreds and even thousands of containers, which makes it the cat's meow. You may wonder about the use cases of Docker, especially in an OpenStack environment. Well, as mentioned previously, Docker is based on containers that are not a replacement for virtual machines, but which are very specific to certain deployments. Containers are very lightweight and fast, which may be a good option for the development of new applications and even to port older application faster. Imagine a virtual machine abstraction that can be shared with any application along with its own specific configuration requirements without them interfering with each other. Docker can do this, but in terms of containers where applications run natively on the Linux kernel and each kernel is segmented from one another to form the operating system. Uniquely, it might be possible to save the state of a container as an image that can be shared though a central image registry. This makes Docker awesome as it creates a portable image across infrastructures and reveals the barrier of building bridges between different clouds, in other words, hybrid clouds.

As this is an introduction to the Havana release, Docker is going to be an important tool for OpenStack, which might stand beside virtual machines in an OpenStack environment.

To read more about Docker, check the following reference: https://www.docker.com/whatisdocker/. The Docker driver documentation for OpenStack can be found here: http://docs.openstack.org/havana/config-reference/content/docker.html.

On the other hand, most OpenStack nova-compute deployments run KVM as the main hypervisor. The fact is that KVM is best suited for workloads that are natively stateless using libvirt.

KVM is the default hypervisor for OpenStack Compute. You can check out your compute node from /etc/nova/nova.conf in the following lines:

```
compute_driver=libvirt.LibvirtDriver
libvirt_type=kvm
```

For proper, error-free hypervisor usage, it might be required to first check whether KVM modules are loaded from your compute node:

```
# lsmod | grep kvm
 kvm_intel or kvm_amd
```

Otherwise, you may load the required modules via:

```
# modprobe -a kvm
```

To make your modules persistent at reboot, which is obviously needed, you can add the following lines to the /etc/modules file when your compute node is an Intel-based processor:

```
kvm
kvm-intel
```

Note that kvm-intel can be replaced by kvm-amd in the case of an AMD-based processor.

Our further compute deployments will be based on KVM.

Changing the color of the hypervisor

While we have decided to use KVM for nova-compute, it would be great to check how OpenStack could support this wide range of hypervisors by means of nova-compute drivers. You might be suggested to run your OpenStack environment with two or more hypervisors. It can be a user requirement to choose a typical hypervisor in order to use its native one. This will help the end user resolve the challenge of native platform compatibility, and then we can calibrate the usage of the virtual machine between environments. This would be a great topic in hybrid cloud environment.

The next figure depicts the integration between nova-compute and KVM, QEMU, and LXC by means of libvirt tools and XCP through APIs. On the other hand, vSphere, Xen, or Hyper-V can be managed directly via nova-compute.

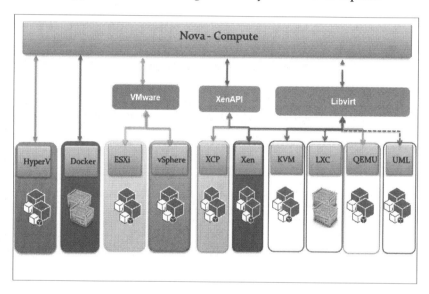

Let s take an example and see how such wonderful multihypervisor capability can be factored in to your OpenStack environment. If you already have a VMware vSphere running in your infrastructure, this example will be suitable for you if you plan to integrate vSphere with OpenStack. Practically, the term **integration** on the hypervisor level refers to the OpenStack driver that will be provided to manage vSphere by nova-compute. Eventually, OpenStack exposes two compute drivers that have been coded:

- `vmwareapi.VMwareESXDriver`: This allows nova-compute to reach the ESXi host by means of the vSphere SDK

- `vmwareapi.VMwareVCDriver`: This allows nova-compute to manage multiple clusters by means of a single VMware vCenter server

Imagine the several functions we will gain from such an integration using the OpenStack driver with which we attempt to harness advanced capabilities, such as vMotion, high availability, and **Dynamic Resource Scheduler (DRS)**. It is important to understand how such an integration can do the magic.

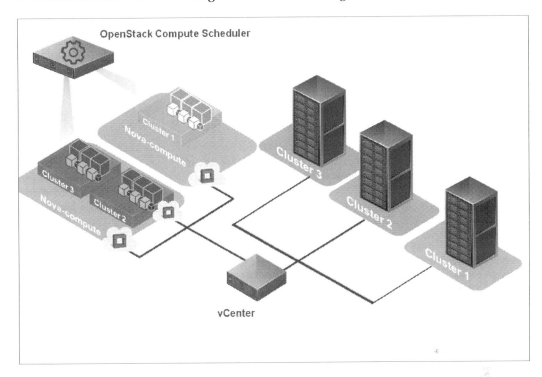

vMotion is a component of VMware vSphere that allows the live migration of a running virtual machine from one host to another with no downtime. VMware's vSphere virtualization suite also provides a load-balancing utility called DRS, which moves computing workloads to available hardware resources.

In a vSphere implementation coupled with OpenStack, nova-scheduler will assume each cluster as a single compute node that has the aggregate of resources of all ESXi hosts managed by that cluster, as shown in the previous figure.

A good practice retrieved from this layout implementation is to place the compute node in a separate management vSphere cluster so that nodes that run nova-compute can take advantage of vSphere HA and DRS. vCenter can be managed by the OpenStack compute nodes only if a management vSphere cluster is created outside the OpenStack cluster.

One common use case for host aggregates is when you want to support scheduling instances to a subset of compute hosts because they have a specific capability.

Our previous example can be thought of as the following if we seek a heterogeneous hypervisor deployment in an OpenStack installation using KVM and vSphere ESXi.

It is important to guarantee that particular VMs are spun up on their specific vSphere cluster, which exposes more hardware requirements. To do this, OpenStack facilitates such requirements by means of host aggregates. They are used with nova-scheduler in order to place VMs on a subset of compute nodes based on their rank capabilities in an automated fashion.

A brief example can be conducted with the following steps:

1. Create a new host aggregate; this can be done through Horizon. Then, select **Admin project**. Point to the **Admin** tab and open **System Panel**. Click on the **Host Aggregates** category and create new host named vSphere-Cluster_01.

2. Assign the compute nodes managing the vSphere clusters within the newly created host aggregate.

3. Create a new instance flavor and name it vSphere.extra with particular VM resource specifications.

4. Map the new flavor to the vSphere host aggregate.

This is amazing because any user requesting an instance with the vSphere.extra flavor will be forwarded only to the compute nodes in the vSphere-Cluster_01 host aggregate.

Therefore, it will be up to vCenter to decide which ESXi server should host the virtual machine.

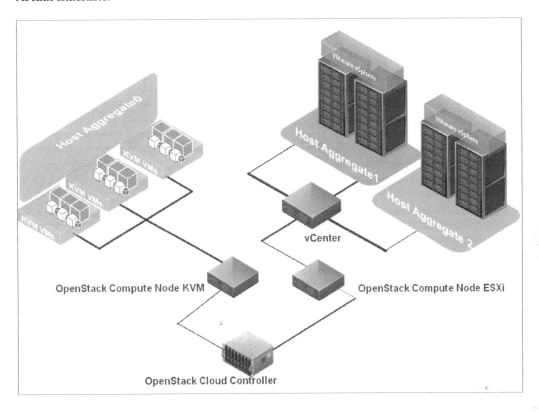

At this point, we consider that running multiple hypervisors in a single OpenStack installation is possible using host aggregates or the terminology of cells. Then, if you factor in hypervisors' varieties, do not get confused by the fact that a single hypervisor is running with an individual compute node.

Eventually, the previous figure might consider that the VM instances running on KVM can be hosted directly on a nova-compute node, whereas the vSphere with vCenter on OpenStack requires a separate vCenter server host where the VM instances will be hosted on ESXi.

Storing instances' alternatives

Compute nodes have been sized with the total CPU and RAM capacity, but we did not cover the disk space capacity. Basically, there are many approaches to doing this but it might expose other trade-offs: capacity and performance.

External shared file storage

The disks of running instances are hosted externally and do not reside in compute nodes. This will have many advantages, such as the following:

- Ease of instance recovery in the case of compute node failure
- Shared external storage for other installation purposes

On the other hand, it might present few drawbacks, such as the following:

- Heavy I/O disk usage affecting the neighboring VM
- Performance degradation due to network latency

Internal nonshared file storage

In this case, compute nodes can satisfy each instance with enough disk space. This has two main advantages:

- Unlike the first approach, heavy I/O won't affect other instances running in different compute nodes
- Performance increase due to direct access to the disk I/O

However, some further disadvantages can be seen, such as the following:

- Inability to scale when additional storage is needed
- Difficulties in migrating instances from one compute node to another
- Failure of compute nodes automatically leading to instance loss

In all cases, we might have more concerns for reliability and scalability. Thus, adopting the external shared file storage would be more convenient for our OpenStack deployment. Although there are some caveats to the external instances' disk storage that must be considered, performance can be improved by reducing network latency.

Cooking the compute node

Deploying the compute node via Chef is much simpler than understanding the resource requirements needed for a node. Basically, the compute node will run nova-compute together with the networking plugin agent. What you should understand at this stage of automated deployment is how to conduct your controller to communicate with the compute node when you run Chef.

You got it: create a correct network mapping in your environment file.

Let's refresh our memory about the compute spot against the controller:

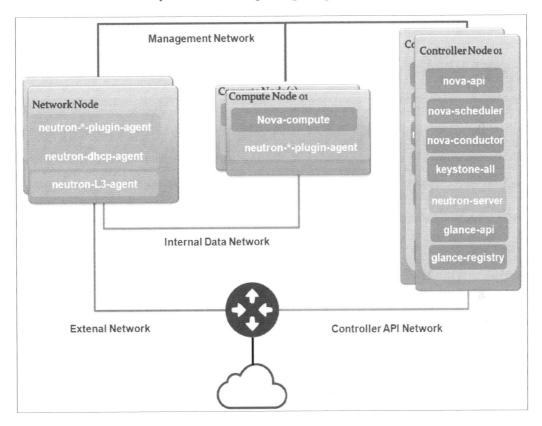

We have already defined a role in the cookbook that automates the installation of the cloud controller instances in *The cloud controller* section. We will do this for the compute node as well by defining a new role named `packtpub-os-compute`.

The next cookbook design will highlight a complete independent compute node setup regardless of the presence of the cloud controller in the environment. Thus, the design might be tempted to show all dependencies as the compute node will be deployed out of the box. As was claimed in our Chef cloud controller installation, many roles can use other recipes within a given role. The same aspect applies to our compute node. Basically, a compute node that runs nova-compute will depend on the image, identity, and network services besides the common services and attributes that describe the OpenStack environment, such as endpoint mapping. If you intend, for example, to start the deployment of the compute node for the first time, its cookbooks must be uploaded. On the other hand, you can create a berks file that defines the list of required cookbook dependencies in your compute node cookbook. Do not be surprised if you find some cookbooks from the Chef community, which may include the same dependencies. This indicates good design as it is considered as a nonmonolithic block with which you can deploy services independently but by sharing the same dependencies. We have our primary cookbooks already uploaded. Adding new ones will depend on the existing ones if you would like to customize your OpenStack deployment. In addition, any updates to recipes will be taken into consideration by Chef. Chef is smart enough to claim that it is already added and there is no need to upload it again, but just to use it. This is another reusability aspect of Chef deployments. You may feel the difference between the first deployment in Chef and the subsequent ones from the perspectives of speed and fewer errors. The Chef compute node cookbook design may look like the following:

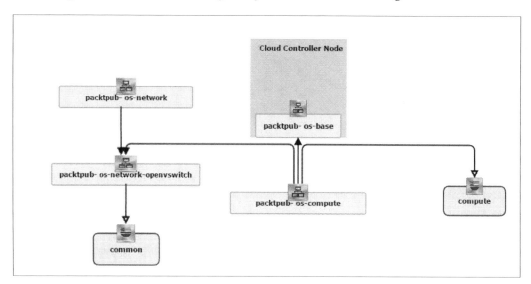

The open vSwitch agent service can also run optionally on compute nodes. In this way, scalability of open vSwitch is achieved in case of compute node failure.

The new `packtpub-os-compute` Chef role can be defined as the following:

```
name "packtpub-os-compute"
description "PacktPub scalable compute node role"
run_list(
  "role[packtpub-os-compute-worker]",
  "role[packtpub-os-network-openvswitch]"
)
```

To upload the new role to your Chef environment, run the following command from the Chef workstation using the Knife command line:

```
packtpub@workstation$  knife role from file /home/packtpub/chef-
cookbooks/roles/packtpub-os-compute.json
```

Preparing for plan B

One of the most critical tasks for a system administrator or cloud operator is to plan a backup. Building infrastructure and starting in production without a disaster recovery background is considered highly risky and you will need to start taking immediate actions. We may find a bunch of property software in the cloud computing area that does the job, such as the VMware backup solution.

However, backing up open source clouds will not be that easy. OpenStack does not, for instance, support any special tool for backup. As it is merely a collection of components combined to deliver services, an OpenStack operator should think how to map the components used in its infrastructure and prepare a backup strategy for each; the strategy should be easy, efficient, and autorecovery-enabled.

Thus, you should not miss the first question: what do we need to back up and how do we perform such a mission?

At first glance, you might be tempted to think that backing up the cloud controller will be centered on configuration files and databases.

Back up with backup-manager

Considering that there are many backup methods, you may wonder how to choose the right tool for your system.

One of these methods involves using the backup-manager tool: a simple command-line backup that is available for most Linux distributions. You can install it on your nodes and configure it easily from one central file. If you are using CentOS 6 or earlier, you will need to enable your EPEL repository:

```
packtpub@cc01$ sudo rpm -Uvh http://mirrors.kernel.org/fedora-epel/6/
i386/epel-release-6-8.noarch.rpm.
```

Import the GPG key, as follows:

```
packtpub@cc01$ sudo rpm --import /etc/pki/rpm-gpg/RPM-GPG-KEY-EPEL-6
```

Install the `backup-manager` package:

```
packtpub@cc01$ sudo yum install backup-manager
```

The main configuration file for backup-manager is `/etc/backup-manager.conf`. You can edit the file by defining each section by the backup methods and their associated variables. We can start by listing the directories and files that we want to back up:

```
export BM_TARBALL_DIRECTORIES="/var/lib/nova /etc/keystone
   /etc/cinder /etc/glance /var/lib/glance /var/lib/glance/images
   /etc/mysql"
```

> Note that we have excluded the `/var/lib/nova/instances` file from the backup folder list, as it contains running KVM instances. It might result in nonproper bootable images once you have restored them from the backup. For safety reasons, it might be possible to save the image states first by means of snapshots and backing up the generated image files in the next step.

Then, we specify the backup methods, such as `mysql` using `mysqldump` and `tarball` to define the list of directories of corresponding tarballs:

```
export BM_ARCHIVE_METHOD="tarball mysql"
```

The next line will point to where you can store the backups:

```
export BM_REPOSITORY_ROOT="/var/backups/"
```

You may plan for a redundancy plan by uploading the archived backup to a secondary server using `rsync`. You can use your Swift cluster to provide more data redundancy across the SWIFT rings.

 Backing up your nodes' configuration files locally needs continuous monitoring, especially for disk space consumption. Try to keep an eye on your monitoring system to prevent a full disk space state in your nodes.

Next, we will explain how files will be compressed using gzip, for example:

```
export BM_MYSQL_FILETYPE="gzip"
```

Optionally, you can define the SSH account to upload your archives remotely:

```
export BM_UPLOAD_SSH_USER="root"
```

Next, we move to backing up our SQL databases. You can use the traditional method using `mysqldump`. We can continue with backup-manager and add the following sections to `/etc/backup-manager.conf`:

```
export BM_MYSQL_DATABASES="nova glance keystone dash mysql cinder"
export BM_MYSQL_ADMINPASS="Define the root password in /root/.my.cnf"
```

The downside of this approach is the plaintext presentation of the password of databases. Thus, if you intend to secure the database, ensure that the permissions are restricted for `/etc/backup-manager.conf`, including the root user.

What about compute nodes? In fact, it implies the same folder, `/var/lib/nova/`, and excludes the subdirectory instances where the live KVM resides. Backing up the instances themselves is also possible by either creating a snapshot from Horizon or by installing a backup tool in the instance itself.

Simple recovery steps

For a safe and successful recovery process, you can follow the next set of simple steps:

1. Stop all the services that you intend to recover. For example, for a full Glance recovery in your cloud controller, run these commands:

   ```
   packtpub@cc01$ stop glance-api
   ```

   ```
   packtpub@cc01$ stop glance-registry
   ```

2. Import the `glance` backed-up database:

```
packtpub@cc01$ mysql glance < glance.sql
```

3. Restore the `glance` directories:

```
packtpub@cc01$ cp -a/var/backups/glance /glance/
```

4. Start all `glance` services:

```
packtpub@cc01$ service start mysql
packtpub@cc01$ glance-api start
packtpub@cc01$ glance-registry start
```

Summary

In this chapter, you learned how to distribute services among cloud controllers by taking future deployment based on fundamental concepts about high availability and service clustering into consideration. You also learned how a cloud controller is composed and how it functions in an OpenStack environment. By breaking down the cookbooks we uploaded on our Chef server, you covered an example that showed how you could play with roles to define your own services for them to be reusable with other recipes. You should also have learned the importance of compute node requirement from a hardware perspective by refining the decision related to hypervisor selection and how to conduct the best storage outfit for your compute nodes.

Another important topic was highlighted, which investigates how to back up your OpenStack environment. This is not something to ignore; as your OpenStack installation grows, the size of disk usage per node may increase dramatically and can bring it down quite easily. In this case, we have to look at the storage approaches existing in OpenStack and how to harness them to be useful for different purposes, which will be covered in the next chapter.

4
Learning OpenStack Storage – Deploying the Hybrid Storage Model

"As is our confidence, so is our capacity."

–William Hazlitt

Competing as a large cloud enterprise requires a reliable, scalable, and robust storage solution. The next generation of data centers aims to leverage the power of cloud storage. The storage infrastructure in the data center has been simplified by the means of software-defined storage. With OpenStack, managing storage through the software stack in the data center becomes easier. Additionally, OpenStack provides several storage types that need more understanding in order to make the right choice with regard to which storage solution will suffice for all the workload requirements.

The mission of this chapter is to make the readers self-confident about the design of their storage in the OpenStack environment. In this chapter, we will learn how to use Swift and Cinder. Additionally, we will introduce Ceph, a new cloud storage solution that is seamlessly integrated with OpenStack.

In this chapter, we will go through the following topics:

- Understanding the different storage types in OpenStack
- A few best practices under the umbrella of storage systems
- Simplifying the Swift architecture and explaining how to do it
- Bringing Cinder under the microscope and demonstrating its use case
- Getting to know Ceph and ways to integrate it within OpenStack

Understanding the storage types

Which storage technology will fit into your OpenStack cloud implementation? To answer this question, it is necessary to differentiate between different storage types, which will make sense of each use case of your further decision. The fact that OpenStack clouds can work in tandem with many other open source storage solutions might be an advantage, but on the other hand, it can be overwhelming.

Thus, you are tasked in the beginning as you have to decide what you need—persistent or ephemeral storage?

Ephemeral storage

For the sake of simplicity, we will start with the nonpersistent storage, which is called *ephemeral* storage. As its name suggests, a user who actively uses a virtual machine in the OpenStack environment will lose the associated disks once the VM is terminated.

Persistent storage

Persistent storage means that the storage resource is always available. Powering off the virtual machine does not affect the data. We can divide it into two persistent storage options in OpenStack—object and block storage with the code names Swift and Cinder, respectively. We did talk about Swift and Cinder in *Chapter 1, Designing OpenStack Cloud Architecture*, in a nutshell. Let's dive into each storage OpenStack-aware and see how the two different concepts are used to dump different purposes.

Object storage is not NAS/SAN

Object storage allows a user to store data in the form of objects by using the RESTful HTTP APIs. If you compare an object storage system to traditional NAS or SAN storage, it might be claimed that object storage is much better than the latter. You can refer to an object as a file representation in a traditional way. Let's take a closer look at how they differ:

- Objects are stored in a flat and vast namespace. Unlike a traditional storage system, they do not preserve any specific structure or a particular hierarchy.
- The stored objects are not user friendly.
- Accessing the **Object Storage Devices (OSDs)** by using an API such as REST or SOAP cannot be done via any file protocol such as BFS, SMB, or CIFS.
- Object storages are not suitable for high-performance requirements or structured data that is frequently changed, such as databases.

A spotlight on Swift

Swift was one of the first OpenStack projects. It was developed by NASA and Rackspace, and the former contributed towards the project by developing the code of the block storage of the OpenStack ecosystem. A few major changes to the storage came about in a very short span of time.

Firstly, the emergence of web and mobile applications fundamentally changed data consumption. The second major change was introduced in the **Software Defined Storage (SDS)**, which enables a large distributed storage system to be built by a basic commodity storage. This dramatically reduces the cost of deploying data into an application as the individual component is not reliable.

Swift is an object storage system. This means that it treats immediate consistency before eventual consistency. This allowed Swift to gain HA, redundancy, throughput, and capacity.

By adopting Swift as a cloud storage solution, you can enjoy several benefits, some of which are as follows:

- **Scalability**: Swift is designed as a distributed architecture that allows the performance to scale
- **On-demand**: Swift offers an on-demand storage with a centralized management way
- **Elasticity**: The dynamic ways to use data allow you to increase and decrease its available resources as needed

The Swift architecture

By relying on Swift for the logical software management of data instead of some specialized vendor hardware, you gain incredible flexibility and features related to deployment scaling that are unique to a storage system.

This is the essence of what an SDS is all about. However, what happens under the hood is really interesting. Swift is fundamentally a new type of storage system. It is a *monotonic* system rather than a distributed system, which means that it scales out and tolerates failures without compromising the data availability. Swift does not attempt to be like other storage systems; it doesn't mimic their interfaces. Instead, it changes how the storage works.

The Swift architecture is very distributed, which prevents any **Single Point Of Failure (SPOF)**. It is also designed to scale horizontally.

The components of Swift consist of the following:

- **The Swift proxy server**: This accepts the incoming requests via either the OpenStack Object API, or just the raw HTTP. It accepts file uploads, modifications to metadata, or container creation. In addition, it also serves files or container listings to the web browser. The proxy server may also rely optionally on the cache, which is usually deployed with memcached which improves performance.

- **The account server**: This manages the account that is defined with the object storage service. It describes the storage area that defines its own descriptive information (metadata) and the list of containers in the account.

- **The container server**: This manages a mapping of containers in the account server. A container refers to the user-defined storage area in an account server. It defines a list of stored objects in the container. A container can be conceptually similar to a sample folder in a traditional filesystem.

- **The object server**: This manages an actual object within a container. The object storage defines where the actual data and its metadata is stored. Note that every object must belong to a container.

> Metadata provides descriptive information about the object. It is stored as key-value pairs. For example, a database backup can contain information about the backup time and backup tool.

Also, there are a number of processes that perform the housekeeping task on the large data stores. The most important of these are the replication services, which ensure consistency and availability through the cluster. Other post-processing processes include auditors, updaters, and other reapers.

> Auditors, updaters, replicators, and reapers are background daemons that are run by Swift. Note that these processes can be high resource consumers, which can be noticed by the increase in the disk I/O traffic metric. It is recommended to adjust a few settings in every object and container configuration file. For example, it is possible to limit the number of background processes running simultaneously on each node by adding a **concurrency** value in each replicator, reaper, updater, or section. To see more about the Swift object, container, and server configurations, check the following link: http://docs.openstack.org/havana/config-reference/content/object-server-conf.html.

Fire and forget

What makes Swift an amazing *handler* of objects in a storage system is the way it treats the blob data and gives access via the OpenStack API.

It just clears the question: *Where is my file and how can I access it?* You would instead change the question to: *Do I have the unique object ID of the corresponding file?*

If the answer is yes, then you should really not care about the location of the file. Make it simple. Exchanging OID with your OSD is enough!

Indexing the data

Searching, retrieving, and indexing the data in an OSD is done via the extensive usage of metadata. Although a typical NAS storage uses the metadata, you should consider the fact that the metadata in OSD is stored with the object itself in key-value pairs. What makes it pretty wonderful is that the OSD keeps tagging the object even if it is sliced or chunked with its metadata for storage efficiency reasons.

A rich API access

The proxy Swift process is the only process that can communicate outside a storage cluster, and what it does is listen and speak to a specific HTTP.

Thanks to the RESTful HTTP API, we will be able to access the OSDs. On the other hand, Swift provides language-specific libraries and APIs in PHP, Java, Python, and so on.

Let's see what the HTTP request looks like within the Swift API:

- **GET**: This downloads objects with metadata and lists the contents of the containers or accounts
- **PUT**: This uploads objects, creates containers, and overwrites the metadata headers
- **POST**: This updates the metadata (accounts or containers), overwrites the metadata (objects), and creates containers if they do not exist
- **DELETE**: This deletes objects or empty containers
- **HEAD**: This retrieves header information, which includes the metadata for the account, container, or object

An object request always requires an authentication token. Therefore, authentication can be configured through the WSGI middleware, which is typically Keystone.

 Objects stores can be mounted and accessed via NFS, SMB, or CIFS if their corresponding stores provide a NAS interface.

Physical design considerations

The hallmark of Swift usage is that it requires you to look after your data durability and availability. By default, a Swift cluster storage design considers a replica of three.

Therefore, once the data is written on a replica, it is spread across two other replicas, which increases the availability of your data on one hand. On the other hand, you will need more storage capacity. In addition, referring to the first logical design in *Chapter 1*, *Designing OpenStack Cloud Architecture*, we have dedicated a network for storage.

That was by purpose firstly for logical network design organization and secondly to mitigate the load on the network by dedicating a separate storage handler. Imagine a situation where one of the storage nodes with 50 TB fails when you need to transfer this huge blob of data remotely to accomplish the required three-replica design. It can take a few hours, but we need it *immediately*! Thus, take into account the bandwidth precisely between your storage servers and proxies. This is a good reason to put the spotlight on the physical design and the way the data is organized in Swift.

In the first stage, we saw that the accounts, containers, and objects form the term *data* in Swift, which will need physical storage. In this stage, the storage node will be constructed first. Remember that Swift aims to isolate failures, which makes the cluster wider in terms of grouping according to the nodes. Thus, Swift defines a new hierarchy that helps you abstract the logical organization of data from the physical one:

- **Region**: Being in a geographically distributed environment, data can be held in multiple nodes that are placed in different regions. This is the case with a **multi-region cluster** (**MRC**). A user can suffer due to higher latency that comes with the different servers being placed away from each other in each region. To do so, Swift supports a performance read/write function called **read/write affinity**. Based on the latency measurements between the connections, Swift will favor the data that is closer to read. On the other hand, it will try to write data locally to transfer the data to the rest of the regions asynchronously.

- **Zone**: Regions encapsulate zones, which define the availability level that Swift aims to provide. A grouping or a set of hardware items, such as a rack or storage node, can refer to a zone. You can guess the rest—zoning to isolate hardware failure from the other neighbors.

 It is recommended to use five zones and start with at least one zone in a given cluster.

- **Storage nodes**: The logical organization continues the storage abstraction from the region which is the highest level, zones within region until we find the storage servers which define the zone. A set of storage nodes forms a cluster that runs the Swift processes and stores an account, a container, the object data, and its associated metadata. What makes Swift unique is a special storage organizer aware is possibly used to define how your set of nodes would be grouped by criteria.

- **Storage criteria**: Depending on how the zones are set within the available regions, Swift allows us to customize the way you wish to distribute data across a single region or multiple regions on specific storage hardware or a defined replica cluster.

- **Storage device**: This is the smallest grain of the Swift abstraction data classification. The storage device can be the internal storage node's device or connected via an external stack of a collection of disks in a drive enclosure.

> The drives that are used in Swift can be set in a **Just a Bunch of Disks (JBOD)** regardless of the configuration and can be accessed from the host computer as a separate drive unlike RAID, which treats a collection of drives as a single storage unit.

The following figure shows the hierarchy in Swift:

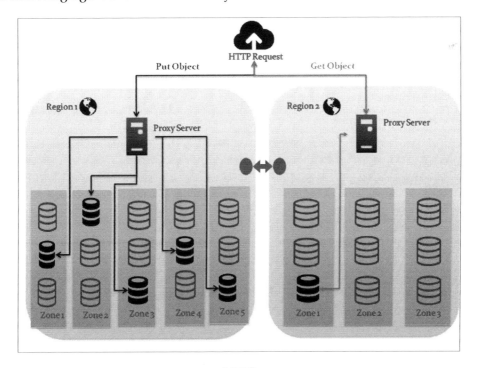

Where is my data?

Ultimately, considering an MRC and looking for some sample data across a bunch of storage servers fires up a pertinent question: how could Swift do that?

Whether the request was to read or write, the Swift servers need to map the data names to physical locations, which are called *rings*. We can summarize the concept of the rings as follows:

- Assign accounts, containers, and objects in separate rings
- Logical partition of the storage device in the ring
- Update the ring by redistributing the partitions in case or add/remove a device to/from the cluster respectively

> It is recommended to use 100 partitions for each device per zone.

Practically, a ring is a bunch of tables that are distributed to every node in the cluster. So, why do these tables exist everywhere? The answer is simple. This is because Swift replicates data everywhere!

> There are various rings present in a cluster. When a process needs to find an account, a container, or an object, it first looks for the data in all the locations on every separate ring.

Does this not make sense? When a process needs to find some account-related data, it first starts looking in a local copy of the rings, which points to all the locations on the account ring for the data. For example, the rings in Swift use the hash functions to determine how to retrieve or store an object. When using several drives in a multiregion Swift environment, complicated hashing functions can be used to accomplish such data location.

For example, a simple method to determine where to store an object can use an MD5 algorithm by getting the hash of the object storage location in an account server, as follows:

```
md5 ("/account_server01/container01/objectID") =
    f46aaa8067cbeb944b547a0fbc3012a2
```

The ring will define the MD5 hash to a hexadecimal representation, which will give a value of 65485316749524531527494523854500245 0045.

Next, we'll proceed with a modulo operation by dividing its value by the available number of drives. Assuming that we have three drives, it might give the following result:

```
33211519859701979615983889907105997419 % 3 = 2
```

The remainder of the former division will map the drive ID, which is 2.

Swift uses the ring-builder tool to create builder files by account/container/object storage that contains information such as the replica count, partition power, and the location of the storage drives within the cluster.

> The total number of partitions that exist in your cluster can be obtained by using the following partition power formula:
>
> *Total_partitons_per_cluster = 2 [partition power]*
>
> Here, the partition power is a random integer.

The following figure shows the ring mechanism:

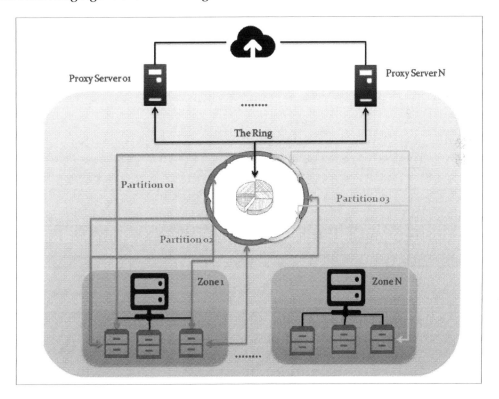

Let's sum up our understanding of Swift in a real write-show example, as illustrated in the previous figure:

1. Get the list of drives by the proxy servers from the ring.
2. Associate the objects to write the data.
3. Devices acknowledge for the ability to perform write operations.

Swift hardware

Basically, we want to know how many proxy and storage nodes (containers, accounts, and objects) we will need. Note that we can logically group containers, accounts and/or objects in a node to form a storage tier. Note that the racks formed by a set of storage tiers that are logically sharing a physical point of failure, such as a connection to a standalone switch, will be grouped into the same zone. Let's take a look at an example of the deployment that we intend to have:

- 50 TB of object storage
- Cluster replica of 5
- The Swift filesystem is XFS
- A hard drive of 2.5 TB
- 30 hard drive slots per chassis

With a few basic calculations, we can conclude how many storage nodes we will need.

Starting with an important point concerning the factor or the XFS overhead gives a value of 0.5 percent, which gives a factor of 1.0526.

 A nice post can be found at http://rwmj.wordpress.com/2009/11/08/filesystem-metadata-overhead/. In this, several filesystem metadata overheads are compared.

On the other hand, by assuming a cluster of five replicas, the total storage capacity can be calculated in the following way:

```
50 * 5 replicas = 250 TB
```

Next, we will get the total raw storage that is needed to calculate the size of the drive, as follows:

```
250 TB * 1.0526 = 263 TB
```

Now, we need to determine the number of hard drives that are required, as follows:

```
[263 / 2.5] = 105.2 => 106 drives
```

Finally, the total number of storage nodes will be calculated in the following way:

```
106/30 = 3.533333 => 4 nodes
```

We can use one proxy node per four tier nodes.

> If the number of storage nodes increases and has a value of more than six in high workload traffic, you ought to add more proxy server processes.

Where to place what

Most probably, you will feel more comfortable when it comes to choosing the CPU or RAM capacity based on our previous calculations in *Chapter 1, Designing OpenStack Cloud Architecture*. What will be the case in large distributed storage systems?

We can go for the advanced CPU calculations as we have to make our proxy servers and storage nodes a good outfit for the commodity hardware that we plan to deploy in the OpenStack storage system. We will not spend a lot of money while maintaining the minimum capacity requirements. Let's just make it run.

The proxy server in the Swift cluster will forward the client's request and send back the responses across the storage nodes, which might increase the CPU utilization.

Storage nodes will perform intensive disk I/O operations, while affording more CPUs is highly recommended with regards to the Swift process handler for the replication and auditing of data.

Thus, with more drives per node, more CPUs are needed. Let's optimize the approach based on the CPU calculation in *Chapter 1, Designing OpenStack Cloud Architecture*. So, we already have 106 drives that are distributed in 4 nodes.

Assuming that we intend to use a CPU of 2 GHz processors with a ratio of cores to drives of 3:4, we can calculate the number of cores that we will need, as follows:

```
(27 drives * 3/4 (core.GHz/drive))/2 GHz = 10.125 cores
```

> The CPU cores can be obtained by using the following formula:
> *(Total_Number_Drives * (core:drive ration)) / GHz_Cores*

As was claimed previously, Swift recommends the use of the XFS filesystem, where it caches its nodes in the RAM. More RAM implies more caching, and therefore, a faster object access. On the other hand, you might need to cache all nodes in the RAM because you have to take care that your network limitation does not lead to a bottleneck. We will start with 2 GB RAM per server.

Finally, the most particular spec that comes now is the disks. Basically, the proxy nodes will not require any additional drive, but we need to find a cost/performance fit for the storage nodes.

Eventually, the account and container servers can be deployed with the use of SSDs, which will boost the speed during the localization of the data.

On the other hand, the object storage servers can be satisfied by utilizing the SATA/ATA disks with 6 TB disks, for example. Note that the object storage server is complaining of a low IOPS. Thus, you should add more disks till you get an acceptable value of IOPS.

The Swift network

Our first network design assumes that an additional network is dedicated for the storage system. In fact, we should remind ourselves that we are talking about a large infrastructure. More precisely, Swift is becoming a big house with small rooms in our OpenStack deployment. However, Cinder can still provide a big room in a fairly small house.

For this reason, we will extend the Swift network by deriving more subnets, as follows:

- **The front-cluster network**: Proxy servers handle communication with the external clients over this network. Besides, it forwards the traffic for the external API access of the cluster.

- **The storage cluster network**: It allows communication between the storage nodes and proxies as well as inter-node communication across several racks in the same region.

- **The replication network**: We do care about the development of our infrastructure size, right? Therefore, we will plan for the same for the multiregion clusters, where we dedicate a network segment for replication-related communication between the storage nodes.

The Swift network is shown in the following figure:

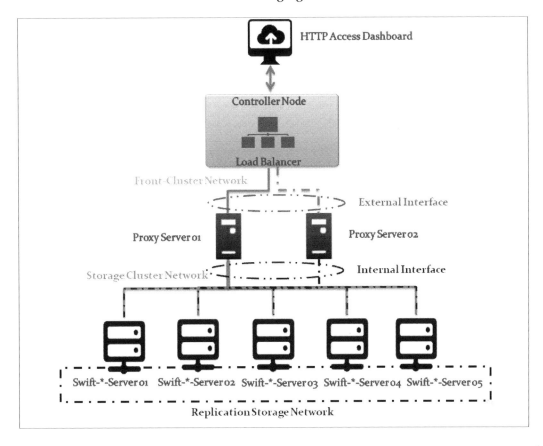

HTTP Access Dashboard

Controller Node

Load Balancer

Front-Cluster Network

External Interface

Proxy Server 01

Proxy Server 02

Storage Cluster Network

Internal Interface

Swift-*-Server 01 Swift-*-Server 02 Swift-*-Server 03 Swift-*-Server 04 Swift-*-Server 05

Replication Storage Network

Cooking Swift

The cookbooks uploaded to the Chef server in *Chapter 2, Deploying OpenStack – DevOps and OpenStack Dual Deal*, include as well the Swift cookbook named `cookbook-openstack-object-storage`.

> If you did not upload the Swift cookbook, you can download it and add to your Chef cookbook repository from GitHub: `https://github.com/openstack/cookbook-openstack-object-storage/tree/stable/havana`.

For a large environment, it is recommended to split the proxy and storage layers, as shown in the previous figure. Optionally, we can assign, for each storage node, a triple Swift server: account, container and object role while keeping dedicated nodes for the Swift proxy server. From our Chef server, we can assign the following roles.

A Swift storage node role, add this code:

```
name "packtpub-os-object-storage"
description "Swift Triple Servers Roles"
run_list(
  "role[packtpub-os-base]",
  "role[packtpub-os-object-storage-account]",
  "role[packtpub-os-object-storage-container]",
  "role[packtpub-os-object-storage-management]",
  "role[packtpub-os-object-storage-object]"
  )
```

A Swift proxy node role can be as follows:

```
name "packtpub-os-object-storage-proxy"
description "Swift Proxy Server Role"
run_list(
  "role[packtpub-os-base]",
  "recipe[openstack-object-storage::proxy-server]"
  )
```

Upload both roles to Chef server via `knife` command line:

```
$ knife role from file roles/packtpub-os-object-storage.rb
$ knife role from file roles/packtpub-os-object-storage-proxy.rb
```

For the sake of simplicity, we can run the Swift proxy server on the cloud controller. Most importantly, the Swift proxy server should have access to the storage network. The next code shows an update of our Chef environment file to support Swift in our first test environment:

```
...
"override_attributes": {
    ...........
          "object-storage": {
          "zone": "1",
          "swift_hash": "877c0688aa47",
          "authmode": "keystone",
          "authkey": "swauthkey",
          "auto_rebuild_rings": false,
          "git_builder_ip": "127.0.0.1",
```

```
        "network": {
        "proxy-cidr": "192.168.47.0/24",
        "object-cidr": "192.168.47.0/24"
            }
        },
.....
    }
}
```

We modify next our Vagrant file which will include a new `packtpub-os-object-storage-proxy` role on the cloud controller node. We will add five Swift storage nodes. The Vagrant file will be updated as the following:

```
...
chef_environment = "vagrant-packtpub"

    controller_run_list = [
      "role[packtpub-os-base-controller]",
      ...
      "role[packtpub-os-object-storage-proxy]"
    ]
...
    swift_run_list = [
      "role[packtpub-os-object-storage]"
    ]
...
# Swift 5 Storage Nodes

(1..5).each do |j|
  config.vm.define "storage_node#{j}" do |node|
        config.vm.provider "virtualbox" do |node|
            node.name = "storage_node#{j}"
            node.vm.box = "opscode-centos-6.5"
            node.vm.network "private_network", ip: "192.168.47.11#{j}"
      end
  end
    node.vm.provision :chef_client do |chef|
      chef.run_list = swift_run_list
      chef.environment = chef_environment
      chef.chef_server_url = "https://chef.packtpub.com:443"
      chef.validation_key_path = "/home/packtpub/chefrepo/.chef/chef-
validator.pem"
    end
end
...
```

After saving the Vagrantfile, update the controller node role and bring the new Swift nodes up by running the following commands:

```
# export VAGRANT_VAGRANTFILE=vagrant-packtpub
# vagrant reload --no-provision controller1
# vagrant up
```

This commands give the following output:

```
Bringing machine 'storage_node1' up with 'virtualbox' provider...
Bringing machine 'storage_node2' up with 'virtualbox' provider...
Bringing machine 'storage_node3' up with 'virtualbox' provider...
Bringing machine 'storage_node4' up with 'virtualbox' provider...
Bringing machine 'storage_node5' up with 'virtualbox' provider...
```

Next, run the following command:

```
# vagrant provision
```

Running the preceding command gives the following result:

```
==> storage_node1: Running provisioner: chef_client...
==> storage_node1: Detected Chef (latest) is already installed
==> storage_node1: Creating folder to hold client key...
==> storage_node1: Uploading chef client validation key...
Generating chef JSON and uploading...
==> storage_node1: Running chef-client...
```

Joining Cinder

Now, we will talk about block storage. We made a small comparison between Swift and Cinder in *Chapter 1, Designing OpenStack Cloud Architecture*. Since we are building the infrastructure, we need to decide on the best outfit storage. Without doubt, we have seen that Cinder is fully integrated into OpenStack Compute, where users are able to manage their own storage needs by managing the volumes and the associated snapshots of these volumes.

It is imperative to check the use case of Cinder in our storage design. Like object storage, block storage is mainly a tool for persistent storage. Under the hood, volumes expose a raw block of storage that can be attached to instances and which can store data permanently. On the other hand, Cinder manages snapshots. Keep in mind that the former is a point-in-time copy of a volume, whereas you might be able to make *fast and temporary* backups by fully copying a volume's data and storing the same in the backup system. However, the concept of the snapshot can be misunderstood when you rely on it purely for long-term backup purposes.

Fundamentally, block storage becomes an essential requirement for virtual infrastructure within OpenStack that is in favor of ephemeral storage. We should be glad that Cinder provides a block device that uses iSCSI, NFS, and Fiber Channel. Alternatively, we can even make it compatible with some other vendor backend storage connectivity. Moreover, Cinder helps you manage the quotas by limiting the tenant's usage. You can limit the quota usage by total storage utilized including snapshots, total of volumes available, or total number of snapshots taken. The following example shows the current default quota for the `packtpub_tenant` tenant by using the following command line:

```
# cinder quota-defaults packtpub_tenant
+-----------+-------+
|  Property | Value |
+-----------+-------+
| gigabytes |  1000 |
| snapshots |   50  |
|  volumes  |   50  |
+-----------+-------+
```

The limiting of the quotas for the `packtpub` tenant can be done in the following way:

```
# cinder quota-update --volumes 20 packtpub_tenant
# cinder quota-update --gigabytes 500 packtpub_tenant
# cinder quota-update --snapshots 20 packtpub_tenant
# cinder quota-show packtpub_tenant
+-----------+-------+
|  Property | Value |
+-----------+-------+
| gigabytes |  500  |
| snapshots |   20  |
|  volumes  |   20  |
+-----------+-------+
```

Choosing the storage

While dealing with the different storage systems within OpenStack, you may wonder which outfit would be the best for your storage solution. Based on our previous discussions, you should proceed into the next stage and discard a few questions and scenarios to validate your choice.

Why should your environment support block storage and why not object storage? Should you rely on the compute nodes to store your persistent storage drives? Alternatively, will the external nodes be more convenient, taking your budget into consideration? What about performance? Do the internal users need only reliable storage? Should they turn a blind eye to its performance capabilities? Do you need real redundant storage to meet the requirements of data-loss scenarios?

As you can see, we throttled a lot of questions. This can be done to a great extent. Does it sound like an investigation series? Let's keep it simple and bring our case under the microscope. Keep in mind that it will be one of many possibilities. If you intend to over engineer your profiled storage design, you may expect complexity, which may lead to an unknown state. To avoid such confusion, we can make a choice based on the strategy of using simplicity.

We will assume that block storage is recommended for our OpenStack environment for the following reasons:

- It provides persistent storage for virtual machines, which guarantees more consistency than Swift
- It offers a better read/write and input/output storage performance for the virtual machine volumes
- It resolves the trade-off between performance and availability through the use of external storage when a storage backend is supported by Cinder
- It has the snapshot facility to create new volumes for read/write usage

Suddenly, you might be tempted to think that we should not use Swift; the answer to this will be *no*! There are several reasons behind arguing in favor of Swift, some of which are as follows:

- Swift is a good fit if you wish to store large blobs of data, which includes a large number of images
- It is suitable for the backing up of archive storage, which brings the infrastructure-related data in a safe zone
- It is a very cost-effective storage solution that prevents the need to use an external RAID-specific controller

- With Swift, we can access specific user data from anywhere; it can serve as a *Google data search engine*

CAP under scope

OpenStack is designed to facilitate the integration of several existing storage architectures in the enterprise. In fact, you may have noticed that we escalated such choices to resolve the CAP theorem.

Eric Brewer of UC Berkeley proposed a theory in 2000, which states the impossibility of a distributed system to guarantee that the following three important points will be implemented:

- **Consistency**: Return the same data once a request has been launched, which presumes that the clients will see the operations occurring in the same order
- **Availability**: Return an acknowledgement once a request has been launched within a response
- **Partition tolerance**: This is the ability to resist total or partial connectivity network failures of the system

 Read more about the CAP theorem at
`http://en.wikipedia.org/wiki/CAP_theorem.`

Therefore, such a choice aspires to bring the challenge that a storage system might face to a great CAP's narrowed implication opportunity.

Swift belongs to the AP class. We have seen how it was architecturally designed to provide HA and be a good option for partition tolerance by cluster zoning.

On the other hand, although Swift and Cinder store slightly different OpenStack data, the volumes of the virtual machines are very critical in the first place. They need a very high performance bias along with a consistency level, which is something that Cinder is good at. Thus, we will not take the risk and wait for a scenario where a write operation to all the nodes in your cloud storage are not reflected simultaneously.

Stirring up the storage

Once validated, the topology for any system design will go through a hardware planning phase. For Swift, we will talk about object storage. We are highly redundant to respect the native requirements of its architecture. Let's examine an example of hardware selection.

Cinder can do more

By relying on Swift to manage object storage on commodity servers instead of specialized vendor hardware, we gain a lot of flexibility at a low cost. However, when we arrive to spend some time on our block storage, we face a few other options.

Block storage differs from object storage with regard to the consistency. In a cloud environment, where machines depend on their volumes to run, it might be obvious to treat this case in a different way. If you already have a special vendor storage solution deployed in your infrastructure, you can change the way of starting from scratch, which might not only be time consuming, but also expensive. The awesome thing about Cinder in OpenStack is that it supports many storage array suppliers. The former exposes block storage by means of Cinder drivers, such as Dell, Hitachi, IBM, VMware, HP, NetApp, and so on.

> You can check the Cinder support matrix at
> `https://wiki.openstack.org/wiki/CinderSupportMatrix`.

Cinder provides the available block storage driver support by the vendor product. The functions that are enabled by OpenStack release code names. Note that most of the suppliers provide support for protocols such as iSCSI in the first place then Fiber Channel and NFS. In our case, we will deploy block storage with the EMC plugin. As shown in the next figure, you will need an EMC **Storage Management Initiative Specification** (**SMI-S**) server to initiate the (CMI) clients operation over HTTP in the backend.

In our case, the integration of an SMI-S server is very useful if we wish to provide a common point to manage the heterogeneous storage devices in our OpenStack environment. Starting with the EMC storage, for example, you will be able to manage the additional SMI-S-enabled storage property from a unique web-based console instead of rushing between each vendor-native management interface.

CMI stands for **Clariion Message Interface** and is used for communication between the storage processors.

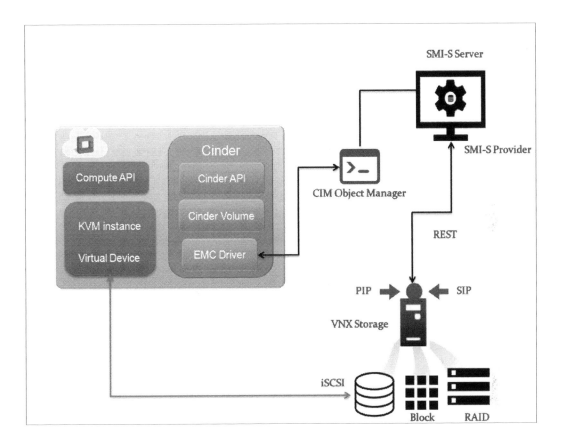

You will need to create a thin `PacktPub` OpenStack storage pool.

On your SMI-S server, you will need to install some Python dependency packets, which can be done in the following way:

```
# yum install -y libgcc_s.so.1 glibc.i686 *pywbem*
compat-libstdc++-33.x86_64  libstdc++-devel-*
```

From the EMC website, get the SMI-S install package and install it as follows:

```
# tar -xvf se7628-Linux-i386-SMI.tar
# ./ se7628_install.sh -install -host
```

Deploy the SMI-S server and configure the storage array in the following way:

```
# cd /opt/emc/ECIM/ECOM/bin/
#   ./TestSmiProvider
    (localhost:5988) ? addsys
    Add System {y|n} [n]: y
    ArrayType (1=Clar, 2=Symm) [1]:
    One or more IP address or Hostname or Array ID
    Elements for Addresses
    IP address or hostname or array id 0 (blank to quit): 192.168.1.102
    IP address or hostname or array id 1 (blank to quit): 192.168.1.103
    IP address or hostname or array id 2 (blank to quit):
    Address types corresponding to addresses specified above.
    (1=URL, 2=IP/Nodename, 3=Array ID)
    Address Type (0) [default=2]:
    Address Type (1) [default=2]:
    User [null]: adminpack
    Password [null]: adminpack
    ++++ EMCAddSystem ++++
```

On the Cinder node, check whether you have the following package installed:

```
# yum install -y libgcc_s.so.1 glibc.i686 *pywbem*
compat-libstdc++-33.x86_64  libstdc++-devel-*
```

Do not forget to tell Cinder about its backend by editing the /etc/cinder/cinder.conf file:

```
            iscsi_target_prefix = iqn.1992-04.com.emc
            iscsi_ip_address = 192.168.1.104
            volume_driver =
             cinder.volume.drivers.emc.emc_smis_iscsi.EMCSMISISCSIDriver
            cinder_emc_config_file = /etc/cinder/cinder_emc_config.xml
```

Also, we need to tell it which storage pool and which array to use with the following commands:

```
# touch   /etc/cinder/cinder_emc_config.xml
# Edit   /etc/cinder/cinder_emc_config.xml
```

Append the following configuration to the XML file:

```
<?xml version='1.0' encoding='UTF-8'?>
<EMC>
<StorageType>OpenStack</StorageType>
<EcomServerIp>192.168.1.110</EcomServerIp>
<EcomServerPort>5985</EcomServerPort>
<EcomUserName>admin</EcomUserName>
<EcomPassword>adminpass</EcomPassword>
</EMC>
```

After restarting the Cinder service, try to test it as follows:

```
#    cinder create --display-name packtpub01  5
#    cinder list
```

For the preceding code, we will get the following output:

```
+--------------------------------------+-----------+--------------+------+-------------+----------+-------------+
|                  ID                  |  Status   | Display Name | Size | Volume Type | Bootable | Attached to |
+--------------------------------------+-----------+--------------+------+-------------+----------+-------------+
| e0d836be-3ac1-4893-b2a4-34469eac9973 | available |  packtpub01  |  5   |    None     |  false   |             |
+--------------------------------------+-----------+--------------+------+-------------+----------+-------------+
```

The Cinder use case

Managing the different storage pools from one centralized management interface makes Cinder send only the volume management requests to your existing storage system. At this point, you should realize how OpenStack is open to seamlessly integrating the existing pieces in your infrastructure without you having to go through a nightmare when you wish to deploy what you exactly need.

Obviously, you may have a running OpenStack storage with one or multiple backends where Cinder stands happily. However, there are some limitations that you must take into consideration. As a system designer, you may come across different knobs that you might have to twiddle around with in a distributed storage environment. It starts when you move to the production. A database administrator may suddenly discover that its Red Hat box has almost reached 95 percent at home partition. You don't have the time to book a flight and go to Singapore to add a new storage array to the ESX server in the data center, create a new virtual disk, and attach it through the vSphere client. Even worse, it is Christmas! The trading server will expect a peak load the day after, where the database size will increase by gigabytes and you can't go offline. You have an evening to handle the situation and then join the Christmas dinner!

This kind of situation puts a system administrator under tons of pressure, where everybody expects to hear things such as: it will work! Between the words, a lot of words! Stop blaming your monitoring system, which does not send such notifications on time, and look at the situation from a different perspective. Realize that virtualization can remove the limits of hardware access for the endpoint machines, where the cloud computing paradigm just uses it to give a hand and give exactly what you need without wasting resources. You will need to add a new disk and your current case to extend an existing home partition. For example, traditionally creating a new `/dev/sda5` primary partition and assigning it to your home partition via LVM will resolve the issue in a few minutes. In a virtual environment, a precondition needs to be satisfied first, which is the price that you have to pay to derive benefits from the cloud technology. For example, if you intend to extend the virtual disk size from your vSphere client while the machine is running, you will need to check whether it is *thin provisioned*. In case it is *thick provisioned*, you will need to reboot the machine after resizing the disk in the right partition. For this reason, storage in production should be carefully handled and managed by keeping a margin of surprises that might happen.

In our deployment scenario, it is worth differentiating the types of volume that are provisioned in OpenStack by using Cinder and VNX as a backend, as follows:

- **Thin provisioning**: In this, the volume is virtually provisioned and can be allocated as needed.

- **Thick provisioning**: Here, the volume is allocated during the volume creation and is fully provisioned.

- **Deduplicated provisioning**: Here, the volumes are virtually provisioned and made deduplication-aware. In this case, the storing of volumes in the VNX devices will be done in a more efficient way by eliminating the duplicated segments in the incoming data and storing only the unique one.

- **Compressed provisioning**: In this, the volumes are virtually compressed and made compression-aware. In this case, the block storage devices may gain more capacity with better, efficient usage by freeing up a greater amount of valuable storage space with lower performance overheads. The compressed provisioning applies to all the volumes, unlike the deduplication provisioning.

The next example depicts how to create a thin volume named `ThinVol01` with the `storagetype: provisioning=thin` spec value. Keep in mind that without specifying the volume type, the driver will create a thick one by default.

```
$ cinder type-create "ThinVolume"
$ cinder type-key "ThinVolume" set storagetype:provisioning=thin
```

The preceding command will produce the following output:

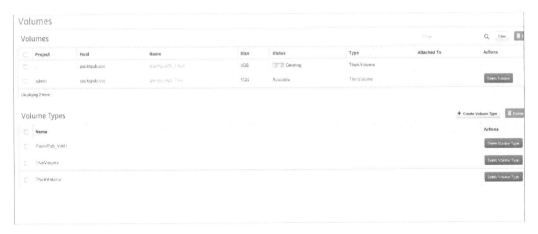

Depending on the driver configured against OpenStack, you will be requested to check each approach for what sort of limitations you will face during the production phase. For example, you will not be able to extend a thick volume, which is associated with a snapshot. It is very important to know in advance what kind of volume you are using in order to avoid an error state. On the other hand, the matrix that was cited earlier is very useful to bear in mind all the storage management functionalities. Some of them are not supported directly by Cinder, but you can use them from the native backend resource storage management.

Beyond Cinder – Ceph

Look carefully at the matrix mentioned previously, and you will find Ceph! It is not just a driver that has to be installed and configured as a backend for Cinder. It is more of a standard open source distributed storage. Ceph can be used for object storage through its S3 API as well as the Swift API. If you intend to gather all the pieces from the object and network block devices, you should consider Ceph. Moreover, it is being developed to expose the filesystem interface, which is on the way towards receiving support from the production. The concept of Ceph as a scalable storage solution is *almost* the same as Swift that replicates data across the commodity storage nodes. Do you think that is all? Of course not. Ceph is a good data consolidator that enables you to grab both the object and block storages in a single system. You can even use it as a backend to glance at images. If it is agreed that Cinder is still recommended in our block storage solution as we need its API, will you go for Ceph rather than Swift for the object storage backend? Well, this will be a difficult question to answer if you do not verify how Ceph is being architected in a nutshell.

Here's the architecture of Ceph:

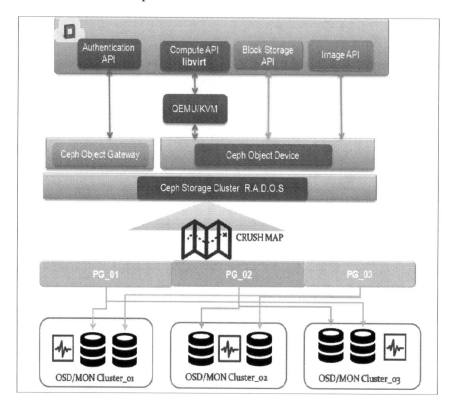

The main core of Ceph is the **Reliable Autonomic Distributed Object Store (RADOS)**, which is responsible for the distribution and replication of objects across the storage cluster. As illustrated in the previous figure, a block storage layer provides a **RADOS Block Device (RBD)** for the object's backend. The amazing part in this architecture is that the RBD devices are thinly provisioned within the RADOS objects and thanks to the `librbd` library, objects can be accessed by means of QEMU drivers, which make the magical link between Ceph and OpenStack. Unlike Swift, Ceph defines other basic components as follows:

- **Object Storage Devices (OSDs)**: This corresponds to the physical disks, which can be a directory residing on a regular filesystem, such as XFS or Btrfs. OSDs run the OSD daemon for the RADOS service, which will take care of the replication, coherency, and recovery of objects.

A Linux filesystem such as XFS or ext4 is required for the Ceph production environment, but Btrfs hasn't been proven to be a stable filesystem that is suitable for a production environment. Refer to the official Ceph website, `http://ceph.com/docs/master/rados/configuration/filesystem-recommendations/`, for recommendation-related updates.

- **Placement groups (PGs)**: A PG helps you map OSDs for performance and scalability reasons. It performs object replication by the pool as well. Every PG that is assigned in a pool will replicate the object into multiple OSDs within the same pool.

- **Pool**: You can compare a pool in Ceph to the concept of rings in Swift. It defines the number of PGs that are not shared. Furthermore, it provides hash maps for objects in OSDs.

- **The CRUSH maps**: Based on the defined criteria, a CRUSH algorithm defines how objects in OSDs will be distributed. Its main purpose is to ensure that the replicated objects will not end up on the same disks, hosts, or shelves. Besides OSD, Ceph introduces the following servers:

  - **The monitor daemon server (MON)** mainly focuses on checking the state of consistency of the data in each node that runs an OSD

  - **The metadata server (MDS)** is required for the Ceph filesystem to store their metadata if you intend to build a POSIX file on top of objects

Ceph can be integrated seamlessly with OpenStack. It has emerged as a reliable and robust storage backend for OpenStack that defines a new way of provisioning the boot-from-volume instances. This new method of provisioning is named *thin provisioning*. Eventually, Ceph compromises on a nice concept, the **copy-on-write** cloning feature, allowing many VMs to start instantly from the templates. This shows a great improvement at the threading level along with an amazing I/O performance boost.

Thousands of VMs can be created from a single master image derived from a Glance image stored in a Ceph block device and booted by using Cinder, which requires only the space needed for their subsequent changes:

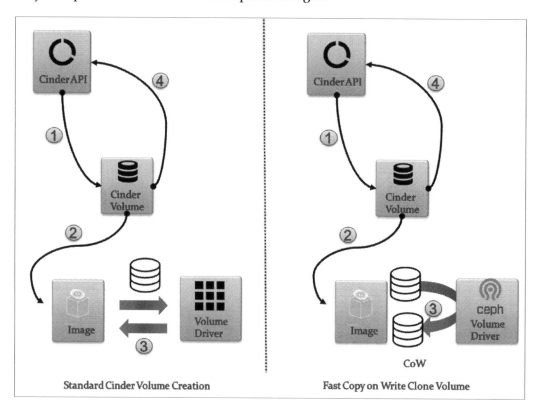

Standard Cinder Volume Creation   Fast Copy on Write Clone Volume

 To boot the virtual machines in Ceph either from an ephemeral backend or from a volume, you must use a RAW image for Glance, which is the supported format in Ceph.

The creation of the standard Cinder volume and fast copy-on-write clone volume require you to use the Cinder API to forward a create image request from a defined image at the Glance storage (**1**). The Cinder volume service tries to locate the image under question in the Glance image store (**2**) and forwards its volume reference back to the API (**4**). Using the standard way to boot an instance, as shown in the **Standard Cinder Volume Creation** section in the previous figure, an image has to be pulled from Glance and streamed to the compute node, which is extremely slow (**3**). The new approach in the **Fast Copy on Write Clone Volume** section (**3**) gives the functionality to make snapshot of images while they are being imported. Thus, it might be easier and a more sophisticated to create clones from them as well as for volume from an image.

Ceph in OpenStack

We have been using Cinder and its driver-enabled support for Ceph. We already have an overview of OSDs, which are the workhorses for object and block storage. Moreover, partitions can be created for the OSD nodes and assigned different storage pools. Keep in mind that this setup can be an example from many others. The common point that you should stick to is the way you distribute the Ceph components across the OpenStack infrastructure. In this example, we made the ceph-mon daemon run in the controller node, which makes sense if you intend to centralize all the management services from a logical perspective. The ceph-osd nodes should run in the replica in separate storage nodes. The compute nodes need to know which Ceph node will clone the images or store the volumes that require a Ceph client to run on them.

From the network perspective, the ceph-osd nodes will join the private storage subnetwork while keeping the nodes that are running the Ceph daemons in the management network.

A simple integration model with OpenStack can be depicted in the following way:

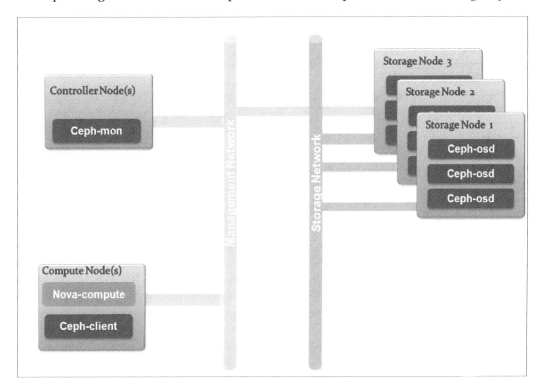

Cooking Ceph

Let's go back to our kitchen and check out the recipes that we have to prepare at this stage. As we have many options to handle either the object or block storage, we will try to sum both of them as a storage backend for OpenStack. Cooking time! We will point to the basic Ceph cookbooks from the main repository of the Opscode cookbook market. You can add the Ceph cookbook to your Chef workstation, as follows:

```
packtpub@workstation$ cd /home/packtpub/chef-repo
```

```
packtpub@workstation /home/packtpub/chef-repo $  git clone
https://github.com/ceph/ceph-cookbooks.git ceph
```

> The Apache cookbook is required as a cookbook dependency for Ceph. It might not have to be uploaded again because it already exists since the first install of the Berks cookbook dependency.

Upload the Ceph cookbooks again. The Chef server will then take care of it:

```
packtpub@workstation/home/packtpub/chef-repo$  knife cookbook upload ceph
```

Let's exploit another flexible feature in Chef—the multienvironment support. We created a basic environment that defines the distribution of the basic components and services of OpenStack in *Chapter 2, Deploying OpenStack – DevOps and OpenStack Dual Deal*. At this point, you will have two options. You can define a separate environment that was purely written for Ceph, and then proceed by modifying the current OpenStack configuration setup. Alternatively, you can use an environment file, to which you can add a Ceph subenvironment section and make some other changes to this file. Since Chef won't be bothered to rerun as many times as we want for the same environment, we will go for the second option. We would like to make more sense for the automation part. Moreover, when your infrastructure exposes dozens of nodes, you should avoid the *nano* way. Trusting your environment file will give you an *easy life*. On the other hand, it might not be wise to adopt such an approach when you only need to modify a few settings or integrate a small plugin that needs only a little modification within a limited number of attributes in your existing environment. Depending on your needs, automation always helps but without a *blind eye*. Let's bring our new environment file into action and highlight the spot of Ceph that is shown in bold, as follows:

```
{
  "name": "vagrant-packtpub",
    "description": "PacktPub Testing Environment for Ceph Integration
in OpenStack."
```

```
    "cookbook_versions": {
    },
    "json_class": "Chef::Environment",
    "chef_type": "environment",
    "default_attributes": {
      "ceph": {
        "config": {
          "mon_initial_members": [
            "controller1"
          ],
          "fsid": " 9ee348be-ef99-ea3e-7a7a-bb133abcef48",

          "osd": {
            "osd journal size": "1000"
          },
          "global": {
            "public network": "172.16.24.0/8",
            "storage network": "192.168.47.0/24"
          }
        },
        "openstack": true,
        "monitor-secret": "BASkSuJPonHgFHaaZixurLvTvAz4PRo5IKYGts=="
      }
    },
    "override_attributes": {
      ...........
          "image": {
            "api": {
              "bind_interface": "eth1",
            "default_store": "rbd",
            "store_pool": "images"
            },
          ........... . .
          "block-storage": {
          "volume": {
            "provider": "ceph",
            "rbd_pool": "volumes"
          }
          }
  .... . .
  }
}
```

We added three Ceph nodes, which have to be deployed within the two interfaces for each node. In the next execution of the Chef client, Cinder and Glance will be aware that we will use Ceph as the backend storage.

 To get the **filesystem ID (fsid)** and the monitor secret key, you will need to run the following commands from the ceph-common package:

```
# uuidgen -r
# ceph-authtool --name=monitor-secret --gen-key
```

As we covered in the previous chapter along with Chef deployment, we again intend to create a different set of roles for Ceph.

Basically, we need OSD and MON in the first place, which can be performed from the Chef web interface or via Knife in the following way:

```
$ nano roles/ceph-osd.json
{
  "name": "ceph-osd",
  "description": "Ceph Object Storage Device",
  "run_list": [
    "recipe[ceph::repo]",
    "recipe[ceph::osd]"
  ]
}
$ nano roles/ceph-mon.json
{
  "name": "ceph-mon",
  "description": "Ceph Monitor",
  "run_list": [
    "recipe[ceph::repo]",
    "recipe[ceph::mon]"
  ]
}
```

You will need to upload the following roles to the Chef server via the knife command line:

```
$ knife role from file roles/ceph-osd.rb
$ knife role from file roles/ceph-mon.rb
```

Do not forget to upload any newly created or
updated environment to the Chef server using the
Knife command line:

```
# knife environment from file <path>
```

For each OSD host, you can assign `ceph-osd` as well as `ceph-mon` if you intend
to run it in the same or a separate node. In our example, we can fire the `ceph-mon` daemon to run on the cloud controller by just adding the `ceph-mon` role to its
Chef run-list. On the other hand, it can be useful to run multiple OSDs in the same
node by running a `ceph-osd` daemon for each disk in your box from the global file
environment, as follows:

```
. . . . . . .
    "ceph": {
        "config": {
        . . . . . . .
    }
            "osd_devices": {
              "0": {
                  "device": "/dev/sdb",
                  "zap": true
              },
              "1": {
                  "device": "/dev/sdc",
                  "journal": "/dev/sdc"
              }
          }
      }
. . . . . . .
```

You can run OSDs with the Ceph node by editing the node settings of each Ceph
node, as follows:

```
{
  "chef_environment": " vagrant-packtpub ",
  "run_list": [
    "recipe[ceph::repo] ",
    "role[ceph-osd] "
  ],
  "normal": {
        "ceph": {
    "osd_devices": [
        {
            "device": "/dev/sdb",
            "journal": "/dev/sdb"
        }
    ]
  }
}
```

```
    },
    "name": "ceph01"
}
```

Let's update the Vagrant file, which will include a new `ceph-mon` role on the cloud controller node. For the sake of simplicity, we will include an additional node that runs three OSDs. The Vagrant file will be updated in the following way:

```
...
chef_environment = "vagrant-packtpub"

    controller_run_list = [
      "role[packtpub-os-base-controller]",
      ...
      "role[ceph-mon]"
    ]
...

    Ceph_run_list = [
      "role[ceph-osd]"
    ]
# Ceph 3 OSDs Node

  config.vm.define :ceph1 do |cephpp|
    cephpp.vm.hostname = "ceph1"
    cephpp.vm.box = "opscode-centos-6.5"
    cephpp.vm.box_url =
    "http://opscode-vm-bento.s3.amazonaws.com/vagrant/virtualbox/
opscode_centos-6.5_chef-provisionerless.box"
    cephpp.vm.network "private_network", ip: "192.168.47.100"
     file_to_disk = "./tmp/cephpp.osd_data.vdi"
  (0..2).each do |osd|
        config.vm.provider :virtualbox do |vb|
          vb.customize ['modifyvm', :id, '--memory', '2048',
'--cpus', '2']
          vb.customize ['createhd', '--filename', disk_file,
'--size', 4048]
          vb.customize ['storageattach', :id, '--storagectl',
'SATA Controller', '--port', 3+d, '--device', 0, '--type',
'hdd', '--medium', disk_file]
        end
      end
    cephpp.vm.provision :chef_client do |chef|
      chef.run_list = Ceph_run_list
      chef.environment = chef_environment
      # Where to find our Chef Server by providing the
          authorization key
      chef.chef_server_url = "https://chefserver.packtpub.com:443"
```

```
    chef.validation_key_path = "/home/packtpub/chef
      repo/.chef/chef-validator.pem"
    end
  end
```

The last thing that you have to do is just *push the button*. Chef will update the new role for the cloud controller in your Vagrant box, as follows:

```
# export VAGRANT_VAGRANTFILE=vagrant-packtpub

# vagrant reload --no-provision controller1

# vagrant up ceph
```

The following is the output for the preceding commands:

```
==> default: Running provisioner: chef_client...
==> default: Detected Chef (latest) is already installed
==> default: Creating folder to hold client key...
==> default: Uploading chef client validation key...
Generating chef JSON and uploading...
==> default: Running chef-client...
==> default: stdin: is not a tty
```

A new Ceph node with an address of `192.168.47.100` will be created. This node resides in the same private VB network. This will mimic the storage network in real production. Thus, you will have to change it to fit your network IP address.

You can check out the newly created Ceph node by issuing the following command:

```
# vagrant ssh ceph01
```

You can check whether the Ceph service is running in `ceph01`, as follows:

```
# ceph -s
```

For the preceding code, you will get the following result:

```
cluster eae38b90-9c9f-411d-b2ce-f4447a510aed
 health HEALTH_ERR 192 pgs stuck inactive; 192 pgs stuck unclean; no osds
 monmap e1: 1 mons at{ceph01=192.168.47.100:6789/0},election epoch 2, quorum 0 ceph01
 osdmap e1: 0 osds: 0 up, 0 in
  pgmap v2: 192 pgs, 3 pools, 0 bytes data, 0 objects
        0 kB used, 0 kB / 0 kB avail
            192 creating
```

Storing images in Ceph

It is possible to use Ceph as a storage backend to store an operating system image for instances.

The following steps show how one can configure Glance to use Ceph as an alternative for the storage of images:

1. On the new Ceph instance, create a new Ceph pool for OpenStack Glance, as follows:

    ```
    # ceph osd pool create images 128
    ```

2. On the cloud controller node, configure OpenStack Glance to use the RBD store in /etc/glance/glance-api.conf, as follows:

    ```
    # nano /etc/glance/glance-api.conf
    rbd_store_user=glance
    rbd_store_pool=images
    ```

     To enable the copy-on-write cloning feature, set the direct_url = True directive in /etc/glance/glance-api.conf.

3. Save the configuration file and restart the glance-api service, as follows:

    ```
    #/etc/init.d/glance-api restart
    ```

     It is possible to reload the cloud controller configuration by commenting out the rbd_store_user and rbd_store_pool lines in the OpenStack image cookbook's attributes file.

4. On the cloud controller node, download a new image for Glance testing, as follows:

    ```
    # wget http://cloud.centos.org/centos/7/images/CentOS-7-
    x86_64-GenericCloud.qcow2.xz
    ```

5. Create a new Glance image from the downloaded image in the following way:

    ```
    # glance image-create --name="CentOS-7-image" --is-public=True
    --disk-format-qcow2 --container-format=ovf < CentOS-7-x86_64-
    GenericCloud.qcow2.xz
    ```

The preceding command yields the following output:

```
+------------------+-------------------------------------------+
| Property         | Value                                     |
+------------------+-------------------------------------------+
| checksum         | 4f26676bcbb6bd4ac97ba295e0c53285          |
| container_format | ovf                                       |
| created_at       | 2015-05-12T19:35:58                       |
| deleted          | False                                     |
| deleted_at       | None                                      |
| disk_format      | qcow2                                     |
| id               | 5c15e35b-c4a9-4fff-9197-a09e77d4f90a      |
| is_public        | True                                      |
| min_disk         | 0                                         |
| min_ram          | 0                                         |
| name             | CentOS-7-image                            |
| owner            | c4ea3292ca234ddea5d50260e7e58193          |
| protected        | False                                     |
| size             | 286675084                                 |
| status           | active                                    |
| updated_at       | 2015-05-12T19:36:06                       |
| virtual_size     | None                                      |
+------------------+-------------------------------------------+
```

6. You can check out the image ID in the `images` Ceph pool by issuing the following query:

```
# rados -p images ls
```

For the preceding code, we will get the following output:

```
rbd_id.5c15e35b-c4a9-4fff-9197-a09e77d4f90a
```

The CentOS image is stored in Ceph, which refers to the CentOS image ID that is shown in the Glance image output. The object that the Glance image recently stored and imported from Ceph is identified with the help of the `rbd_id.Image_Glance_ID` format.

> Note that it is possible to configure Cinder and Nova to use Ceph as well. You will need to create a new Ceph pool and edit the `/etc/cinder/cinder.conf` file to specify the RBD driver for Cinder. Instances in OpenStack can be booted directly into Ceph which requires defining optionally in the /etc/nova/nova.conf file the ephemeral backend for Nova. To read more about this specific setup, you may follow this useful link `http://ceph.com/docs/master/rbd/rbd-openstack/`.

Summary

In this chapter, we covered a vast topic pertaining to storage in OpenStack. By now, you should be more familiar with the different storage types. We delved into a variety of aspects of Swift as a former object storage solution for OpenStack.

Moreover, you should now be comfortable moving beyond the block storage component for OpenStack. You will be able to understand what fits better in your storage design against Cinder. We discussed the different use cases for the OpenStack storage solutions and picked up an example from the many possibilities. You should now be able to take into consideration several factors such as filesystem, storage protocol, storage design, and performance.

Finally, the last section of this chapter talked about how one can mix and deploy a block, object, and filesystem storage in a system called Ceph. Thus, thanks to its APIs, you can seize the wide range of opportunities that are provided by OpenStack. On the other hand, making the right decision for your own storage solution is on you. Remember that any storage use case will depend on your needs or, in other words, the needs of your end users.

However, do you think that only a good storage design will be enough to make your OpenStack cloud perfect? The answer to this might be yes if you noticed that it depends on your network design and security considerations, which will be the topic of the next chapter.

5
Implementing OpenStack Networking and Security

"To have security, plan ahead."

–A Sicilian Proverb

The first networking concepts in OpenStack introduced you to some easy ways to manage networking by the means of the nova-network daemon. Different network providers such as FlatManager, FlatDHCPManager, and VlanManager are used to construct the network configurations for the internal and external OpenStack networks. These network managers eventually included a bridging tool as a default gateway for instances in a compute node.

On the other hand, for management and security reasons, it might be considered limited for the following reasons:

- **Flat network**: This is a single IP pool and layer 2 domain without tenant isolation
- **VLAN network**: This requires manual VLAN configuration on the layer 2 device (switch) for port tagging and trunking

You might have noticed the different existing networks that were deployed in a large OpenStack infrastructure and the need to isolate traffic for better performance. Moreover, securing the OpenStack engine nodes—the user's instances—is without doubt a *must*. Many use cases have demonstrated that ignoring such a topic might expose your environment to serious vulnerabilities. Keep in mind that a user who has access to an instance in a compute node may take control of other instances and could even gain access to the other nodes in production if you haven't implemented a network security plan.

In this scenario, you may wonder about the drawbacks of mono-tenancy in a flat network setup. You may be tempted to think that VLANs can resolve the issue since they are the only way to provide multitenancy, which is great. However, what about ACLs? Are you ready to manage a very complex VLANed network manually?

In this chapter, we will discuss the following topics:

- Understanding how Neutron facilitates the network management in OpenStack
- Using security groups to enforce a security layer for instances
- Discovering the majesty of the Neutron plugins and using Open vSwitch
- Enabling and using Firewall as a Service in an OpenStack environment
- Enabling and using VPN as a Service in an OpenStack environment

We compared the native Nova network manager and Neutron in a nutshell in *Chapter 1, Designing OpenStack Cloud Architecture*. It is obvious that Neutron is much more powerful for management, especially for the security background. Some of the advantages of Neutron are as follows:

- More controlled IP addressing and multi-tier networks
- The management of multiple private networks
- Great network topology customization, which is achieved by supporting virtual, hardware, or mixed networks
- The introduction of new capabilities such as security groups and namespace to separate domains

The story of an API

By analogy, the OpenStack compute service provides an API that provides a virtual server abstraction to imitate the compute resources. The network service and compute service perform in the same way, where we come to a new generation of virtualization in network resources such as network, subnet, and ports, and can be continued in the following schema:

- **Network**: As an abstraction for the layer 2 network segmentation that is similar to the VLANs
- **Subnet**: This is the associated abstraction layer for a block of IPv4/IPv6 addressing per network

- **Port**: This is the associated abstraction layer that is used to attach a virtual NIC of an instance to a network

- **Router**: This is an abstraction for layer 3 that is used to perform routing between the networks

- **Floating IP**: This is used to perform static public IP mapping from external to internal networks

Security groups

Imagine a scenario where you have to apply certain traffic management rules for a dozen compute node instances. Therefore, assigning a certain set of rules for a specific group of nodes will be much easier instead of going through each node at a time. Security groups enclose all the aspects of the rules that are applied to the ingoing and outgoing traffic to instances, which includes the following:

- The source and receiver, which will allow or deny traffic to instances from either the internal OpenStack IP addresses or from the rest of the world

- Protocols to which the rule will apply, such as TCP, UDP, and ICMP

- Egress/ingress traffic management to a Neutron port

In this way, OpenStack offers an additional security layer to the firewall rules that are available on the compute instance. The purpose is to manage traffic to several compute instances from one security group. You should bear in mind that the networking security groups are more granular-traffic-filtering-aware than the compute firewall rules since they are applied on the basis of the port instead of the instance. Eventually, the creation of the network security rules can be done in different ways.

 For more information on how iptables works on Linux, `https://www.centos.org/docs/5/html/Deployment_Guide-en-US/ch-iptables.html` is a very useful reference.

Iptables are empowered by means of security groups to perform traffic filtering. Iptables define a certain number of tables containing chains of rules that determine how packets will be manipulated: packet filtering, mangling, and NAT ruling. Basically, packets traverse rules sequentially within four tables:

- A filter table used to filter packets

- A NAT table used for Network Address Translation

- A mangle table used for an intentional alteration of the data in packet headers

- Raw tables are used to configure packets to be exempted from connection tracking

Tables consist of chains. Every network packet received on any interface of a computer must at least traverse one chain. Chains can be listed briefly as the following:

- The INPUT chain is used by filter and mangle tables for packets coming to the local host.

- The OUTPUT chain is used by all the tables and defines the outgoing traffic leaving the host.

- The FORWARD chain is used by the filter and mangle tables for packets routed through the local host.

- The PREROUTING chain is used by NAT, mangle, and raw tables. The network packet is altered before routing. It defines how the destination IP address of the packet will be translated to match the routing on the localhost called **Destination NAT (DNAT)**. It is useful for floating IP functionality.

- The POSTROUTING chain is used by NAT and mangle tables. The network packet is altered after routing. It defines how the source IP address of the packet will be translated to match the routing on the destination server called **Source NAT (SNAT)**.

The last piece of the picture is the rule in the chain which determines the packet-filtering process. A rule is specified by multiple conditions (**matches**) that the packet must satisfy so that the rule can be applied; and a **target** that defines which action should be taken (in case the match conditions are met). If the condition is not met, it moves to the next rule.

The following are the possible values of a target:

- ACCEPT: This denotes that the packet is accepted

- DROP: This denotes that the packet is dropped

- RETURN: This denotes that the control will be returned to the calling chain
- SNAT: This denotes that the target rewrites the source IP address
- DNAT: This denotes that the target rewrites the destination IP address

> A complete list of possible target values in iptables can be found here:
> http://www.iptables.info/en/iptables-targets-and-jumps.html

Managing the security groups using Horizon

From Horizon, in the **Access and Security** section, you can add a security group and name it, for example, as PacktPub_SG. Then, a simple click on **Edit Rules** will do the trick. The following example illustrates how this network security function can help you understand how traffic—both in ingress/egress—can be controlled:

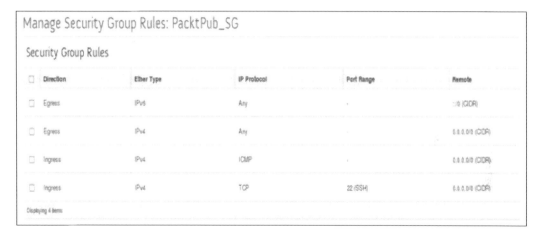

The previous security group contains four rules. The first and the second lines are rules to open all the outgoing traffic for IPv4 and IPv6 respectively. The third line allows the inbound traffic by opening the ICMP port, while the last one opens port 22 for SSH for the inbound interface. You might notice the presence of the CIDR fields, which is essential to know. Based on CIDR, you allow or restrict traffic over the specified port. For example, using CIDR of **0.0.0.0/0** will allow traffic for all the IP addresses over the port that was mentioned in your rule. For example, a CIDR with 32.32.15.5/32 will restrict traffic only to a single host with an IP of 32.32.15.5. If you would like to specify a range of IP addresses in the same subnet, you can use the CIDR notation, 32.32.15.1/24, which will restrict traffic to the IP addresses starting from 32.32.15.*; the other IP addresses will not stick to the latter rule.

The naming of the security group must be done with a unique name per project.

Managing the security groups using the Neutron CLI

The security groups also can be managed by using the Python Neutron command-line interface. Wherever you run the Neutron daemon, you can list, for example, all the present security groups from the command line in the following way:

```
# neutron security-group-list
```

The preceding command yields the following output:

```
+------------------------------------------+------------+---------------------------------+
| id                                       | name       | description                     |
+------------------------------------------+------------+---------------------------------+
| 6973081d-2f21-4268-abcb-3e5beddc12e6     | default    | default                         |
| 8d472279-d071-4610-a99d-6b19e1de0109     | default    | default                         |
| f3c3dbc1-93b7-471e-a5fc-e78b4e053be5     | PacktPub_SG | default Security Group PacktPub |
+------------------------------------------+------------+---------------------------------+
```

To demonstrate how the PacktPub_SG security group rules that were illustrated previously are implemented on the host, we can add a new rule that allows the ingress connections to ping (ICMP) in the following way:

```
# neutron security-group-rule-create --protocol icmp --direction
ingress PacktPub-SG
```

The preceding command produces the following result:

```
Created a new security_group_rule:
+-------------------+--------------------------------------+
| Field             | Value                                |
+-------------------+--------------------------------------+
| direction         | ingress                              |
| ethertype         | IPv4                                 |
| id                | 84297cf5-cd2f-469b-ad5b-7f8961fe5737 |
| port_range_max    |                                      |
| port_range_min    |                                      |
| protocol          | icmp                                 |
| remote_group_id   |                                      |
| remote_ip_prefix  |                                      |
| security_group_id | f3c3dbc1-93b7-471e-a5fc-e78b4e053be5 |
| tenant_id         | c4ea3292ca234ddea5d50260e7e58193     |
+-------------------+--------------------------------------+
```

The following command line will add a new rule that allows ingress connections to establish a secure shell connection (SSH):

```
# neutron security-group-rule-create --protocol tcp --port-range-max
22 --direction ingress PacktPub-SG
```

The preceding command gives the following output:

```
Created a new security_group_rule:
+--------------------+--------------------------------------+
| Field              | Value                                |
+--------------------+--------------------------------------+
| direction          | ingress                              |
| ethertype          | IPv4                                 |
| id                 | 6b9550f4-b27b-446f-b582-9c895c56abc5 |
| port_range_max     | 22                                   |
| port_range_min     | 22                                   |
| protocol           | tcp                                  |
| remote_group_id    |                                      |
| remote_ip_prefix   |                                      |
| security_group_id  | f3c3dbc1-93b7-471e-a5fc-e78b4e053be5 |
| tenant_id          | c4ea3292ca234ddea5d50260e7e58193     |
+--------------------+--------------------------------------+
```

 By default, if none of the security groups have been created, the port of instances will be associated within the default security group for any project where all the outbound traffic will be allowed and blocked in the inbound side.

You may conclude from the output of the previous command line that it lists the rules that are associated with the current project ID and not by the security groups.

Managing the security groups using the Nova CLI

The Nova command line also does the same trick if you intend to perform the basic security group's control, as follows:

```
$ nova secgroup-list-rules default
```

Since we are setting Neutron as our network service controller, we will proceed by using the networking security groups, which will reveal additional traffic control features. If you are still using the compute API to manage the security groups, you can always refer to the nova.conf file for each compute node to set security_group_api = neutron.

To associate the security groups to certain running instances, it might be possible to use the Nova client in the following way:

```
# nova add-secgroup test-vm1 PacktPub_SG
```

The following command line illustrates the new association of the `PacktPub_SG` security group with the `test-vm1` instance:

```
# nova show test-vm1
```

The following is the result of the preceding command:

```
| progress        | 0                                |
| security groups | default, PacktPub_SG             |
| status          | ACTIVE                           |
| tenant_id       | c4ea3292ca234ddea5d50260e7e58193 |
| updated         | 2015-04-27T11:22:08Z             |
| user_id         | c6167606b452492a8bf396c4ab2584b0 |
```

One of the best practices to troubleshoot connection issues for the running instances is to start checking the iptables running in the compute node. Eventually, any rule that was added to a security group will be applied to the iptables chains in the compute node. We can check the updated iptables chains in the compute host after applying the security group rules by using the following command:

```
# iptables-save
```

The preceding command yields the following output:

```
-A neutron-openvswi-if7fabcce-f -m state --state RELATED,ESTABLISHED -j RETURN
-A neutron-openvswi-if7fabcce-f -p tcp -m tcp --dport 22 -j RETURN
-A neutron-openvswi-if7fabcce-f -p icmp -j RETURN
-A neutron-openvswi-if7fabcce-f -s 10.10.10.3/32 -p udp -m udp --sport 67 --dport 68 -j RETURN
```

The highlighted rules describe the direction of the packet and the rule that is matched. For example, the inbound traffic to the `f7fabcce-f` interface will be processed by the `neutron-openvswi-if7fabcce-f` chain.

> It is important to know how iptables rules work in Linux. Updating the security groups will also perform changes in the iptable chains. Remember that chains are a set of rules that determine how packets should be filtered. Network packets traverse rules in chains, and it is possible to jump to another chain. You can find different chains per compute host, depending on the network filter setup.

If you have already created your own security groups, a series of iptables and chains are implemented on every compute node that hosts the instance that is associated within the applied corresponding security group. The following example demonstrates a sample update in the current iptables of a compute node that runs instances within the `10.10.10.0/24` subnet and assigns `10.10.10.2` as a default gateway for the former instances IP ranges:

```
-A neutron-openvswi-of7fabcce-f -m state --state RELATED,ESTABLISHED -j RETURN
-A neutron-openvswi-of7fabcce-f -j RETURN
-A neutron-openvswi-of7fabcce-f -j neutron-openvswi-sg-fallback
-A neutron-openvswi-sf7fabcce-f -s 10.10.10.2/32 -m mac --mac-source FA:16:3E:7E:79:64 -j RETURN
```

The last rule that was shown in the preceding screenshot dictates how the flow of the traffic leaving the `f7fabcce-f` interface must be sourced from `10.10.10.2/32` and the `FA:16:3E:7E:79:64` MAC address. The former rule is useful when you wish to prevent an instance from issuing a MAC/IP address spoofing. It is possible to test ping and SSH to the instance via the router namespace in the following way:

```
# ip netns exec router qrouter-5abdeaf9-fbb6-4a3f-bed2-7f93e91bb904
ping 10.10.10.2
```

The preceding command provides the following output:

```
PING 10.10.10.2 (10.10.10.2) 56(84) bytes of data.
64 bytes from 10.10.10.2: icmp_seq=1 ttl=64 time=340 ms
64 bytes from 10.10.10.2: icmp_seq=2 ttl=64 time=0.593 ms
64 bytes from 10.10.10.2: icmp_seq=3 ttl=64 time=0.583 ms
```

The testing of an SSH to the instance can be done by using the same router namespace, as follows:

```
# ip netns exec router qrouter-5abdeaf9-fbb6-4a3f-bed2-7f93e91bb904
ssh cirros@10.10.10.2
```

The preceding command produces the following output:

```
The authenticity of host '10.10.10.2 (10.10.10.2)' can't be established.
RSA key fingerprint is 0c:91:40:1e:f4:1e:53:67:4c:60:c3:d4:90:25:02:93.
Are you sure you want to continue connecting (yes/no)? yes
Warning: Permanently added '10.10.10.2' (RSA) to the list of known hosts.

$
```

An example of a web server DMZ

In the current example, we will show a simple setup of a security group that might be applied to a pool of web servers that are running in the **Compute01**, **Compute02** and **Compute03** nodes. We will allow inbound traffic from the Internet to access **WebServer01**, **AppServer01**, and **DBServer01** over HTTP, HTTPS, and MySQL. This is depicted in the following diagram:

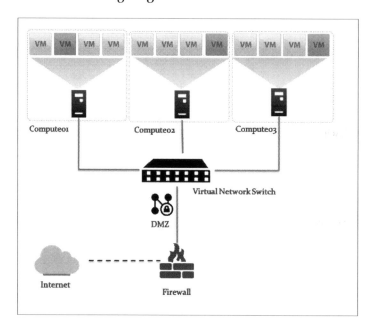

Let's see how we can restrict the traffic ingress/egress via the Neutron API:

```
$ neutron security-group-create DMZ_Zone --description "allow web traffic
from the Internet"
```

```
$neutron security-group-rule-create --direction ingress --protocol tcp
--port_range_min 80 --port_range_max 80 DMZ_Zone --remote-ip-prefix
0.0.0.0/0
```

```
$neutron security-group-rule-create --direction ingress --protocol tcp
--port_range_min 443 --port_range_max 443 DMZ_Zone --remote-ip-prefix
0.0.0.0/0
```

```
$neutron security-group-rule-create --direction ingress --protocol tcp
--port_range_min 3306 --port_range_max 3306 DMZ_Zone --remote-ip-prefix
0.0.0.0/0
```

From Horizon, we can see the following security rules group have been added:

Creating a new security group, DMZ_Zone, will actually update the iptables rules running on the compute node that hosts the instance. For example, we can see on the compute node the new iptables rules by running the following command line:

```
# iptables-save
```

The output of the iptables list is quite long; for the sake of simplicity, we will go only through the fitter chain list.

Eventually the ingress/egress network will traverse first the **FORWARD** chain as the following:

```
-A FORWARD -j neutron-filter-top
-A FORWARD -j neutron-openvswi-FORWARD
-A FORWARD -j nova-filter-top
-A FORWARD -j nova-network-FORWARD
-A FORWARD -j nova-api-FORWARD
```

The rules defined in both chains neutron-filter-top and neutron-openvswi-FORWARD will be processed. Then, iptables return to the calling FORWARD chain, which defines the following chain:

```
-A FORWARD -j neutron-openvswi-FORWARD
```

The previous rule will cause to jump to the **neutron-openvswi-FORWARD** chain. Therefore, it will jump to the **neutron-openvswi-sg-chain** chain, as the following:

```
-A neutron-openvswi-sg-chain -m physdev --physdev-out tap6919f23b-34 --physdev-is-bridged -j neutron-openvswi-i6919f23b-3
-A neutron-openvswi-sg-chain -m physdev --physdev-in tap6919f23b-34 --physdev-is-bridged -j neutron-openvswi-o6919f23b-3
-A neutron-openvswi-sg-chain -j ACCEPT
```

The first rule denotes the direction of the traffic entering the **tap6919f23b-34** interface.

The external traffic entering the **tap6919f23b-34** interface will be processed and treated by the **neurotn-openvsw-i6919f23b-3** chain, as the following:

```
-A neutron-openvswi-i6919f23b-3 -p tcp -m tcp --dport 80 -j RETURN
-A neutron-openvswi-i6919f23b-3 -p tcp -m tcp --dport 443 -j RETURN
-A neutron-openvswi-i6919f23b-3 -p tcp -m tcp --dport 3306 -j RETURN
```

The previous rules reflect the creation of the DMZ_Zone security group, which was configured previously in the Horizon dashboard.

 When the Open vSwitch or the Linux Bridge plugins are used, tap devices are created to connect the guest instance on the host as virtual network interface cards. More details will be covered in *Chapter 8, Extending OpenStack – Advanced Networking Features and Deploying Multi-tier Applications.*

Firewall as a Service

One of the most important reasons behind keeping Neutron in the scope of network management is that several extensions are offered by this component. These extensions are not available in the native Nova networking service. **Firewall as a Service (FWaaS)** is one such extension. It can be deployed in your network map. Thus, it can provide advanced management control over your virtual infrastructure. Can a firewall be abstracted in the software layer? Indeed, the awesomeness of the virtualization technology is not only limited to the computing part but also to network virtualization. This is the style of OpenStack! You can see that such a Cloud solution is not a typical hypervisor, but it encloses all aspects of infrastructure management, including network services. FWaaS is definitely an extension for Neutron. As an administrator, you will be able to define your security perimeter from a logical layer.

This includes the following options:

- Applying the rules to the ingress and egress network of tenants that are within their associated routers
- Managing the firewall policies based on a set of proper rules

You may be tempted to think that this is exactly the same as a standard firewall appliance. It's even more! Neutron in OpenStack provides a firewall that is defined for each tenant. Tenants can share the firewall policies between them. Thus, the common firewall rules are still applicable to several OpenStack tenants. But how does it work? Nothing is kept secret; firewalls in Neutron keep the same firewalling aspect by filtering the traffic using iptables. Eventually, we will see how the security groups in a network make life easier by applying a collection of rules to a certain number of compute nodes. Similarly, the rules regarding the firewall are implemented by using the Neutron namespace.

> Each tenant has its own private networks, routers, firewalls, and load balancers that are isolated by Neutron. It uses a set of logical containers, which are called network namespaces, that identify any network object by its tenant.

You might ask the following question: Do I need to enable such a firewall service? Well, it depends on the way you see your security policy. If you intend to operate on a router level and define a traffic-filtered perimeter, you should think about FWaaS. Moreover, it is tough for a multi-tier architecture to manage the filtering of traffic, especially when it is fronted by a load-balancing capability.

In addition to this, the application of security groups might not be enough to have the global filtering of traffic enabled across the Neutron router since they operate at the instance/port level. The following figure illustrates a simple FWaaS setup in the OpenStack environment:

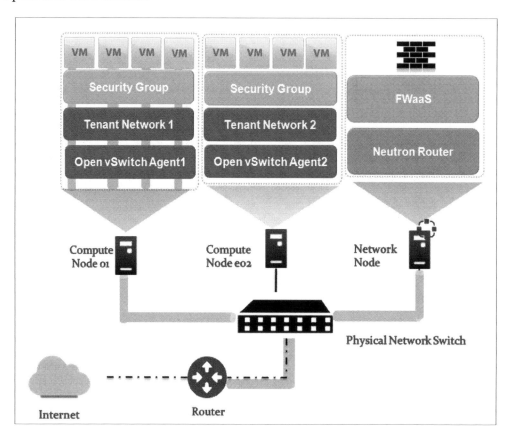

Coupling a firewall with Neutron

Like Cinder, several plugins are exposed to relate some other backend implementation of the OpenStack block storage API requests. Similarly, the Neutron API supports a variety of plugins by using the Linux VLANs and firewalls. Initially, FWaaS in Neutron is available, but it needs to be activated. Let's do this.

In the Neutron node conf file named `neutron.conf`, insert the following lines:

```
service_plugins = firewall
[service_providers]
service_provider =
  FIREWALL:Iptables:neutron.agent.linux.iptables_firewall.OVSHybridIpt
ablesFirewallDriver:default
[fwaas]
driver =
  neutron.services.firewall.drivers.linux.iptables_fwaas.
IptablesFwaasDriver
enabled = True
```

To enable firewall management from the dashboard, change the controller node in `/usr/share/openstack-dashboard/openstack_dashboard/local/local_settings.py` by using the following setting:

```
'enable_firewall' = True
```

Then, you need to restart `neutron-server` and the web server that runs Horizon in the following way:

```
root@packtpub# /etc/init.d/neutron-server restart
root@packtpub# service httpd restart
```

From Horizon, we can see that the new FWaaS section joined the OpenStack management interface, as shown in the following screenshot:

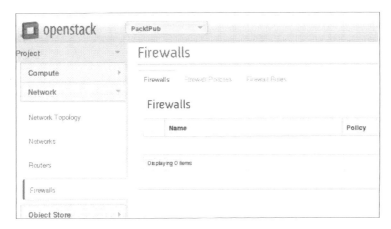

Basically, if you intend to create a firewall, you will need to create a router in the first place, which will apply the firewall setup. Note that FWaaS is a distributed implementation of a firewall per tenant. The firewall will be applied to a router that was created in the same project. You will be able to manage your firewall rules and policies from Horizon or via the Neutron's command line.

 The FWaaS feature was introduced in the Havana release.

Starting the configuration of a firewall in OpenStack is very straightforward. For example, we can apply the rules to allow the ICMP and SSH traffic to go back and forth. You can do the same on security groups level both the ingress/egress directions but will be only in the instance- or port-filtering level. For example, in the VPN site-to-site setup, you will need to allow certain ports in both the L3 devices. We can prepare our rules for the instance and apply them to our first firewall in data center 01.

Let's create the firewall rule, as follows:

```
$neutron firewall-rule-create --protocol icmp --action allow --name FW01
```

Next, we will need to specify a firewall policy in the following way:

```
$neutron firewall-policy-create --firewall-rules FW01 FWpolicy01
```

The last step will require the creation of a firewall named FWaaS, as follows:

```
$neutron firewall-create FWpolicy01 --name FWaaS
```

 The creation of the firewall will remain in a pending state until a router is created and interfaced to it.

The Neutron plugin

Ultimately, the goal of implementing networking plugins in OpenStack is to use the advanced functionalities that the native OpenStack network is not able to perform. You may remember that the basic network model is able to isolate different networks by using VLANs, which is great! But what about exploiting some other features that are present in both layer 2 and 3 by performing the operation of tunneling? One of the supported plugins in OpenStack is Open vSwitch. If anything, it is crucial to understand how to use and configure it in order to validate its use case. **Software Defined Network (SDN)** is the most recent network paradigm technology that has proven its amazing ease with regard to the network configuration and management. In a nutshell, the SDN concept is based on the separation of the hardware levels, which can be the device that is meant to forward the packets and the network intelligence layer or the decision maker layer that abstracts the network infrastructure to a software controller.

 In SDN, the packet forwarding device can be an Ethernet switch while its control logic is decoupled. The device can be programmed by using an open interface such as OpenFlow.

Keep in mind that Open vSwitch is an SDN-aware technology. It is a new, revolutionary way to write a program that can be used to customize and manage your network. Since we are moving in to the new *era* of network virtualization, it essentially provides switching services to virtual networks within the OpenStack environment.

We have already seen at the start of this chapter the extensions that were brought by the Neutron API. Basically, Open vSwitch is one of the most well-supported and stable plugins together with the Linux Bridge plugin. Both of these plugins provide a layer 2 switching. There is more! If you are wondering how one can make a virtual switch population talk to another physical one, Open vSwitch will support this mix. Open vSwitch officially supports the following:

- 802.1Q VLANs and trunking
- Port aggregation
- Tunneling: VXLAN and GRE
- NetFlow
- sFLOW
- OpenFlow
- STP and LCAP
- KVM, Xen, XenServer, and VirtualBox

There can be more than one plugin

Many third-party vendors such as VMware, Juniper, IBM, Cisco, Nicira, and many others have developed and integrated their vendor plugins in order to allow a Neutron interface with their network resources.

You are lucky if you already have some vendor switches in your current infrastructure. Thus, it is beneficial to integrate it into Neutron and extend the network functionality. However, how about using the multiplugins simultaneously? This is a tricky question! Using Open vSwitch with the Linux Bridge plugins at the same time can be very fruitful if you wish to exploit a majority of the advanced networking features that are supported by both. The recent OpenStack releases support simultaneous Neutron plugins, which alleviate such problems by introducing the Modular Layer 2 plugin.

Thankfully, there is no more vendor lock-in. You can mix and bring hardware from different supported Neutron vendors in the same OpenStack infrastructure. Therefore, any plugin that is being created and integrated can be accessed via any existing L2 agent.

> Since it was not possible to use both the Linux Bridge and Open vSwitch plugins simultaneously, they have been deprecated in the IceHouse release. The Modular Layer 2 plugin is currently a new replacement, allowing the utilization of several plugins at the same time. To read more about ML2, refer to the following link http://docs.openstack.org/juno/config-reference/content/networking-options-plugins-ml2.html.

Empowering the traffic isolation

Now that we measured the network security requirement by using Neutron, we can move ahead and extend the first network design in *Chapter 1, Designing OpenStack Cloud Architecture*.

Due to the pluggable architecture of the OpenStack networking, we will integrate Open vSwitch and test the network isolation on an instance level. Before we delve into the details, let's refresh our knowledge of the overall network topology by introducing two different logical networks:

- **Tenant networks**: By default, they are created in isolation and not shared with any other network that is associated within a user project in OpenStack

- **Provider networks**: In order to connect to the non-OpenStack resources, provider networks can be served by the administrator to map to a specific physical device in the data center

Let's assume that we would like to bring our network design into an existing physical setup. In other words, we want to create provider and tenant networks using the VLAN IDs that correspond to the real VLANs in the data center. We only need one OVS bridge to customize the connection between the following:

- Instances in an OpenStack environment
- Load balancers and firewalls
- A network device residing on the same VLAN layer 2

The next illustration depicts the existence of two tenants, A and B, each has a network with one router and one subnet. The Neutron router connects the tenants to the physical switch to interface the public Internet. Under the hood, it is possible to route securely between tenant networks using VLAN (*802.1q tagged*) and GRE-based networks. Without the Neutron router, both tenant networks are effectively isolated from each other.

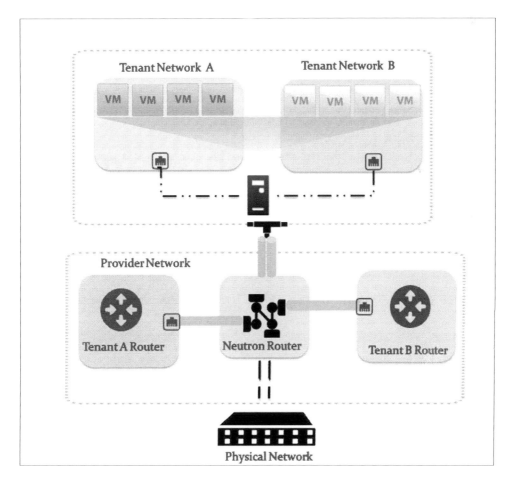

VPN as a Service – a case study

As business grows, it might be needed to expand to the multisite endpoints. In OpenStack, it can be referred to as a multicell endpoint that can provide access to the different regions of the same OpenStack infrastructure. Of course, the implementation of a VPN setup—whether it is a simple SSL one or an IPSEC solution—will empower the security of traffic across the Internet. We have worked around the host security level and brought different isolated networks in order to avoid traffic congestion and improve the security of the internal network of the OpenStack environment. The following case study will sum up the different aspects that were covered previously and take things a step further by protecting the integrity of data by using the tunneling and encryption basis. A fruitful Neutron extension provides **VPN as a Service (VPNaaS)** again, thanks to virtualization! Now, if you plan to connect two machines in different tenants that are geographically located in different data centers, then you should consider OpenStack, which makes life easier and offers a simple step-by-step configuration. VPNaaS is proven to be extension capable not only to build a site-to-site VPN connection between two private networks, but also to implement several VPN connections per tenant. Thus, you can create as many VPNs as you want, which brings to you a real, extensible network. Let's go to Horizon and study an example that helps you run a hybrid application.

General settings

The next figure depicts two different OpenStack sites, and we intend to link their associated tenants. You may remember that a project in Horizon presents a tenant description that includes its private networks, routers, and subnets.

> Add an admin user to each project in the **Admin** role. This will allow you to fully perform administrative tasks in Horizon. Additionally, you can create different users per project and assign a service type to it using an admin account.

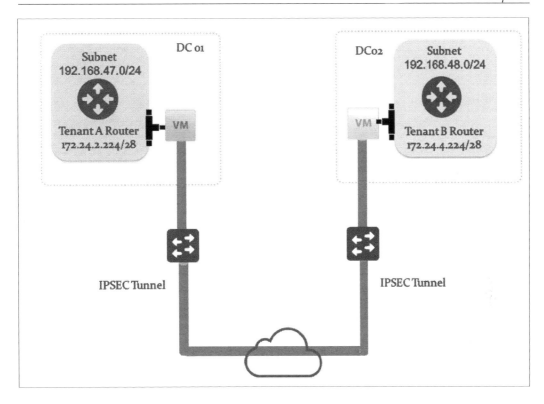

Let's create our first project named `PackPub01` in `DC01` and a second project called `PacktPub02` in `DC02`.

Based on the previous illustration, we intend to let the machines in both the OpenStack subnets talk to each other. Note that each subnet is frontended by a gateway router. Each project's network has a defined subnet that serves local IP addresses, whereas a router connects to the external public interface of each network. The connection between both the public IP addresses will be encrypted by the means of VPNaaS. In other words, the traffic between the networks will be tunneled.

The following screenshot shows a basic network topology for DC01:

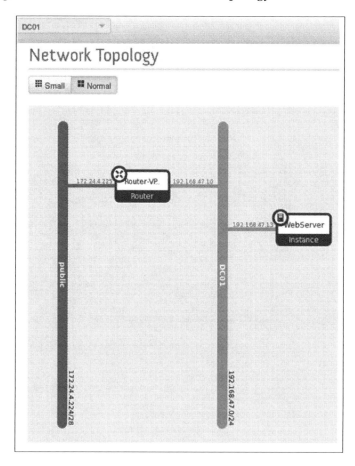

DC02 will have the same network topology by bridging the 192.168.48.0/24 local subnet to the Internet via an external router interface, which is depicted in the following screenshot:

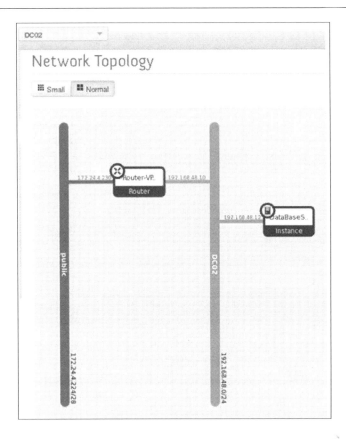

 Subnets in different tenant projects must have nonoverlapping IP address ranges.

We have configured the setup from Horizon. Let's bring VPNaaS shining in our interface by using the following three steps:

1. In order to create a full site-to-site IPsec VPN, we will use Openswan IPsec implementation for Linux. Neutron supports Openswan by providing a driver, which needs to be configured. Additionally, we will need the `neutron-plugin-vpn-agent` package to be installed on both network nodes in each site as follows:

   ```
   # yum install openswan openstack-neutron-vpn-agent
   ```

2. Start the `ipsec` service:

```
# /etc/init.d/ipsec start
```

3. Configure the Neutron agent file to use the openswan driver as follows:

```
# nano /etc/neutron/vpn_agent.ini

[vpnagent]

...

vpn_device_driver=neutron.services.vpn.device_drivers.ipsec.
OpenSwanDriver

...
```

4. Enable VPNaaS in Neutron by activating its plugin in /etc/neutron/ neutron.conf, as follows:

```
service_plugins =........... ,vpnaas
```

5. In the same file, enable the VPN service provider to use the Openswan driver in the service_providers section as the following:

```
#service_provider=VPN:openswan:neutron.services.vpn.service_
drivers.ipsec.IPsecVPNDriver:default
```

6. Next, we will add a VPNaaS module interface in /usr/share/openstack-dashboard/openstack_dashboard/local/local_settings.py in the following way:

```
'enable_VPNaaS': True,
```

7. Finally, restart neutron-server and neutron-vpn-agent services, and the web server, as follows:

```
# /etc/init.d/httpd restart
# /etc/init.d/neutron-server restart
# /etc/init.d/neutron-vpn-agent restart
```

 To read more about Openswan, check the official website: https://www.openswan.org/

VPNaaS configuration

We will start by configuring VPN on DC01.

Creating the Internet Key Exchange policy

In Horizon, we can create the **Internet Key Exchange (IKE)** policy in the first VPN phase. The following screenshot shows a simple IKE setup of an OpenStack environment that is located in the DC01 site:

An IKE policy can also be created by using the Neutron command line, as follows:

```
# neutron vpn-ikepolicy-create --auth-algorithm
sha1 --encryption-algorithm aes-256  --ike-version v2
--lifetime units=seconds,value=3600 --pfs group5
--phase1-negotiation-mode  main --name PP-IKE-Policy
```

Creating an IPSec policy

The creation of an IPSec policy in the OpenStack environment that is located in the DC01 site in Horizon can be done in the following way:

An IPSec policy can also be created by using the Neutron command line, as follows:

```
# neutron vpn-ipsecpolicy-create  --auth-algorithm  sha1
--encapsulation-mode tunnel --encryption-algorithm
aes-256  --lifetime units=seconds,value=36000  --pfs group5
                --transform-protocol esp –name PP_IPSEC_Policy
```

Standard VPN settings such as **Encapsulation mode**, **Encryption algorithm**, **Perfect Forward Secrecy**, and **Transform Protocol** should remain the same in both the sites for phase 1.

 If you face a VPN connectivity problem, a best practice of troubleshooting before filtering or debugging the traffic is to begin checking the existence of any mismatch of the phase 1 and phase 2 settings in both sites.

Creating a VPN service

To create a VPN service, you will need to specify the router facing the external interface and attach the web server instance to the private network in the DC01 site. The router will act as a VPN gateway. We can add a new VPN service from Horizon in the following way:

A VPN service can also be created by using the Neutron command line, as follows:

```
# neutron vpn-service-create --tenant-id
c4ea3292ca234ddea5d50260e7e58193 --name PP_VPN_Service
Router-VPN public_subnet
```

Keep in mind that a VPN service is needed to select the router that will perform your VPN gateway. Note that here, we have exposed our local subnet, `192.168.47.0/24`.

Creating an IPSec site connection

The last step needs some information. Usually, we need to set up an external IP address of the other peer for a VPN site. In OpenStack, you can check it by logging on as an admin and from the `PacktPub02` tenant, clicking on the **Router** section. Here, you will get all of its details, which includes information regarding the external gateway interface, `172.24.4.227`. The **Remote peer subnet(s)** value is the CIDR notation `192.168.48.0/24`. We will finish our first project, the `DC01` VPNaaS connection, by setting the secret preshared key to `AwEsOmEVPn`. The key will be the same for both the sides. The process of setting the key is depicted in the following screenshot:

A VPN service can also be created by using the Neutron command line, as follows:

```
# neutron ipsec-site-connection-create --name PP_IPSEC
---vpnservice-id PP_VPN_Service --ikepolicy-id
PP-IKE-Policy --ipsecpolicy-id PP_IPSEC_Policy
--peer-address 192.168.48.0/24 --peer-id 172.24.4.232
                    --psk AwEsOmEvPn
```

The peer gateway public IPv4 address can be obtained from the router details of DC02. We will need to hit the external interface, as shown in the following screenshot:

Name	Fixed IPs	Status	Type	Admir
(045c2737)	172.24.4.232	DOWN	External Gateway	UP
(e4657c96)	192.168.47.10	DOWN	Internal Interface	UP

To finish the VPN setup, you will need to follow the latter steps, but changing the IP gateway addresses of DC01 and the remote subnet to 192.168.47.0/24. Note that the VPN settings, encryption algorithms and protocols, and the shared password must be the same on both the sides.

A small smoke test can evaluate our setup.

From an instance in DC01, we can ping the DC02 site via 192.168.48.12, as follows:

```
# ping 192.168.48.12
PING 192.168.48.12 (192.168.48.12): 56 data bytes
64 bytes from 192.168.48.12: seq=0 ttl=64 time=1.295 ms
64 bytes from 192.168.48.12: seq=1 ttl=64 time=0.308 ms
64 bytes from 192.168.48.12: seq=2 ttl=64 time=0.284 ms
64 bytes from 192.168.48.12: seq=3 ttl=64 time=0.245 ms
64 bytes from 192.168.48.12: seq=4 ttl=64 time=0.245 ms
```

From an instance in DC02, we can ping the DC01 site via 192.168.47.13, as follows:

```
# ping 192.168.47.13
PING 192.168.47.13 (192.168.47.13): 56 data bytes
64 bytes from 192.168.47.13: seq=0 ttl=64 time=0.737 ms
64 bytes from 192.168.47.13: seq=1 ttl=64 time=0.452 ms
64 bytes from 192.168.47.13: seq=2 ttl=64 time=0.263 ms
64 bytes from 192.168.47.13: seq=3 ttl=64 time=0.241 ms
64 bytes from 192.168.47.13: seq=4 ttl=64 time=0.264 ms
```

Be sure that you have enabled ICMP on the DC02 router to allow pings.

Summary

In this chapter, we delved into the various aspects of networking and security in OpenStack. A major part of the chapter focused on presenting the different security layouts by using Neutron. At this point, you should be comfortable with security groups and their use cases. You should also be aware of the benefits of the Neutron API and the support of several plugins that allow you to diversify the networking hardware setup within OpenStack.

Although we have left the detailed networking implementation for the next few chapters, we went through other network and security functions such as FWaaS. At this stage, you should be able to understand the difference between FWaaS and the security groups and configure both of them at the network and instance level. Finally, a straightforward step-by-step guide showed another awesome point of Neutron by leveraging the networking security using VPNaaS—Neutron is very extensible and powerful. As it is a critical aspect of your OpenStack infrastructure that is responsible for network management, you should consider that Neutron can be a single of failure as well as any other OpenStack engine node in your environment. Thus, you should be sure that everything works like a charm—not only in an event of failure, but also when it's time for surprises.

This will be our next topic—investigating how the OpenStack environment has to be highly available across all layers and services. Also, it should be able to fail over at any sudden issue.

6
OpenStack HA and Failover

"Once we accept our limits, we go beyond them."

–Albert Einstein

So far, you have gained a good knowledge of all the components needed to provide a functional OpenStack infrastructure. In *Chapter 1, Designing OpenStack Cloud Architecture*, we saw one of the many ways to design a complete OpenStack environment. *Chapter 3, Learning OpenStack Clustering – Cloud Controllers and Compute Nodes*, looked at one of the most important logical and physical designs of OpenStack clustering in depth by iterating through cloud controller and compute nodes. Distributing services through the mentioned nodes after considering the standalone storage cluster, as seen in *Chapter 4, Learning OpenStack Storage – Deploying the Hybrid Storage Model*, aims to reduce the downtime for a given service. Many design approaches can fulfill such high-availability goals in OpenStack. On the other hand, HA may not be as simple as the name suggests: it's the effort to eliminate any **Single Point Of Failure (SPOF)** on every layer in your architecture. OpenStack components can be brought and distributed in different nodes while maintaining a sense of *team work*, which OpenStack is good at—again, thanks to our messaging service. In this chapter, we will:

- Understand how HA and failover mechanisms can guarantee OpenStack business continuity
- Look for a workaround on how to make different OpenStack components configured in HA
- Check out different ways to validate a complete HA setup

HA under the scope

On a daily basis, system and network administrators are faced with a new challenge by hitting the same point: *we are aiming to make our infrastructure highly available!*

Meanwhile, the IT manager sticks to his chair, drinking his tea and claims: *our IT system works just fine and our customers are satisfied.* Surprisingly, you get that phone call from the help desk with a struggling voice: *well, the browser said "page not found". Is the application server down?* Obviously, the infrastructure was not as highly available as it should have been. Despite your extra time spent configuring clusters to be in uptime, more often than not, servers might not be reachable and you then face a few *special* events, and you raise this question: *why does it not fail over?* To make sense of an HA infrastructure, on one hand, you should know what HA offers to your environment and how. On the other hand, you should stay close to test scenarios of failing over as exemplified in the following real-life show. Many system administrators feel lucky when they have bought a storage box that is not supposed to fail, and even has this written: *the solution that never shouts I am offline.* They claim that the new NAS box is highly available. Sadly, this is never realized. A power outage takes place and it takes the fancy cluster out of service for a few hours so that it can be restarted. If you realized that you need an extra battery, then you can prevent this physical event failure. Later, you update its software package by clicking on **Update the NAS**. Unfortunately, the developers of the NAS appliance have included a new feature in its HA package that makes the software unstable, but you are not able to not figure that out, as it is a new release and nobody had complained about it previously. After a while, a failover happens but the server is unreachable. It should have worked as intended. But in vain, by checking in the racks, you figured out that eventually, the slave node is becoming the master according to the shining LED light, which gets stuck while blinking! The failover is on its way, but the system is not responsive. There was a software bug in the last release. At this point, the downtime increases again while the bug waits to be fixed. Unluckily, you were the first NAS box client to complain about the new features, which you might have to wait to fix. This might take some time. A real-long unplanned failure could lead to a bigger problem!

The storage system is not highly available anymore. Downtime is the exact *enemy* of HA. Friendly downtime can be planned as you will only need to replace some pieces of hardware. On the other hand, there are many reasons for unexpected downtime, such as problems with hardware and software, or any external condition that leads to the failure of the system.

Do not mix them

We still remember that one of the several purposes of OpenStack clustering is to make sure that services remain running in the case of a node failure. The HA functionality aims to make sure that the different nodes participating in a given cluster work in tandem to satisfy certain downtime. HA, in fact, is a golden goal for any organization where some useful concepts can be used to reach it with minimum downtime, such as the following:

- **Failover**: Migrate a service running on the failed node to a working one (switch between primary and secondary)

- **Fallback**: Once a primary is back after a failed event, the service can be migrated back from the secondary

- **Switchover**: Manually switch between nodes to run the required service

On the other side, we may find a different terminology, which you may have most likely already experienced, that is, **load balancing**. In a heavily loaded environment, load balancers are introduced to redistribute a bunch of requests to less loaded servers. This can be similar to the **high performance clustering** concept, but you should note that this cluster logic takes care of working on the same request, whereas a load balancer aims to relatively distribute the load based on its task handler in an optimal way.

HA levels in OpenStack

It might be important to understand the context of HA deployments in OpenStack. This makes it imperative to distinguish the different levels of HA in order to consider the following in the cloud environment:

- **L1**: This includes physical hosts, network and storage devices, and hypervisors

- **L2**: This includes OpenStack services, including compute, network, and storage controllers, as well as databases and message queuing systems

- **L3**: This includes the virtual machines running on hosts that are managed by OpenStack services

- **L4**: This includes applications running in the virtual machines themselves

The main focus of the supporting HA in OpenStack has been on L1 and L2, which are covered in this chapter. On the other hand, L3 HA has limited support in the OpenStack community. By virtue of its multistorage backend support, OpenStack is able to bring instances online in the case of host failure by means of **live migration**. Nova also supports the **Nova evacuate** implementation, which fires up API calls for VM evacuation to a different host due to a compute node failure. The Nova evacuate command is still limited as it does not provide an automatic way of instance failover. L2 and L3 HA are considered beyond the scope of this book. L4 HA is touched on, and enhanced by, the community in the Havana release. Basically, a few incubated projects in OpenStack, such as Heat, Savana, and Trove, have begun to cover HA and monitoring gaps in the application level. Heat will be introduced in *Chapter 8, Extending OpenStack – Advanced Networking Features and Deploying Multi-tier Applications*, while Savana and Trove are beyond the scope of this book.

> Live migration is the ability to move running instances from one host to another with, ideally, no service downtime. By default, live migration in OpenStack requires a shared filesystem, such as a **Network File System** (**NFS**). It also supports **block live migration** when virtual disks can be copied over TCP without the need for a shared filesystem. Read more on VM migration support within the last OpenStack release at http://docs.openstack.org/admin-guide-cloud/content/section_configuring-compute-migrations.html.

A strict service-level agreement

Normally, if you plan to invest time and money in OpenStack clustering, you should refer to the HA architectural approaches in the first place. They guarantee business continuity and service reliability.

At this point, meeting these challenges will drive you to acquire skills you never thought you could master. Moreover, exposing an infrastructure that accepts failures might distinguish your environment as a *blockbuster* private cloud. Remember that this topic is very important in that all you have built within OpenStack components *must* be available to your end user.

Availability means that not only is a service *running*, but it *is also exposed and able to be consumed*. Let's see a small overview regarding the maximum downtime by looking at the availability percentage or *HA as X-nines*:

Availability level	Availability percentage	Downtime/year	Downtime/day
1 Nine	90	~ 36.5 days	~ 2.4 hours
2 Nines	99	~ 3.65 days	~ 14 minutes
3 Nines	99.9	~ 8.76 hours	~ 86 seconds
4 Nines	99.99	~ 52.6 minutes	~ 8.6 seconds
5 Nines	99.999	~ 5.25 minutes	~ 0.86 seconds
6 Nines	99.9999	~ 31.5 seconds	~ 0.0086 seconds

Basically, availability management is a part of IT best practices when it comes to making sure that IT services are running when needed, which reflects your **service-level agreement (SLA)**:

- Minimized downtime and data loss
- User satisfaction
- No repeat incidents
- Services must be consistently accessible

A paradox may appear between the lines when we consider that eliminating the SPOF in a given OpenStack environment will include the addition of more hardware to join the cluster. At this point, you might be exposed to creating more SPOF and, even worse, complicated infrastructure where maintenance turns into a difficult task.

Measuring HA

The following is a simple tip:

If you do not measure something, you cannot manage it. But what kind of metrics can be measured in a highly available OpenStack infrastructure?

Agreed, HA techniques come across as increasing the availability of resources, but still, there are always reasons you may face an interruption at some point! You may notice that the previous table did not mention any value equal to 100 percent uptime.

First, you may appreciate the nonvendor lock-in hallmark that OpenStack offers on this topic. Basically, you should mark the differences between HA functionalities that exist in a virtual infrastructure. Several HA solutions provide protection to virtual machines when there is a sudden failure in the host machine. Then, it will perform a restore situation for the instance on a different host. What about the virtual machine itself? Does it hang? So far, we have seen different levels of HA. In OpenStack, we have already seen cloud controllers run manageable services and compute hosts, which can be any hypervisor engine and third-rank the instance itself!

The last level might not be a cloud administrator task that maximizes its internal services' availability as it belongs to the end user. However, what should be taken into consideration, is what really affects the instance externally, such as:

- Storage attachment
- Bonded network devices

A good practice is to design the architecture with an approach that is as simple as possible by keeping efficient track of every HA level in our OpenStack cluster.

> Eliminating any SPOF while designing the OpenStack infrastructure would help in reaching a scalable environment.

A good strategy to follow is to design an **untrustworthy SPOF** principle by ruling. This keyword can be found anywhere in any system. In *Chapter 1, Designing OpenStack Cloud Architecture*, within our first design, we highlighted a simple architecture that brings in many instances in order to maximize availability. Nowadays, large IT infrastructures are likely to suffer from database scalability across multiple nodes. Without exception, the database in the OpenStack environment will need to scale as well. We will cover how to implement a database HA solution in more detail later in this chapter.

> High availability in OpenStack does not necessarily mean that it is designed to achieve maximum performance. On the other hand, you should consider the limitations of the overhead result on updating different nodes running the same service.

The HA dictionary

To ease the following sections of this chapter, it might be necessary to remember few terminologies to justify high availability and failover decisions later:

- **Stateless service**: This is the service that does not require any record of the previous request. Basically, each interaction request will be handled based on the information that comes with it. In other words, there is no dependency between requests where data, for example, does not need any replication. If a request fails, it can be performed on a different server.

- **Stateful service**: This is the service where request dependencies come into play. Any request will depend on the results of the previous and the subsequent ones. Stateful services are difficult to manage, and they need to be synchronized in order to preserve consistency.

Let's apply our former definition to our OpenStack services:

Stateful services	Stateless services
MySQL, RabbitMQ	nova-api, nova-conductor, glance-api, keystone-api, neutron-api, nova-scheduler, and web server (Apache/nginx)

Any HA architecture introduces an "active/active" or "active/passive" deployment, as covered in *Chapter 1, Designing OpenStack Cloud Architecture*. This is where your OpenStack environment will highlight its scalability level.

First, let's see the difference between both concepts in a nutshell in order to justify your decision:

- **Active/active**: Basically, all OpenStack nodes running the same stateful service will have an identical state. For example, deploying a MySQL cluster in the active/active mode will bring in a multimaster MySQL node design, which involves any update to one instance that may be propagated to all other nodes. Regarding the stateless services, redundancy will invoke instances to be load-balanced.

- **Active/passive**: In the case of stateful services, a failure event in one node will bring its associated redundant instance online. For example, within database clustering, only one master node comes into play, where the secondary node will act as a listener when failover occurs. It keeps load balancing handling requests within stateless services.

Hands on HA

Chapter 1, Designing OpenStack Cloud Architecture, provided a few hints on how to prepare for the first design steps: *do not lock keys inside your car.* At this point, we can go further due to the emerging different topologies, and it is up to you to decide what will fit best. The first question that may come into your mind: OpenStack does not include native HA components; how you can include them? There are widely used solutions for each component that we cited in the previous chapter in a nutshell.

Understanding HAProxy

HAProxy stands for **High Availability Proxy**. It is a free load balancing software tool that aims to proxy and direct requests to the most available nodes based on TCP/HTTP traffic. This includes a load balancer feature that can be a frontend server. At this point, we find two different servers within an HAProxy setup:

- A frontend server listens for requests coming on a specific IP and port, and determines where the connection or request should be forwarded

- A backend server defines a different set of servers in the cluster receiving the forwarded requests

Basically, HAProxy defines two different load balancing modes:

- **Load balancing layer 4**: Load balancing is performed in the transport layer in the OSI model. All the user traffic will be forwarded based on a specific IP address and port to the backend servers.

  For example, a load balancer might forward the internal OpenStack system's request to the Horizon web backend group of backend servers. To do this, whichever backend Horizon is selected should respond to the request under scope. This is true in the case of all the servers in the web backend serving identical content. The previous example illustrates the connection of the set servers to a single database. In our case, all services will reach the same database cluster.

- **Load balancing layer 7**: The application layer will be used for load balancing. This is a good way to load balance network traffic. Simply put, this mode allows you to forward requests to different backend servers based on the content of the request itself.

Many load balancing algorithms are introduced within the HAProxy setup. This is the job of the algorithm, which determines the server in the backend that should be selected to acquire the load. Some of them are as follows:

- **Round robin**: Here, each server is exploited in turn. As a simple HAProxy setup, round robin is a dynamic algorithm that defines the server's **weight** and adjusts it on the fly when the called instance hangs or starts slowly.

- **Leastconn**: The selection of the server is based on the *lucky* node that has the lowest number of connections.

 It is highly recommended that you use the leastconn algorithm in the case of long HTTP sessions.

- **Source**: This algorithm ensures that the request will be forwarded to the same server based on a hash of the source IP as long as the server is still up.

 Contrary to RR and leastconn, the source algorithm is considered a static algorithm, which presumes that any change to the server's weight on the fly does not have any effect on processing the load.

- **URI**: This ensures that the request will be forwarded to the same server based on its URI. It is ideal to increase the cache-hit rate in the case of proxy caches' implementations.

 Like the source, the URI algorithm is static in that updating the server's weight on the fly will not have any effect on processing the load.

You may wonder how the previous algorithms determine which servers in OpenStack should be selected. Eventually, the hallmark of HAProxy is a healthy check of the server's availability. HAProxy uses health check by automatically disabling any backend server that is not listening on a particular IP address and port.

But how does HAProxy handle connections? To answer this question, you should refer to the first logical design in *Chapter 1*, *Designing OpenStack Cloud Architecture*, which is created with **virtual IP (VIP)**. Let's refresh our memory about the things that we can see there by treating a few use cases within a VIP.

Services should not fail

A VIP can be assigned to the active servers running all the OpenStack services that need to be configured to use the address of the server. For example, in the case of a failover of the nova-api service in controller node 1, the IP address will follow the nova-api in controller node 2, and all clients' requests, which are the internal system requests in our case, will continue to work:

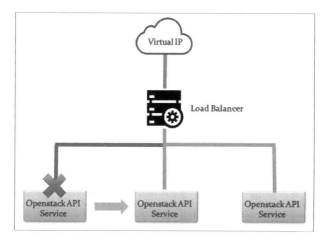

The load balancer should not fail

The previous use case assumes that the load balancer never fails! But in reality, this is an SPOF that we have to arm by adding a VIP on top of the load balancer's set. Usually, we need a stateless load balancer in OpenStack services. Thus, we can undertake such challenges using software similar to Keepalived:

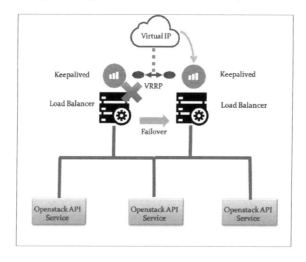

Keepalived is a free software tool that provides high availability and load balancing facilities based on its framework in order to check a **Linux Virtual Server (LVS)** pool state.

 LVS is a highly available server built on a cluster of real servers by running a load balancer on the Linux operating system. It is mostly used to build scalable web, mail, and FTP services.

As shown in the previous illustration, nothing is magic! Keepalived uses the **Virtual Router Redundancy Protocol (VRRP)** protocol to eliminate SPOF by making IPs highly available. VRRP implements virtual routing between two or more servers in a static, default routed environment. Considering a master router failure event, the backup node takes the master state after a period of time.

 In a standard VRRP setup, the backup node keeps listening for multicast packets from the master node with a given priority. If the backup node fails to receive any VRRP advertisement packets for a certain period, it will take over the master state by assigning the routed IP to itself. In a multibackup setup, the backup node with the same priority will be selected within its highest IP value to be the master one.

OpenStack HA under the hood

Deep down in the murky depths of HA, the setup of our magnificent OpenStack environment is much diversified! It may come across as a bit biased to favor a given HA setup, but remember that depending on which software clustering solution you feel more comfortable with, you can implement your HA OpenStack setup.

Let's shine the spotlight brightly on our first OpenStack design in *Chapter 1*, *Designing OpenStack Cloud Architecture*, and take a closer look at the pieces in the HA mode.

Next, we will move on to specific OpenStack core components and end up with exposing different possible topologies.

HA the database

There's no doubt that behind any cluster, lies a story! Creating your database in the HA mode in an OpenStack environment is not negotiable. We have set up MySQL in cloud controller nodes that can also be installed on separate ones. Most importantly, keep it safe not only from water, but also from fire. Many clustering techniques have been proposed to make MySQL highly available. Some of the MySQL architectures can be listed as follows:

- **Master/slave replication**: As exemplified in the following figure, a VIP that can be optionally moved has been used. A drawback of such a setup is the probability of data inconsistency due to delay in the VIP failing over (data loss).

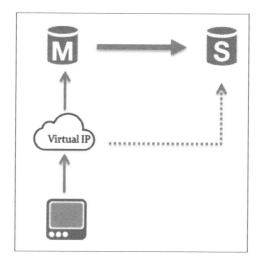

- **MMM replication**: By setting two servers, both of them become masters by keeping only one acceptable write query at a given time. This is still not a very reliable solution for OpenStack database HA as in the event of failure of the master, it might lose a certain number of transactions:

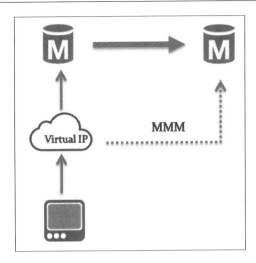

- **MySQL shared storage**: Both servers will depend on a redundant shared storage. As shown in the following figure, a separation between servers processing the data and the storage devices is required. Note that an active node may exist at any point in time. If it fails, the other node will take over the VIP after checking the inactivity of the failed node and turn it off. The service will be resumed in a different node by mounting the shared storage within the taken VIP.

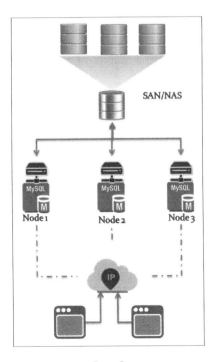

Such a solution is excellent in terms of the uptime, but it may require a powerful storage/hardware system which could be extremely expensive.

- **Block-level replication**: One of the most adopted HA implementations is the **DRBD** replication, which stands for **Distributed Replicated Block Device**. Simply put, it replicates data in the block device, which is the physical hard drive between OpenStack MySQL nodes.

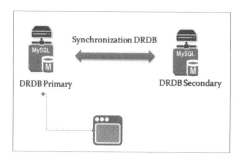

What you need are just Linux boxes. The DRBD works on their kernel layer exactly at the bottom of the system I/O stack.

> With shared storage devices, writing to multiple nodes simultaneously requires a cluster-aware filesystem, such as the Linux **Global File System (GFS)**.

DRBD can be a costless solution, but performance-wise, it cannot be a deal when you rely on hundreds of nodes. This can also affect the scalability of the replicated cluster.

- **MySQL Galera multimaster replication**: Based on multimaster replication, the Galera solution has a few performance challenges within an MMM architecture for the MySQL/innoDB database cluster. Essentially, it uses synchronous replication where data is replicated across the whole cluster. As was stated in our first logical design in *Chapter 1, Designing OpenStack Cloud Architecture*, a requirement of the Galera setup is the need for at least three nodes to run it properly. Let's dive into the Galera setup within our OpenStack environment and see what happens under the hood. In general, any MySQL replication setup can be simple to set up and make HA-capable, but data can be lost during the failing over. Galera is tightly designed to resolve such a conflict in the multimaster database environment. An issue you may face in a typical multimaster setup is that all the nodes try to update the same database with different data, especially when a synchronization problem occurs during the master failure. This is why Galera uses **Certification Based Replication (CBR)**.

Keep things simple; the main idea of CBR is to assume that the database can roll back uncommitted changes, and it is called **transactional** in addition to applying replicated events in the same order across all the instances. Replication is truly parallel; each one has an ID check. What Galera can bring as an added value to our OpenStack MySQL HA is the ease of scalability; there are a few more things to it, such as joining a node to Galera while it is automated in production. The end design brings an active-active multimaster topology with less latency and transaction loss.

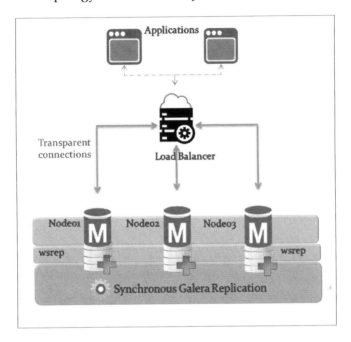

A very interesting point in the last illustration is that every MySQL node in the OpenStack cluster should be patched within a **Write-Set Replication (wsrep)** API. If you already have a MySQL master-master actively working, you will need to install wsrep and configure your cluster.

 Wsrep is a project that aims to develop a generic replication plugin interface for databases. Galera is one of the projects that use wsrep APIs by working on its wsrep replication library calls.

You can download and install Galera from `https://launchpad.net/galera/`. Every node will need a certain number of steps to configure a complete MySQL cluster setup.

HA in the queue

RabbitMQ is mainly responsible for communication between different OpenStack services. The question is fairly simple: no queue, no OpenStack service intercommunication. Now that you get the point, another critical service needs to be available and survive the failures. RabbitMQ is mature enough to support its own cluster setup without the need to go for Pacemaker or another clustering software solution.

The amazing part about using RabbitMQ is the different ways by which such a messaging system can reach scalability using an active/active design with:

- **RabbitMQ clustering**: Any data or state needed for the RabbitMQ broker to be operational is replicated across all nodes.

- **RabbitMQ mirrored queues**: As the message queue cannot survive in nodes in which it resides, RabbitMQ can act in active/active HA message queues. Simply put, queues will be mirrored on other nodes within the same RabbitMQ cluster. Thus, any node failure will automatically switch to using one of the queue mirrors.

> Setting up queue mirroring does not enhance any load distribution across the cluster and only guarantees availability. A good reference on the HA of queues within RabbitMQ can be found here: `https://www.rabbitmq.com/ha.html`.

Like any standard cluster setup, the original node handling the queue can be thought of as a master, while the mirrored queues in different nodes are purely slave copies. The failure of the master will result in the selection of the oldest slave to be the new master.

Keep calm and use HA

So far, we have introduced most of the possibilities that can make our OpenStack environment highly available. OpenStack cloud controller nodes, database clusters, and network nodes can be deployed in redundancy in the following ways:

- MySQL high availability through Galera active/active multimaster deployment and Keepalived

- RabbitMQ active-active high availability using mirrored queues and HAProxy for load balancing

- The OpenStack API services' inclusion of nova-scheduler and glance-registry in cloud controllers nodes in the active-passive model using Pacemaker and Corosync
- Neutrons agents using Pacemaker

Implementing HA on MySQL

In this implementation, we will need three separate MySQL nodes and two HAProxy servers, so we can guarantee that our load balancer will fail over if one of them fails. Keepalived will be installed in each HAProxy to control VIP. Different nodes in this setup will be assigned as the following:

- **VIP**: 192.168.47.47
- **HAProxy01**: 192.168.47.120
- **HAProxy02**: 192.168.47.121
- **MySQL01**: 192.168.47.125
- **MySQL02**: 192.168.47.126
- **MySQL03**: 192.168.47.127

In order to implement HA on MySQL, perform the following steps:

1. First, let's start by installing and configuring our HAProxy servers:

   ```
   packtpub@haproxy1$ sudo yum update
   packtpub@haproxy1$ sudo yum install haproxy keepalived
   ```

2. Check whether the HAProxy is properly installed:

   ```
   packtpub@haproxy1$ haproxy -v
   HA-Proxy version 1.5.2 2014/07/12
   ```

3. Let's configure our first HAProxy node. We start by backing up the default configuration file:

   ```
   packtpub@haproxy1$ sudo cp /etc/haproxy/haproxy.cfg \ /etc/
   haproxy/haproxy.cfg.bak
   packtpub@haproxy1$ sudo nano /etc/haproxy/haproxy.cfg
   global

       log         127.0.0.1 local2
       chroot      /var/lib/haproxy
       pidfile     /var/run/haproxy.pid
   ```

```
    maxconn     1020    # See also: ulimit -n
    user        haproxy
    group       haproxy
    daemon
    stats socket /var/lib/haproxy/stats.sock mode 600 level admin
    stats timeout 2m


defaults
    mode    tcp
    log     global
    option  dontlognull
    option  redispatch
    retries                 3
    timeout queue           45s
    timeout connect         5s
    timeout client          1m
    timeout server          1m
    timeout check           10s
    maxconn                 1020


listen haproxy-monitoring *:80
    mode    tcp
    stats   enable
    stats   show-legends
    stats   refresh         5s
    stats   uri             /
    stats   realm           Haproxy\ Statistics
    stats   auth            monitor:packadmin
    stats   admin           if TRUE


frontend haproxy1    # change on 2nd HAProxy
    bind    *:3306
    default_backend         mysql-os-cluster
```

```
backend mysql-os-cluster
   balance roundrobin
   server   mysql01          192.168.47.125:3306 maxconn 151 check
   server   mysql02          192.168.47.126:3306 maxconn 151 check
   server   mysql03          192.168.47.127:3306 maxconn 151 check
```

4. Start the `haproxy` service:

    `packtpub@haproxy1$ sudo service haproxy start`

5. Repeat steps 1 to 4, replacing `haproxy1` with `haproxy2` in the `frontend` section.

6. Now, we arm our HAProxy servers by adding the VRRP `/etc/keepalived/keepalived.conf` file. But first, we back up the original configuration file:

    `packtpub@haproxy1$ sudo cp /etc/keepalived/keepalived.conf \ /etc/keepalived/keepalived.conf.bak`

    `packtpub@haproxy1$ sudo nano /etc/keepalived/keepalived.conf`

    To bind a virtual address that does not exist physically on the server, you can add the following option to `sysctl.conf` in your CentOS box:

    `net.ipv4.ip_nonlocal_bind=1`

    Do not forget to activate the change using the following:

    `packtpub@haproxy1$ sudo sysctl -p`

    `packtpub@haproxy1$ sudo nano /etc/keepalived/keepalived.conf`

```
vrrp_script chk_haproxy {
   script    "killall -0 haproxy"
   interval 2
   weight    2
}


vrrp_instance MYSQL_VIP {
   interface          eth0
   virtual_router_id 120

   priority          111    # Second HAProxy is 110
   advert_int        1
```

```
virtual_ipaddress {
  192.168.47.47/32 dev eth0
}

track_script {
  chk_haproxy
}
}
```

7. Repeat step 6 by replacing the priority to `110`, for example, in the `HAProxy2` node.

8. Check whether the VIP was assigned to `eth0` in both the nodes:

```
packtpub@haproxy1$ ip addr show eth0

packtpub@haproxy2$ ip addr show eth0
```

9. Now you have HAProxy and Keepalived ready and configured; all we need to do is set up the Galera plugin through all the MySQL nodes in the cluster:

```
packtpub@db01$ wget https://launchpad.net/codership-
mysql/5.6/5.6.16-25.5/+download/MySQL-server-5.6.16_wsrep_25.5-1.
rhel6.x86_64.rpm

packtpub@db01$ wget https://launchpad.net/galera/0.8/0.8.0/ \
+download/galera-0.8.0-x86_64.rpm
```

10. We need to install the previously downloaded `rpm` files using:

```
packtpub@db01$  sudo rpm -Uhv galera-0.8.0-x86_64.rpm

packtpub@db01$ sudo  rpm -Uhv MySQL-server-5.6.16_wsrep_25.5 \
1.rhel6.x86_64.rpm
```

> If you did not install MySQL within Galera from scratch, you should stop the `mysql` service first before proceeding with the Galera plugin installation. The example assumes that MySQL is installed and stopped. More information about the usage of Galera in OpenStack can be found here: `http://docs.openstack.org/high-availability-guide/content/ha-aa-db-mysql-galera.html`.

11. Once the Galera plugin is installed, log in to your MySQL nodes and create a new `galera` user with the `galerapass` password and, optionally, the `haproxy` username for HAProxy monitoring without a password for the sake of simplicity. Note that for MySQL clustering, a new `sst` user must exist. We will set up a new `sstpassword` password for node authentication:

    ```
    mysql> GRANT USAGE ON *.* to sst@'%' IDENTIFIED BY 'sstpassword';

    mysql> GRANT ALL PRIVILEGES on *.* to sst@'%';

    mysql> GRANT USAGE on *.* to galera@'%' IDENTIFIED BY
    'galerapass';

    mysql> INSERT INTO mysql.user (host,user) values ('%','haproxy');

    mysql> FLUSH PRIVILEGES;

    mysql> quit
    ```

12. Configure the MySQL wresp Galera library in each MySQL node in `/etc/mysql/conf.d/wsrep.cnf`.

    For `db01.packtpub.com`, add this code:

    ```
    wsrep_provider=/usr/lib64/galera/libgalera_smm.so
    wsrep_cluster_address="gcomm://"
    wsrep_sst_method=rsync
    wsrep_sst_auth=sst:sstpass
    ```

    Restart the MySQL server:

    ```
    packtpub@db01$ sudo /etc/init.d/mysql restart
    ```

    For `db02.packtpub.com`, add this code:

    ```
    wsrep_provider=/usr/lib64/galera/libgalera_smm.so
    wsrep_cluster_address="gcomm://192.168.47.125"
    wsrep_sst_method=rsync
    wsrep_sst_auth=sst:sstpass
    ```

    Restart the MySQL server:

    ```
    packtpub@db01$ sudo /etc/init.d/mysql restart
    ```

    For `db03.packtpub.com`, add this code:

    ```
    wsrep_provider=/usr/lib64/galera/libgalera_smm.so
    wsrep_cluster_address="gcomm://192.168.47.126"
    wsrep_sst_method=rsync
    wsrep_sst_auth=sst:sstpass
    ```

Restart the MySQL server:

```
packtpub@db01$ sudo /etc/init.d/mysql restart
```

Note that the db01.packtpub.com gcomm:// address is left empty to create the new cluster. The last step will connect to the db03.packtpub.com node. To reconfigure it, we will need to modify our /etc/mysql/conf.d/wsrep.cnf file and point to 192.168.47.127:

```
wresp_cluster_address ="gcomm://192.168.47.127"
```

From the MySQL command line, set your global MySQL settings as follows:

```
mysql> set global wsrep_cluster_address='gcomm://192.168.1.140:4567';
```

13. Check whether the Galera replication is running the way it should be running:

```
packtpub@db01$ mysql -e "show status like 'wsrep%' "
```

If your cluster is fine, you should see something like:

```
wsrep_ready = ON
```

Additional checks can be verified from the MySQL command line. In db01.packtpub.com, you can run:

```
Mysql> show status like 'wsrep%';
|wsrep_cluster_size    | 3 |
|wsrep_cluster_status  | Primary |
|wsrep_connected       | ON |
```

The wsrep_cluster_size node that shows value 3 means that our cluster is aware of three connected nodes while the current node is designated as a wsrep_cluster_status primary node.

Starting from step 9, you can add a new MySQL node and join the cluster.

Note that we have separated our MySQL cluster from the cloud controller, which means that OpenStack services running in the former node, including Keystone, Glance, Nova, and Cinder as well as Neutron nodes, need to point to the right MySQL server. Remember that we are using HAProxy while VIP is managed by Keepalived for MySQL high availability. Thus, you will need to reconfigure the Virtual IP in each service, as follows:

- ○ **Nova**: `/etc/nova/nova.conf`

    `sql_connection=mysql://nova:openstack@192.168.47.47/nova`

- ○ **Keystone**: `/etc/keystone/keystone.conf`

    `sql_connection=mysql://keystone:openstack@192.168.47.47/keystone`

- ○ **Glance**: `/etc/glance/glance-registry.conf`

    `sql_connection=mysql://glance:openstack@192.168.47.47/glance`

- ○ **Neutron**: `/etc/neutron/plugins/openvswitch/ovs_neutron_plugin.ini`

    `sql_connection=mysql://neutron:openstack@192.168.47.47/neutron`

- ○ **Cinder**: `/etc/cinder/cinder.conf`

    `sql_connection=mysql://cinder:openstack@192.168.47.47/cinder`

Remember that in order to edit your OpenStack configuration files, you will need to restart the corresponding services. Ensure that after each restart, the service is up and running and does not show any error in the log files.

If you are familiar with `sed` and `awk` command lines, it might be easier to reconfigure files using them. You can take a look at another useful shell tool to manipulate `ini` and `conf` files; **crudini** can be found at `http://www.pixelbeat.org/programs/crudini/`. To update an existing configuration file, the command line is fairly simple:

`# crudini --set <Config_File_Path> <Section_Name> <Parameter> <Value>`

To update, for example, the `/etc/nova/nova.conf` file showed previously, you can enter the following command line:

`# crudini --set /etc/nova/nova.conf database connection mysql://nova:openstack@192.168.47.47/nova`

Implementing HA on RabbitMQ

In this setup, we will use a node to introduce minor changes to our RabbitMQ instances running in cloud controller nodes. We will enable the mirrored option in our RabbitMQ brokers. In this example, we assume that the RabbitMQ service is running on three OpenStack cloud controller nodes, as follows:

- **VIP**: 192.168.47.47
- **HAProxy01**: 192.168.47.120
- **HAProxy02**: 192.168.47.121
- **Cloud controller 01**: 192.168.47.100
- **Cloud controller 02**: 192.168.47.101
- **Cloud controller 03**: 192.168.47.102

In order to implement HA on RabbitMQ, perform the following steps:

1. Stop RabbitMQ services on the second and third cloud controller. Copy the `erlang` cookie from the first cloud controller and add the additional nodes:

   ```
   packtpub@cc01$  scp /var/lib/rabbitmq/.erlang.cookie\ root @cc02:/
   var/lib/rabbitmq/.erlang.cookie

   packtpub@cc01$  scp /var/lib/rabbitmq/.erlang.cookie\ root @cc03:/
   var/lib/rabbitmq/.erlang.cookie
   ```

2. Set the `rabbitmq` group and user with `400` file permissions in both the additional nodes:

   ```
   packtpub@cc02$ sudo chown rabbitmq:rabbitmq\ /var/lib/rabbitmq/.
   erlang.cookie

   packtpub@cc02$ sudo chmod 400 /var/lib/rabbitmq/.erlang.cookie

   packtpub@cc03$ sudo chown rabbitmq:rabbitmq\ /var/lib/rabbitmq/.
   erlang.cookie

   packtpub@cc03$ sudo chmod 400 /var/lib/rabbitmq/.erlang.cookie
   ```

3. Start the RabbitMQ service in `cc02` and `cc03`:

   ```
   packtpub@cc02$ service rabbitmq-server start

   packtpub@cc02$chkconfig rabbitmq-server on

   packtpub@cc03$ service rabbitmq-server start

   packtpub@cc03$chkconfig rabbitmq-server on
   ```

4. Now, it's time to form the cluster and enable the mirrored queue option. Currently, all the three RabbitMQ brokers are independent and they are not aware of each other. Let's instruct them to join one cluster unit. First, stop the `rabbimqctl` daemon.

On the `cc02` node, run these commands:

```
# rabbitmqctl stop_app
Stopping node 'rabbit@cc02' ...
...done.
# rabbitmqctl join-cluster rabbit@cc01
Clustering node 'rabbit@cc02' with 'rabbit@cc01' ...
...done.
# rabbitmqctl start_app
Starting node 'rabbit@cc02' ...
... done
```

On the `cc03` node, run the following commands:

```
# rabbitmqctl stop_app
Stopping node 'rabbit@cc03' ...
...done.
# rabbitmqctl join-cluster rabbit@cc01
Clustering node 'rabbit@cc03' with 'rabbit@cc01' ...
...done.
# rabbitmqctl start_app
Starting node 'rabbit@cc03' ...
... done
```

5. Check the nodes in the cluster by running them from any RabbitMQ node:

```
# rabbitmqctl cluster_status
Cluster status of node 'rabbit@cc03' ...
[{nodes, [{disc, ['rabbit@cc01','rabbit@cc02',
        'rabbit@cc03']}]},
  {running_nodes, ['rabbit@cc01','rabbit@cc02',
                  'rabbit@cc03']},
  {partitions, []}]
...done.
```

6. The last step will instruct RabbitMQ to use mirrored queues. By doing this, mirrored queues will enable both producers and consumers in each queue to connect to any RabbitMQ broker so that they can access the same message queues. The following command will sync all the queues across all cloud controller nodes by setting an HA policy:

```
# rabbitmqctl set_policy HA '^(?!amq\.).*' '{"ha-mode":"all", "ha-sync-mode":"automatic" }'
```

 Note that the previous command line settles a policy where all queues are mirrored to all nodes in the cluster.

7. Edit its configuration file in each RabbitMQ cluster node to join the cluster on restarting /etc/rabbitmq/rabbitmq.config:

```
[{rabbit,
  [{cluster_nodes, {['rabbit@cc01', 'rabbit@cc02', 'rabbit@cc03'],
ram}}]}].
```

8. We can proceed to set up a load balancer for RabbitMQ. We need to only add a new section in both the haproxy1 and haproxy2 nodes and reload the configurations:

```
listen rabbitmqcluster 192.168.47.47:5670
  mode tcp
  balance roundrobin
    server cc01 192.168.47.100:5672 check inter 5s rise 2 fall 3
    server cc02 192.168.47.101:5672 check inter 5s rise 2 fall 3
    server cc03 192.168.47.102:5672 check inter 5s rise 2 fall 3
```

Note that we are listening on the VIP 192.168.47.47. Reload the configuration on both HAProxy nodes:

```
# service haproxy reload
```

Using VIP to manage both HAProxy nodes as a proxy for RabbitMQ might require you to configure each OpenStack service to use the 192.168.47.47 address and the 5670 port. Thus, you will need to reconfigure the RabbitMQ settings in each service in the VIP, as the following:

○ **Nova**: /etc/nova/nova.conf:

```
# crudini --set  /etc/nova/nova.conf   DEFAULT rabbit_host
192.168.47.47
```

```
# crudini --set  /etc/nova/nova.conf   DEFAULT rabbit_port
5470
```

- ◦ **Glance**: `/etc/glance/glance-api.conf`:

  ```
  # crudini --set  /etc/glance/glance-api.conf  DEFAULT
  rabbit_host 192.168.47.47
  ```

  ```
  # crudini --set  /etc/glance/glance-api.conf  DEFAULT
  rabbit_port 5470
  ```

- ◦ **Neutron**: `/etc/neutron/neutron.conf`:

  ```
  # crudini --set  /etc/neutron/neutron.conf  DEFAULT rabbit_
  host 192.168.47.47
  ```

  ```
  # crudini --set  /etc/neutron/neutron.conf  DEFAULT rabbit_
  port 5470
  ```

- ◦ **Cinder**: `/etc/cinder/cinder.conf`:

  ```
  # crudini --set  /etc/cinder/cinder.conf  DEFAULT rabbit_
  host 192.168.47.47
  ```

  ```
  # crudini --set  /etc/cinder/cinder.conf  DEFAULT rabbit_
  port 5470
  ```

Implementing HA on OpenStack cloud controllers

Moving on to the setting up of highly available OpenStack cloud controllers requires a way of managing the services running in the former nodes. Another alternative for the high-availability game is using Pacemaker and Corosync. As a native high-availability and load-balancing stack solution for the Linux platform, Pacemaker depends on Corosync to maintain cluster communication based on the messaging layer. Corosync supports multicast as the default network configuration communication method. For some environments that do not support multicast, Corosync can be configured for unicast. In multicast networks, all the cluster nodes are connected to the same physical network device, it will be necessary to make sure that at least one multicast address is configured in the configuration file. Corosync can be considered as a message bus system that allows OpenStack services running across different cloud controller nodes to manage quorum and cluster membership to Pacemaker. But how does Pacemaker interact with these services? Simply put, Pacemaker uses **Resource Agents (RAs)** to expose the interface for resource clustering. Natively, Pacemaker supports over 70 RAs found in `http://www.linux-ha.org/wiki/Resource_Agents`.

In our case, we will use native OpenStack RAs, including:

- The OpenStack compute service
- The OpenStack identity service
- The OpenStack image service

 There is a native Pacemaker RA to manage MySQL databases and VIP, which you can use as an alternative for the MySQL Galera replication solution.

In order to implement HA on OpenStack cloud controllers, perform the following steps:

1. Install and configure Pacemaker and Corosync on cloud controller nodes:

   ```
   # yum update
   # yum install pacemaker corosync
   ```

   Corosync allows any server to join a cluster using active-active or active-passive fault-tolerant configurations. You will need to choose an unused multicast address and a port. Create a backup for the original Corosync configuration file and edit /etc/corosync/ corosync.conf as follows:

   ```
   # cp /etc/corosync/corosync.conf /etc/corosync/corosync.conf.bak
   # nano /etc/corosync/corosync.conf
   Interface {
       ringnumber: 0
   bindnetaddr: 192.168.47.0
   mcastaddr: 239.225.47.10
   mcastport: 4000
   ....}
   ```

 In the case of a unicast network, you might be needed to specify the addresses of all nodes that are allowed as members of the OpenStack cluster, in the Corosync configuration file. There is no need for a multicast cluster. A sample example template can be found at http://docs.openstack.org/high-availability-guide/content/_set_up_corosync_unicast.html.

Generate an authorization key on the `cc01` node to enable communication between cloud controller nodes:

```
# sudo corosync-keygen
```

Copy the generated `/etc/corosync/authkey` and `/etc/corosync/corosync.conf` files to other nodes in the cluster:

```
# scp /etc/corosync/authkey /etc/corosync/corosync.conf\
packpub@192.168.47.101:/etc/corosync/
```

```
# scp /etc/corosync/authkey /etc/corosync/corosync.conf\
packpub@192.168.47.102:.etc/corosync/
```

Start the Pacemaker and Corosync services:

```
# service pacemaker start
```

```
# service corosync start
```

A good way to check the setup is to run the following command:

```
# crm_mon -1
```

```
Online: [cc01 cc02 cc03]
```

```
First node (cc01)
```

> By default, Corosync uses **Shoot The Other Node In The Head (STONITH)** option. It is used to avoid a split-brain situation where each service node believes that the other(s) is (are) broken and it is the elected one. Thus, in the case of a STONITH death match, the second node, for example, shoots the first one to ensure that there is only one primary node running. In a simple two nodes Corosynced environment, it might be convenient to disable it by running:
>
> ```
> # crm configure property stonith-enabled= "false"
> ```

On `cc01`, we can set up a VIP that will be shared between the three servers. We can use `192.168.47.48` as the VIP with a 3-second monitoring interval:

```
# crm configure primitive VIP ocf:heartbeat:IPaddr2 params \
ip=192.168.47.48 cidr_netmask=32 op monitor interval=3s
```

We can see that the VIP has been assigned to the `cc01` node. Note that the use of the VIP will be assigned to the next cloud controller if `cc01` does not show any response during 3 seconds:

```
# crm_mon -1
```

```
Online: [ cc01 cc02]
```

```
VIP     (ocf::heartbeat:IPaddr2):    Started cc01
```

Optionally, you can create a new directory to save all downloaded resource agent scripts under `/usr/lib/ocf/resource.d/openstack`.

> Creating a new VIP will require you to point OpenStack services to the new virtual address. You can overcome such repetitive reconfiguration by keeping both IP addresses of the cloud controller and the VIP. In each cloud controller, ensure that you have exported the needed environment variables as follows:
>
> ```
> # export OS_AUTH_URL=http://192.168.47.48:5000/v2.0/
> ```

2. Set up RAs and configure Pacemaker for Nova.

    First, download the resource agent in all the three cloud controller nodes:

    ```
    # cd /usr/lib/ocf/resource.d/openstack
    # wget https://raw.github.com/leseb/OpenStack-ra/master/nova-api
    # wget https://raw.github.com/leseb/OpenStack-ra/master/nova-cert
    # wget https://raw.github.com/leseb/OpenStack-ra/ \
    master/nova-consoleauth
    # wget https://raw.github.com/leseb/OpenStack-ra/ \
    master/nova-scheduler
    # wget https://raw.github.com/leseb/OpenStack-ra/master/nova-vnc
    # chmod a+rx *
    ```

> You can check whether the Pacemaker is aware of new RAs or not by running this:
>
> ```
> # crm ra info ocf:openstack:nova-api
> ```

Now, we can proceed to configure Pacemaker to use these agents to control our Nova service. The next configuration creates `p_nova_api`, a resource to manage the OpenStack nova-api:

```
# crm configure primitive p_nova-api ocf:openstack:nova-api \
    params config="/etc/nova/nova.conf" op monitor interval="5s"\
timeout="5s"
```

Create `p_cert`, a resource to manage the OpenStack nova-cert:

```
# crm configure primitive p_cert ocf:openstack:nova-cert \
    params config="/etc/nova/nova.conf" op monitor interval="5s"\
timeout="5s"
```

Create p_consoleauth, a resource to manage the OpenStack nova-consoleauth:

```
# crm configure primitive p_consoleauth ocf:openstack: \
nova-consoleauth params config="/etc/nova/nova.conf" \
 op monitor interval="5s" timeout="5s"
```

Create p_scheduler, a resource to manage the OpenStack nova-scheduler:

```
# crm configure primitive p_scheduler ocf:openstack:nova-scheduler \
    params config="/etc/nova/nova.conf" op monitor interval="5s" \
timeout="5s"
```

Create p_novnc, a resource to manage the OpenStack nova-vnc:

```
# crm configure primitive p_ novnc ocf:openstack:nova-vnc \
    params config="/etc/nova/nova.conf" op monitor interval="5s" \
timeout="5s"
```

3. Set up RA and configure Pacemaker for Keystone:

   Download the resource agent in all three cloud controller nodes:

   ```
   # cd /usr/lib/ocf/resource.d/openstack
   # wget https://raw.github.com/madkiss/ \
   openstack-resource-agents/master/ocf/keystone
   ```

   Proceed to configure Pacemaker to use the downloaded resource agent to control the Keystone service. The next configuration creates p_keysone, a resource to manage the OpenStack identity service:

   ```
   # crm configure primitive p_keystone ocf:openstack:keystone \
   params config="/etc/keystone/keystone.conf" op monitor
   interval="5s"\ timeout="5s"
   ```

4. Set up RA and configure Pacemaker for Glance.

   Download the resource agent in all three cloud controller nodes:

   ```
   # cd /usr/lib/ocf/resource.d/openstack
   # wget https://raw.github.com/madkiss/ \
   openstack-resource-agents/master/ocf/glance-api
   # wget https://raw.github.com/madkiss/ \
   openstack-resource-agents/master/ocf/glance-registry
   ```

Proceed to configure Pacemaker to use the downloaded resource agent to control the Glance API service. The next configuration creates `p_glance-api`, a resource to manage the OpenStack Image API service:

```
# crm configure primitive p_glance-api ocf:openstack:glance-api \
params config="/etc/glance/glance-api.conf" op monitor
interval="5s"\ timeout="5s"
```

Create `p_glance-registry`, a resource to manage the OpenStack glance-registry:

```
# crm configure primitive p_glance-registry \
ocf:openstack:glance-registry params config="/etc/glance/ \
glance-registry.conf " op monitor interval="5s" timeout="5s"
```

5. Set up RA and configure Pacemaker for the Neutron server:

   Download the resource agent in all three cloud controller nodes:

   ```
   # cd /usr/lib/ocf/resource.d/openstack
   # wget https://raw.github.com/madkiss/ \
   openstack-resource-agents/master/ocf/neutron-server
   ```

   Now, we can proceed to configure Pacemaker to use these agents to control our Neutron server service. The next configuration creates `p_neutron-server`, a resource to manage the OpenStack networking server:

   ```
   # crm configure primitive p_neutron-server ocf:openstack: \
   neutron-server params config="/etc/neutron/neutron.conf" \
   op monitor interval="5s" timeout="5s"
   ```

   Check whether our Pacemaker is handling our OpenStack services correctly:

   ```
   # crm_mon -1
   Online: [ cc01 cc02 cc03 ]
   VIP (ocf::heartbeat:IPaddr2): Started cc01
   p_nova-api (ocf::openstack:nova-api):
   Started cc01
   p_cert (ocf::openstack:nova-cert):
   Started cc01
   p_consoleauth (ocf::openstack:nova-consoleauth):
   Started cc01
   ```

```
p_scheduler (ocf::openstack:nova-scheduler):

Started cc01

p_nova-novnc (ocf::openstack:nova-vnc):

Started cc01

p_keystone (ocf::openstack:keystone):

Started cc01

p_glance-api (ocf::openstack:glance-api):

Started cc01

p_glance-registry (ocf::openstack:glance-registry):

Started cc01

p_neutron-server (ocf::openstack:neutron-server):

Started cc01
```

To use private and public IP addresses, you might need to create two different VIPs. For example, you will have to define your endpoint as follows:

```
keystone endpoint-create --region $KEYSTONE_REGION \
--service-id $service-id --publicurl \ 'http://PUBLIC_
VIP:9292' \
--adminurl 'http://192.168.47.48:9292' \
--internalurl 'http://192.168.47.48:9292'
```

Implementing HA on network nodes

Extending our OpenStack deployment will necessitate the network controller be brought to its own cluster stack. As we have concluded previously, Neutron is very extensible in terms of the plugin and network configuration. Whichever network setup you imply, a network controller will have to sit on three different networks:

- Management network
- Data network
- External network or Internet (Internet access for instances)

To ensure a fault-tolerant network controller cluster, we will use Pacemaker to avoid any SPOF in the overall OpenStack environment:

1. Set up RA and configure Pacemaker for the Neutron L3 agent.

   Download the resource agent in all three cloud controller nodes:

   ```
   # cd /usr/lib/ocf/resource.d/openstack
   # wget https://raw.github.com/madkiss/ \
   openstack-resource-agents/master/ocf/neutron-agent-l3
   ```

   > The Neutron L3 agent provides layer 3 and **Network Address Translation** (**NAT**) forwarding to allow instances, access to the tenant networks.

   Proceed to configure Pacemaker to use the downloaded resource agent to control Neutron agent L3. The next configuration creates p_neutron-l3-agent, a resource to manage the OpenStack Image API service:

   ```
   # crm configure primitive p_neutron-l3-agent ocf:openstack: \
   neutron-l3-agent params config="/etc/neutron/neutron.conf"\
   plugin_config= "/etc/neutron/l3_agent.ini" \
   op monitor interval="5s" timeout="5s"
   ```

2. Set up RA and configure Pacemaker for the Neutron DHCP agent.

   Download the resource agent in all three cloud controller nodes:

   ```
   # cd /usr/lib/ocf/resource.d/openstack
   # wget https://raw.github.com/madkiss/ \
   openstack-resource-agents/master/ocf/neutron-agent-dhcp
   ```

   > By default, the Neutron DHCP agent uses dnsmasq to assign IP addresses to instances.

   Proceed to configure Pacemaker to use the downloaded resource agent to control the Neutron DHCP agent. The next configuration creates p_neutron-dhcp-agent, a resource to manage the OpenStack DHCP agent:

   ```
   # crm configure primitive p_neutron-dhcp-agent ocf:openstack: \
   neutron-dhcp-agent params config="/etc/neutron/neutron.conf"\
   plugin_config= "/etc/neutron/dhcp_agent.ini" \
   op monitor interval="5s" timeout="5s"
   ```

3. Set up RA and configure Pacemaker for the Neutron metadata agent.

   Download the resource agent in all three cloud controller nodes:

   ```
   # cd /usr/lib/ocf/resource.d/openstack
   # wget https://raw.github.com/madkiss/ \
   openstack-resource-agents/master/ocf/neutron-metadata-agent
   ```

 The Neutron metadata agent enables instances on tenant networks to reach the Compute API metadata.

   Proceed to configure Pacemaker to use the downloaded resource agent to control the Neutron metadata agent. The next configuration creates p_neutron-metadata-agent, a resource to manage the OpenStack metadata agent:

   ```
   # crm configure primitive p_neutron-metadata-agent ocf:openstack:\
   neutron-metadata  agent params config="/etc/neutron/neutron.conf" \
   plugin_config= "/etc/neutron/metadata_agent.ini" \
   op monitor interval="5s" timeout="5s
   ```

Summary

In this chapter, you learned some of the most important concepts about high availability and failover. You also learned the different options available to build a redundant OpenStack architecture with a robust resiliency. You will know how to diagnose your OpenStack design by eliminating any SPOF across all services. We highlighted different open source solutions out of the box to arm our OpenStack infrastructure and make it as fault-tolerant as possible. Different technologies were introduced, such as HAProxy, database replication such as Galera, Keepalived, Pacemaker, and Corosync. This completes the first part of the book that aimed to cover different architecture levels and several solutions to end up with an optimal OpenStack solution for a medium and large infrastructure deployment.

Now that we have crystallized the high availability aspect in our private cloud, we will focus on building a multinode OpenStack environment in the next chapter and dive deeper into orchestrating it. You can call it *my first production day*.

7
OpenStack Multinode Deployment – Bringing in Production

"The value of an idea lies in the using of it."

–Thomas A. Edison

The ultimate goal of this book is to get you from where you are today to the point where you can confidently build an operational OpenStack environment in a production environment. While going through the previous chapters, you may notice the diversity of services and components that exist in OpenStack that are still under intensive development and which are constantly extending their respective features. Of course, most readers will appreciate that moving OpenStack from a small test environment to a production setup is not an easy task.

Generally, a complete production setup can be pretty tough to create. It is time to collect the pieces to form our first big picture. You will realize that different implementations of OpenStack are suited for the wallets of different organizations. *Chapter 1, Designing OpenStack Cloud Architecture*, introduced sample resources and the hardware computation that is related to the OpenStack nodes to get ready for a "production day". On the other hand, a major challenge might appear at this stage that was not detailed in previous chapters: How do we connect the pieces? As you may have noted, going through a networking setup needs a lot of preparation and detailed planning.

In this chapter, you will learn how to perform the following operations:

- Proceed gradually and decide a first physical layout of your first production day
- Define the OpenStack production network topology
- Set up your first production environment by using bare metal provisioning tools
- Automate the OpenStack setup by using Chef in production
- Integrate a failover mechanism into the production setup

The next section will deal with an example of a sample setup derived from a specific design layout. Thus, it is fundamental to bear in mind that you should select the solution that will fit your needs, the hardware that you will be able to offer, and the size of your infrastructure for your first private cloud deployment. You can always go through the previous chapters to review the component that can be chosen or replaced by another. Also, do not forget to follow the happenings in the OpenStack community. Let's start our first production day, which needs some preparation and a lot of enthusiasm.

Confirming the multinode setup

We can divide our physical setup into the following two categories:

- **OpenStack node role assignment**: The number of nodes as well as the services that will be running into each one
- **OpenStack node provisioning**: The way we will conduct the installation of each one from the bare metal level

By combining our multinode setup with a bare metal provisioning that configures the physical servers on a hardware level and a services categorization by using a group of nodes, we have an end-to-end approach that can quickly install a primary OpenStack private cloud in a wide range of hardware.

Assigning physical nodes

Depending on the number of physical machines that you would like to deploy, take into consideration the best practices and recommendations that were discussed in the previous chapters while building your first OpenStack production environment. In the current example, the following nodes need to be installed:

- Three controller nodes
- Three compute nodes

- Three Ceph OSD nodes
- Two network nodes (Is the health of the L3 agent stable in the Juno release? This will be covered in the next chapter.)

Node type	Services	Network interfaces
Cloud controller 1	MySQL Active wsrep_1 RabbitMQ Active Mirror_1 Horzion nova-* cinder-* keystone-* glance-* neutron-server	2 x 10G network ports 1 x 40G network port
Cloud controller 2	MySQL Active wsrep_2 RabbitMQ Active Mirror_2 Horzion nova-* cinder-api keystone-* glance-* neutron-server	2 x 10G network ports 1 x 40G network port
Cloud controller 3	MySQL Active wsrep_3 RabbitMQ Active Mirror_3 Horzion nova-* cinder-api keystone-* glance-* neutron-server standby	2 x 10G network ports 1 x 40G network port
Compute 1	nova-compute neutron-openvswitch-agent Ceph client	2 x 10G network ports 1 x 40G network port
Compute 2	nova-compute neutron-openvswitch-agent Ceph client	2 x 10G network ports 1 x 40G network port

Node type	Services	Network interfaces
Compute 3	nova-compute	2 x 10G network ports
	neutron-openvswitch-agent	1 x 40G network port
	Ceph client	
Storage 1	ceph-osd	2 x 10G network ports
	ceph-mon	1 x 40G network port
Storage 2	ceph-osd	2 x 10G network ports
	ceph-mon	1 x 40G network port
Storage 3	ceph-osd	2 x 10G network ports
	ceph-mon	1 x 40G network port
Network 1	L2 Agent Active	2 x 10G network ports
	L3 Agent Active	1 x 40G network port
	DHCP Agent Active	
Network 2	L2 Agent Standby	2 x 10G network ports
	L3 Agent Standby	1 x 40G network port
	DHCP Agent Standby	

Preparing the OpenStack Initiator

Chapter 2, Deploying OpenStack – DevOps and OpenStack Dual Deal, cited a few ways that can be used to deploy the OpenStack software by the means of system management tools such as Chef, Puppet, and many others. We have seen in-depth how to use Chef to install the OpenStack software across different nodes. Moving to a larger environment, you will need a second level of automation to provision your operation system software across all the nodes. Basically, you will need a tool or a system that makes it quick and easy to set up physical hardware, on which you can deploy your OpenStack private cloud infrastructure. Several solutions such as Cobbler, Kickstart, Razor, and **Extreme Cluster/Cloud Administration (xCAT)** are able to do the job. In the sample setup, we will use xCAT as a **Master Initiator Node (MIN)** for the OpenStack environment. Again, feel free to use any other tool instead of xCAT.

In our setup, xCAT can perform the following tasks:

- Provision operating systems such as CentOS
- Manage the remote system and power
- Run and serve network services such as DNS, DHCP, and TFTP

Furthermore, xCAT is capable of identifying the nodes by the means of network autodiscovery, which will be covered later during the installation process. It will be amazing to bring the Chef server into action, but this time, this process will be performed in the second stage. Once the operating system for each node in our network is installed, xCAT triggers some post-install scripts to bootstrap the Chef environment. The Chef server will take over and bring each OpenStack server to its final configuration state, as described in the Chef role list.

The xCAT supports **Preboot Execution Environment** (**PXE**) as a network boot method. It is necessary that all the nodes supporting PXE boot the network before the local drive during the first operating system setup. Be sure that all the NICs for your nodes support PXE.

We have chosen the MIN and Chef server to run the following services with an appropriate number of network interfaces. For the sake of simplicity, we will run the Chef workstation in the same node as that of the Chef server. It is recommended to separate your workstation in a different node. This is more convenient for a better cookbook's development environment, as was discussed in *Chapter 2, Deploying OpenStack – DevOps and OpenStack Dual Deal*.

Node type	Services	Network interfaces
Master initiator	xcatd	2 x 10G network ports
	TFTP	
	DHCP	
	DNS	
	Conserver	
	Kickstart	
	Post-provision	
Chef server	Chef server	2 x 10G network ports
	Knife	

The network topology

At first, choosing the right network setup can be challenging, especially in a large environment, when you consider different networks and node clusters. Generally, a good practice for a first successful step is to make it as simple as possible. Overengineering a network setup might bring more troubleshooting tasks while running in production rather than extending it. Thus, we will go for a simpler setup in two phases—the OpenStack network mode and the physical network topology.

The OpenStack network mode

We will proceed with our setup by using Neutron as the OpenStack network manager. We intend to take advantage of the several technologies that are offered by Neutron, which includes switching and routing first and load balancing the features later on. Basically, we aim to separate traffic for each tenant in a private network and enable the VM for each tenant to reach the default gateway of the router device that faces the public network. The former "per tenant routers with private networks" setup might be suitable for the following two main reasons:

- Configuration enables deployment of multi-tier applications per tenant by keeping each tier on a separate network

- Providing a network-level separation leverages the degree of security

The physical network topology

Even though we decided on how we will conduct the OpenStack network management, picking up the right network devices to connect the "pieces" is very essential for the formation of the "puzzle".

Firstly, how many networks do we need in the overall setup? Let's refresh our memory by going to *Chapter 1, Designing OpenStack Cloud Architecture*, where we had a look at an example within at least four networks—the external, management, VM internal, and storage network. Remember that combining or adding more networks in your infrastructure depends on your choice and the hardware limits and may affect your network performance output. Since we introduced the MIN bare metal provisioning node, which needs connectivity to all the nodes along with the Chef server, a fifth network named `Administration` will be added to our overall setup. The following list summarizes our OpenStack networks:

- The administration network

- The management OpenStack network

- The storage network

- The external network

- The VM internal/private network

We can map multiple logical networks to a single physical NIC when we start setting up the hardware connectivity devices, such as switches and routers. At this point, you should think in terms of higher requirements in order to avoid a slowdown of the network. This makes it imperative to install enough network hardware to satisfy the different former networks as well as the multiple tenant networks that are involved in the OpenStack environment, in which, considered as VLANs. In addition, you should think about the capability of the HA network devices by using double links.

 Switching the redundancy setup is highly recommended, but it is beyond the scope of the book. Refer to *vendor configuration cookbook* to set up the L2 and L3 network redundancy functionality for switches and routers devices.

The following switches are required for the current setup:

- 1 x 40 GbE for internal VM/private, storage, and management networks
- 1 x 1 GbE switch for the external network
- 1 x 1 GbE switch for the administrative network

 As your network grows, it is recommended to choose switches of the 48 ports and consider uplinks and aggregation switches.

The next step is to identify the different VLANs across our network layout. In other words, each network card that is connected to a specific port in a given switch must be properly configured to the VLAN that it belongs to. The VLAN configuration differs from one vendor device to another. It is highly recommended to understand the basics of tagged and untagged concepts. Let's see how it works in a nutshell before delving deeper into the deployment. As you may have noted, we have five different types of network traffic across more than one network device. However, we need a way to separate the packet's traffic since they pass through the same port. In other words, we need to tell which packet belongs to which VLAN through the different switches. Therefore, we marked a port as **tagged** if it is aware about VLAN information or ID. On the other hand, the **untagged** ports perform a normal Ethernet packet without any VLAN identification.

Applying the previous concept to our use case will require the following settings:

- The administration network ports should be marked as untagged since we provide a dedicated switch to connect the nodes for PXE within VLAN ID 3.
- The external network ports should be marked as untagged since we provide a dedicated switch to access the Internet within VLAN ID 4.
- The management network ports will be marked as tagged with VLAN ID 5.
- The storage network ports will be marked as tagged within VLAN ID 6.

- The VM internal network ports will be marked as tagged. The VLAN ID will be assigned for each tenant. To do so, a VLAN range should be planned in advance. We will consider 10 VLANs within a range ID 7-16.

Considering the server-side interface, the ports will be assigned, tagged, and untagged, as follows:

Node name	Network name	Network interface	VLAN tagging	VLAN ID
MIN (xCAT)	Admin (PXE)	eth0	untagged	3
	External (Internet)	eth1	untagged	4
Chef server	Admin (PXE)	eth0	untagged	3
	External (Internet)	eth1	untagged	4
Controller	Admin (PXE)	eth0	untagged	3
	External (Internet)	eth1	untagged	4
	Management	eth2	tagged	5
	Storage	eth2	tagged	6
	Internal VM	eth2	tagged	7-16
Compute	Admin (PXE)	eth0	untagged	3
	External (Internet)	eth1	untagged	4
	Management	eth2	tagged	5
	Storage	eth2	tagged	6
	Internal VM	eth2	tagged	7-16
Storage	Admin (PXE)	eth0	untagged	3
	Management	eth1	tagged	5
	Storage	eth1	tagged	6
	Internal VM	eth1	tagged	7-16
Network	Admin (PXE)	eth0	untagged	3
	External (Internet)	eth1	untagged	4
	Management	eth2	tagged	5
	Internal VM	eth2	tagged	7-16

 Ensure that each node that is connected to the 40 GbE switch via eth2 is equipped with a 40 GbE adapter.

The general layout of our minimal physical setup can be illustrated in the following way:

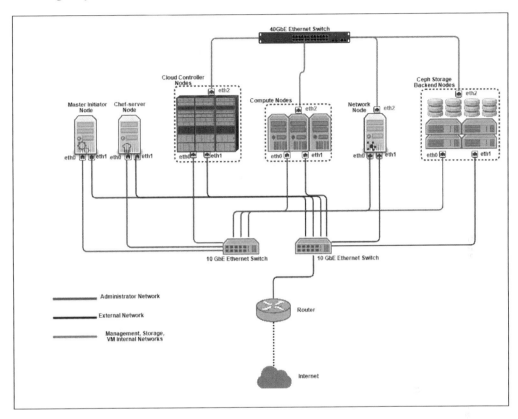

Each cloud network will use a different IP range. Let's see an example to get an idea of our setup:

Network name	Subnet /IP range
Administrative network	47.147.0.0/16
External network	94.49.0.0/16
Management network	172.16.0.0/16
Storage network	172.17.0.0/16

The VM internal network can be defined after completing the OpenStack setup and moving on to define the tenant networks. Bear in mind that the network and compute node will communicate physically through eth2 in our example, where each tenant will have a separate private network per VLAN. For example, we can define for tenant 1 a VLAN 8 within a private range, `192.168.47.0/24`, tenant 2 will be defined in VLAN 9 within a private range, `192.168.48.0/24`, and so on.

The OpenStack deployment

Now, it is time to cook. We will start by first preparing the MIN to automate the base operating system installation across all nodes.

The MIN installation

The MIN installation is straightforward. First, we should be sure that we fulfill the minimum requirements for our physical machine. Depending on the size of your cluster, we can go for the following hardware specifications:

- 4 CPUs
- 8 GB of memory
- 100 GB free disk space with a RAID setup

 Make sure that you provide redundant power supply for each device or node in your physical infrastructure.

CentOS 6.6 is the chosen Linux distribution for the MIN. We will go through the following steps to bring the MIN up and running:

1. Once the operating system is installed, we will proceed by disabling, for instance, SELinux and iptables. Keep in mind that if you expose the CentOS box to the Internet, disabling the former security tools is not a good idea! In this setup, we will assume that we are running behind a firewall:

   ```
   [packtpub@min ~]$ sudo echo "SELINUX=disabled" > /etc/sysconfig /
   selinux
   [packtpub@min ~]$ sudo iptables stop
   [packtpub@min ~]$ chkconfig iptables off
   ```

   If you intend to rely on iptables for MIN security, you should allow the ports needed for xCAT. You can find them in `http://sourceforge.net/p/xcat/wiki/XCAT_Port_Usage/`.

2. We will need to configure the two NICs for MIN. Let's edit our first network card configuration in `/etc/sysconfig/network-scripts/ifcfg-eth0`, as follows:

```
DEVICE=eth0
ONBOOT=yes
BOOTPROTO=static
IPADDR=47.147.1.10
NETMASK=255.255.0.0
```

The second interface will be connected to the external network by editing `/etc/sysconfig/network-scripts/ifcfg-eth1`, as follows:

```
DEVICE=eth1
ONBOOT=yes
BOOTPROTO=static
IPADDR=94.49.1.10
NETMASK=255.255.0.0
```

Restart the network service, as follows:

```
[packtpub@min ~]$ sudo service network restart
```

3. Set the hostname by editing `/etc/sysconfig/network`, as follows:

```
HOSTNAME=min
```

4. Finish the minimal configuration by restarting the machine by using the following command:

```
[packtpub@min ~]$ sudo reboot
```

5. Now, we will proceed by installing xCAT. By referring to the official xCAT download page, `http://sourceforge.net/p/xcat/wiki/Download_xCAT/`, we will grab a stable distribution, regardless of the xCAT version. You will need `xcat-core-*tar.bz2` and `xcat-dep*tar.bz2`.

Once the distribution is downloaded, extract the bundles in the following way:

```
[packtpub@min install]$ tar jxf xcat-core*tar.bz2
[packtpub@min install]$ tar jxf xcat-dep*tar.bz2
```

The xCAT packages include scripts to resolve package dependencies and help you create the `yum` repositories, which are included in the bundle, by running the following commands, as follows:

```
[packtpub@min install]$ cd xcat-core
[packtpub@min core]$ ./mklocalrepo.sh
[packtpub@min core]$ ./mklocalrepo.sh
```

Now, let's do the magic in one command, as follows:

```
[packtpub@min install]$ yum install xCAT xCAT-server xCAT-client
perl-xCAT
```

The xCAT server is already running. You need to update the next xCAT commands in your path, as follows:

```
[packtpub@min ~]$ . /etc/profile.d/xcat.sh
```

A final test can be performed in the following way:

```
[packtpub@min ~]$ tabdump site
#key,value,comments,disable
"blademaxp","64",,
"fsptimeout","0",,
"installdir","/install",,
.....
```

Congratulations! The xCAT server is running and ready to go. Note that the previous command enquires the site table, which defines the global settings for the entire cluster.

> xCAT uses a database to store the node-related information and details regarding the network's attributes. By default, sqlite3 is used. To update the xCAT tables and attributes, you can use simple xCAT commands such as `tabdump`, `tabedit`, `nodech`, and so on. By default, the database files are stored in `/etc/xcat`.

Besides the installation of the native xCAT packages, we will need to install an extra rpm in MIN for the OpenStack and Chef environment installation, as shown in the following code. You can find the latest rpm version at `http://rpmfind.net/linux/rpm2html/search.php?query=xCAT-OpenStack`:

```
# wget  ftp://ftp.pbone.net/mirror/ftp.sourceforge.net/pub/
sourceforge/x/xc/xcat/yum/2.8/core-snap/xCAT-OpenStack-2.8.6-
snap201409160710.x86_64.rpm
```

```
# mv xCAT-OpenStack-2.8.6-snap201409160710.x86_64.rpm xCAT-
OpenStack.rpm
```

```
# rpm -ivh xCAT-OpenStack.rpm
```

> xCAT-OpenStack is a meta-meta package that is used to manage the xCAT node setup in an OpenStack environment. The xCAT-OpenStack package was developed and maintained by IBM to manage both hardware and software within an OpenStack deployment.

6. We intend to include a DNS server in our MIN.

   Let's define the `packtpub` domain in `/etc/resolv.conf`, as follows:

   ```
   domain packtpub
   nameserver 47.147.1.10
   ```

   Add it to your `/etc/hosts` file, as follows:

   ```
   47.147.1.10 min min.packtpub
   ```

   Alternatively, you can set a list of public DNS as site forwarders in the following way:

   ```
   # chdef -t site forwarders=8.8.8.8,8.8.4.4
   ```

   Now, you only need to run the DNS and test it in the following way:

   ```
   # makedns -n
   Handling localhost in /etc/hosts.
   Handling min in /etc/hosts.
   Getting reverse zones, this may take several minutes for a large
   cluster. Completed getting reverse zones.
   Updating zones.
   Completed updating zones.
   Restarting named
   Restarting named complete
   Updating DNS records, this may take several minutes for a large
   cluster.
   Completed updating DNS records.
   ```

7. We also need to set up our DHCP server, which can be done in the following way:

   ```
   # chdef -t site dhcpinterfaces=eth0
   ```

   Note that we have enforced the DHCP service to run over the `eth0` network interface, which is connected directly to the administrator network.

 xCAT uses rcons to enable the multiple read-only consoles on a cluster server by using the `conserver` package. Optionally, running `conserver` will allow a collaborative way to troubleshoot the server by sharing the console server session between the administrators.

8. The most important stage in the xCAT installation is the process of ensuring the nodes are seen by the MIN when they boot up. This is called autodiscovery. Eventually, when a node boots up, it gets an IP address before the xCAT server knows and populates its MAC address table, then proceeds by updating the DHCP and finishes by provisioning the desired operating system. Autodiscovery won't work without defining a dynamic IP range in advance. This is required since we are not planning to assign a static IP for each node on the `eth0` interface. Let's define a dynamic discovery range on the `47.147.50.1-47.147.50.254` administrative network, as follows:

```
# chdef -t network 47_147_0_0-255_255_0_0
dynamicrange=47.147.50.1-47.147.50.254
```

9. Before provisioning our nodes, we should inform MIN about how we organize them. This is fairly simple and can be accomplished by associating each node to a certain naming group. Automating the provisioning of the nodes within the same role, such as the controller cluster nodes or compute cluster nodes, has proven to be very helpful. To define a `chefserver` node in xCAT, you can use the following code:

```
# mkdef chefserver    groups=chefserver,management,all
```

The previous command line defines a node within the `chefserver` hostname, which belongs to the `chefserver`, `management`, and `all` groups.

You can extend a group node definition by using the xCAT regular expression. For example, instead of manually defining 10 compute nodes that are named `computeXX` (assuming that `XX` is an integer varying in the range 1 to 10), you can simply type the following command line:

```
# mkdef compute[01-10] groups=compute,all
```

We will do the same for the cloud controller nodes, storage nodes, and network nodes, as demonstrated in the following code:

```
# mkdef controller[01-03] groups=controller ,all
# mkdef storage[01-05] groups=storage,all
# mkdef network[01-02] groups=network,all
```

You can check whether your nodes were defined by running the `nodels` command line. You will see the following output:

```
# nodels
chefserver
compute01
compute02
compute03
controller01
```

```
controller02
controller03
network01
network02
storage01
storage02
storage03
storage04
storage05
```

An additional substep requires a DNS setup for our MIN, which can be done by adding your nodes to `/etc/hosts`. However, do you have to type them manually? What about the scenario where you have hundreds of nodes? In this case, a simple trick can optimize the configuration time with zero mistakes. As you may have noted, we have followed a sequential host numbering naming (`node_name + ID_suffix`) as well as IP addressing. This approach can be the simplest and most organized way that can be used to avoid any host naming complication. You will realize the nirvana of the xCAT node management if you check the `hosts` table, as follows:

```
# tabedit hosts
#node,ip,hostnames,otherinterfaces,comments,disable
"min","47.147.1.10",,,,
```

There is only one stored host, the MIN. Adding more lines to the hosts table can help us populate `/etc/hosts/` and the DNS information later on. Using regular expressions can get the job done in one command line. It can be tricky! Let's have a look at a simple input in the hosts table:

```
"controller","|controller(\d+)|47.147.50.($1+0)|","|(.*)|($1).
packtpub|",,,
```

Each line in the hosts table is separated by a comma (`,`). The first column, `controller`, defines the node's group name. The second column is a regular expression, where we take the digit portion (`\d+`) and create an IP address from the hostname by using the same suffix that was already captured in the matching (`\d+`) part. For example, `controller01` would have captured `01` as the digit portion. The IP address creation would take `01` and append `47.147.50.1` by getting rid of the `0` header. The third column, hostnames `'(.*)|($1).packtpub`, will simply grab the first part of the row regular expression, `controller(\d+)`, and add to the `packtpub` prefix. Once you populate the hosts table, you can add nodes to the `/etc/hosts` file by running the following command:

```
# makehosts
```

Now, you will see the new hosts added in the /etc/hosts file, as follows:

```
47.147.50.1 controller01 controller01.packtpub
47.147.50.2 controller02 controller02.packtpub
47.147.50.3 controller03 controller03.packtpub
```

Great! We can do the same for the compute, storage, and network nodes in the following way:

```
# tabedit hosts
```

Add the following lines:

```
"compute","|compute(\d+)|47.147.50.($1+3)|","|(.*)|($1).
packtpub|",,,
"storage","|storage (\d+)|47.147.50.($1+6)|","|(.*)|($1).
packtpub|",,,
"network","|network (\d+)|47.147.50.($1+11)|","|(.*)|($1).
packtpub|",,,
"chefserver","|chefserver (\d+)|47.147.50.($1+13)|","|(.*)|($1).
packtpub|",,,
```

You can pinpoint a certain group of nodes that you wish to add to /etc/hosts by running makehosts <group_name>. For example, the #makehosts controller will add only the cloud controllers' nodes to /etc/hosts.

Let's check out the newly generated /etc/hosts file, as follows:

```
47.147.50.1 controller01 controller01.packtpub
47.147.50.2 controller02 controller02.packtpub
47.147.50.3 controller03 controller03.packtpub
47.147.50.4 compute01 compute01.packtpub
47.147.50.5 compute02 compute02.packtpub
47.147.50.6 compute03 compute03.packtpub
47.147.50.7 storage01 storage01.packtpub
47.147.50.8 storage02 storage02.packtpub
47.147.50.9 storage03 storage03.packtpub
47.147.50.10 storage04 storage04.packtpub
47.147.50.11 storage05 storage05.packtpub
47.147.50.12 network01 network01.packtpub
47.147.50.13 network02 network02.packtpub
47.147.50.14 chefserver chefserver.packtpub
```

Amazing! Now we can map all the IPs that were generated to the DNS that was running in the MIN, as follows:

```
# makedns
```

Check whether your DNS settings are running for example:

```
# host chefserver
chefserver.packtpub has address 47.147.50.14
```

10. The last OpenStack network topology illustrates the three different networks that are connected to each node, Chef server, and the MIN. Basically, each node of the OpenStack cloud environment requires three NICS. Thus, we have to tell the xCAT server about the different network interfaces for each node. We can do this either by using command line or via the `nics` table of xCAT.

For example, considering the two NICs for the Chef server, we can specify via `chdef` which IP address will be assigned to which NIC, as follows:

```
# chdef chefserver nicips.eth0=47.147.50.14
nicips.eth1=94.49.50.14
# lsdef chefserver
Object name: chefserver
    groups=chefserver,management,all
    hostnames=chefserver.packtpub
    ip=47.147.50.14
    nicips.eth1=94.49.50.14
    nicips.eth0=47.147.50.14
    postbootscripts=otherpkgs
    postscripts=syslog,remoteshell,syncfiles
```

Let's populate the `nics` table for all the nodes by using the same regular expression trick of going through each node group and assigning the associated IP range per network interface, as follows:

```
# chdef controller  nicips.eth0='|controller(\d+)|47.147.50.
($1+0)|'\ nicips.eth1='|controller(\d+)|94.49.50.($1+0)|'\
nicips.eth2='|controller(\d+)|172.16.50.($1+0)|'
# chdef compute nicips.eth0='|compute(\d+)|47.147.50.($1+3)|'\
nicips.eth1='|compute(\d+)|94.49.50.($1+3)|'\  nicips.
eth2='|compute(\d+)|172.16.50.($1+3)|'
# chdef storage nicips.eth0='|storage(\d+)|47.147.50.($1+6)|'\
nicips.eth1='|storage(\d+)|94.49.50.($1+6)|'\  nicips.
eth2='|storage(\d+)|172.16.50.($1+6)|'
# chdef network nicips.eth0='|network(\d+)|47.147.50.($1+11)|'\
nicips.eth1='|network(\d+)|94.49.50.($1+11)|'  nicips.
eth2='|network(\d+)|172.16.50.($1+11)|'
```

11. We will also need to set a few postscripts for each node that is defined by xCAT, to set up the network configuration and general setup for each OpenStack cluster node. We will set to `all` group as follows, and `eth1` as the default external interface:

```
# chdef all -p postscripts="confignics -s"
1 object definitions have been created or modified.
# chdef all -p postscripts="configgw eth1"
1 object definitions have been created or modified.
```

12. The next step is to define the cookbook repository. If you check under `/install/chef-cookbooks/` in your MIN, you will find that the xCAT-OpenStack package installation placed a bunch of cookbooks within `version-xcat`, where `version` is an OpenStack release. At the time of writing this book, the cookbooks within xCAT have been designed for OpenStack Grizzly release. Eventually, you will not stick to the default ones. Feel free to create or update cookbooks, roles, and environment files that reside under `/install/chef-cookbooks/`.

For our example, we intend to deploy the Havana release. By default, the cookbooks will be cloned from the StackForge repository in GitHub: `https://github.com/stackforge/openstack-chef-repo`. First, we will create an `xcat-havana` directory under `/install/chef-cookbooks/`, as follows:

```
# mkdir /install/chef-cookbooks/xcat-havana
```

Under `/install/chef-cookbooks/xcat-havana`, clone the former `openstack-chef-repo` repository and proceed to resolve all the cookbooks dependencies, as cited in *Chapter 2, Deploying OpenStack – DevOps and OpenStack Dual Deal, using Berksfile*. We will need cookbooks for Ceph. We will use the official ones, which can be found at `https://github.com/ceph/ceph-cookbook`.

Now that the Chef repository is ready, we should tell the Chef server how our environment would be like. Create a new directory called `cloud_environment`. The cloud environment template will be placed under `/opt/xcat/share/xcat/templates/cloud_environment/`.

> By default, the xCAT-OpenStack package places by default few templates for grizzly release under `/root/rpmbuild/SOURCES/xCAT-OpenStack/share/xcat/templates/cloud_environment/`. It is possible to create a new one named `Havana.rb.tmpl` for example after adjusting few required settings. For the sake of simplicity, you can refer to the code source of this chapter and place the `Havana.rb.tmpl` under the cloud environment directory as demonstrated previously.

13. Now, you can assign roles for each node, as follows:

```
# chdef controller01-controller03 cfgmgr=chef
cfgserver=chefserver\  cfgmgtroles=packtpub-os-base-controller
# chdef compute01-compute03 cfgmgr=chef cfgserver=chefserver\
cfgmgtroles= packtpub-os-compute-worker
# chdef network01-network02 cfgmgr=chef cfgserver=chefserver\
cfgmgtroles=packtpub-os-network
# chdef storage01-storage05 cfgmgr=chef cfgserver=chefserver\
cfgmgtroles=ceph-osd,ceph-mon
```

Every argument in the previous command set is essential. Let's see what we have:

- ○ cfgmgr: This defines which host profile or group in MIN will manage the node's post-script installation
- ○ cfgserver: This defines the name of the configuration host, chefserver
- ○ cfgmgtroles: This defines a list of roles per node/groups from / install/chef-cookbooks/xcat-havana/roles

14. We should tell the Chef server how to load cookbooks and which environment to choose from our MIN. A very simple way is to use a cloud file, which includes all the information and details regarding the setup for the OpenStack environment, as follows:

```
# mkdef all cloud=packtpub  all  extinterface=eth0
admininterface=eth1\ intinterface=eth2 template="/opt/xcat/share/
xcat//templates/cloud_environment/havana.rb.tmpl"  repository="/
install/chef-cookbooks/xcat-havana/"  virttype=kvm
```

Now, we will generate the cloud data file by using the following code:

```
# makeclouddata packtpub
```

We have generated a global description of the cloud named packtpub including all as a group of nodes that were defined previously, named network per interface, template environment, repository path, and the hypervisor type.

15. The final step for the preparation phase involves pinpointing how chefserver will behave once booted. This has something to do with postbootscripts, which was defined in xCAT. We will need the following two scripts:

- ○ The mountinstall postboot script, which is used to mount the OpenStack Chef cookbooks repository in the /install directory
- ○ The loadclouddata script, which is used to load the generated cloud details previously to the Chef server

This can be done in the following way:

```
# chdef chefserver -p postbootscripts=mountinstall,loadclouddata
```

Chef server preinstallation

The nodes that were defined in the MIN can be provisioned and installed by just booting each one in a certain order. Note that the MIN and Chef server will work in tandem. Thus, we should install the second hand of the automated installer process for the `packtpub` cloud deployment. Basically, we will install it using the awesome bare metal tool, xCAT. This will be our first bare metal installation. For a successful installation for any bare metal node, you should verify the following:

- Every node is being defined in the MIN
- Every node has the PXE boot capability
- MIN contains the OS images

CentOS will be our operating system base that is used to run the Chef server node. Furthermore, we will add and use a set of kits that are appropriate for the Chef installer to the CentOS image:

1. On the MIN, download the latest kit for Chef, as follows:

   ```
   # wget http://sourceforge.net/projects/xcat/files/kits/\ chef/
   x86_64/chef-11.4.0-1-rhels-6-x86_64.tar.bz2/download
   # addkit chef-11.4.0-1-rhels-6-x86_64.tar.bz2
   ```

    A software kit is a software bundler for xCAT that combines any specific configuration setup or scripts for an xCAT operating system image or to update a running xCAT node.

2. Check the kit components that were added to your MIN, as follows:

   ```
   #lsdef -t kitcomponent | grep chef
   chef_client_kit-11.4.0-1-rhels-6-x86_64    (kitcomponent)
   chef_server_kit-11.0.6-1-rhels-6-x86_64    (kitcomponent)
   chef_workstation_kit-11.4.0-1-rhels-6-x86_64    (kitcomponent)
   ```

3. Add the previous kit to the OS image for Chef server in the following way:

   ```
   # addkitcomp -i centos-6.5 chef_server_kit,chef_workstation_kit
   ```

To verify which OS image was assigned to which node in the MIN, type the following:

```
# lsdef chefserver -i provmedthod
```

If no images have been assigned, you can create a proper one by visiting http://www-01.ibm.com/support/knowledgecenter/ SSDV85_4.1.0/Admin/tasks/createxcatosimages_rhel.dita.

Discover and cook

Any node in the OpenStack environment is defined in the MIN. The Chef server is not installed yet, but it needs only one click, *push the button*. Before going through the deployment process, you should understand how the MIN works or, in other terms, how it discovers the nodes, which includes the Chef server in the first place. Eventually, this is fairly simple. Remember that we have defined an IP range for the PXE boot, where every node is attached to it via eth0. Of course, we should tell xcat-server which one is doing what.

To do so, we will point the MIN to start the process of node discovery one by one. We will power on our servers sequentially and let MIN do the rest. We will use a node discovery process based on a node range naming criteria in the following way:

```
# nodediscoverstart noderange=chefserver
# nodediscoverstart noderange=controller[01-03]
# nodediscoverstart noderange=compute[01-03]
# nodediscoverstart noderange=network[01-02]
# nodediscoverstart noderange=storage[01-05]
```

Now, time for the Chef server node! First, power on the Chef server node and check from the MIN what is happening, as follows:

```
# tail /var/log/messages
Feb 25 01:48:40 min dhcpd: DHCPDISCOVER from 00:0c:29:98:86:93 via eth0
Feb 25 01:48:41 min dhcpd: DHCPOFFER on 47.147.50.14 to 00:0c:29:98:86:93
via eth0
Feb 25 01:48:41 min dhcpd: DHCPREQUEST for 47.147.50.14 (47.147.1.10)
from 00:0c:29:98:86:93 via eth0
Feb 25 01:48:41 min dhcpd: DHCPACK on 47.147.50.14 to 00:0c:29:98:86:93
via eth0
Feb 25 01:49:04 min xCAT[3309]: xCAT: Allowing nodediscoverls -t seq -l
for root from localhost
Feb 25 01:50:00 min dhcpd: DHCPDISCOVER from 00:0c:29:98:86:93 via eth0
Feb 25 01:50:01 min dhcpd: DHCPOFFER on 47.147.50.15 to 00:0c:29:98:86:93
via eth0
Feb 25 01:50:01 min dhcpd: Wrote 0 class decls to leases file.
Feb 25 01:50:01 min dhcpd: Wrote 0 deleted host decls to leases file.
```

```
Feb 25 01:50:01 min dhcpd: Wrote 0 new dynamic host decls to leases file.
Feb 25 01:50:01 min dhcpd: Wrote 6 leases to leases file.
Feb 25 01:50:01 min dhcpd: DHCPREQUEST for 47.147.50.15 (47.147.1.10)
from 00:0c:29:98:86:93 via eth0
Feb 25 01:50:01 min dhcpd: DHCPACK on 47.147.50.15  to 00:0c:29:98:86:93
via eth0
Feb 25 01:50:01 min CROND[3315]: (root) CMD (/usr/lib64/sa/sa1 1 1)
Feb 25 01:50:09 min xCAT[3316]: xCAT: Allowing getcredentials x509cert
```

Great! The PXE is working. After finishing the image provisioning process with the Chef kit we have added running, we should be able to see the Chef server node running, as follows:

```
    ....
    chefserver: Reading package lists...
    chefserver: Building dependency tree...
    chefserver: Reading state information...
    chefserver: git is already the newest version.
    chefserver: rake in already the newest version.
    chefserver: 0 upgraded, 0 newly installed, 0 to remove and 119 not
      upgraded.
    chefserver: chef-validator
    chefserver: chef-webui
    chefserver: Postscript: install_chef_workstation existed with code 0
    chefserver: Running of postscripts has completed.
```

The cookbook and all the roles should also be uploaded to the Chef server. To check whether your assumption is correct or not, you can use the Knife command line to list the Chef clients in the new Chef server from the MIN, in the following way:

```
# xdsh chefserver 'knife client list'
chef-validator
chef-webui
```

Cooking time

All we need now is the push button. All the pieces that were required for automation have been prepared. Now, the Chef is waiting for the signal that initiates the process of cooking. We will provide nodes to the Chef one by one. Before starting off with bare metal provisioning, it is a good practice to go through the following checklist in order to avoid any surprises during the installation process:

- MIN has connectivity to all the nodes through the layer 2, which is also known as the administrative network

- MIN acts as a DHCP server for the OpenStack nodes

- The OS images exist in the MIN

- No VLAN tagging is performed on a switch for the administrative network

- Set the OpenStack nodes to boot using PXE

- The OpenStack compute nodes have hardware virtualization enabled in the BIOS

Next, we will need to prepare the repository on each OpenStack node to be deployed later. To do so, we will need to install additional packages using package list defined in xCAT. Basically, we intend to create an additional OpenStack repository which will be added to the operating system image. Once deployed, post scripts will update the package list of the new node based on the additional rpm list. For example, we can create a new directory to hold an additional Havana OpenStack RPM as the following:

```
# mkdir -p /install/post/otherpkgs/centos/x86_64
# cd / install/post/otherpkgs/centos/x86_64
# wget https://repos.fedorapeople.org/repos/openstack/EOL/openstack-
havana/rdo-release-havana-9.noarch.rpm
```

By default, xCAT defines several netboot package list under /opt/xcat/share/xcat/ netboot/ for different operating system. We will tell xCAT to take into account of our new OpenStack repository within the CentOS image as the following:

```
# chdef -t osimage centos imagetype=linux  otherpkgdir=/install/post/
otherpkgs/centos/x86_64 otherpkglist=/opt/xcat/share/xcat/netboot/centos/
compute.centos6.pkglist
```

In order to setup the new repository in all xCAT nodes for OpenStack, the otherpkgs postbootscripts should be associated within the 'all' group nodes as the following:

```
# chdef -p -t group all postbootscripts=otherpkgs
```

We can check for example the association of the otherpkgs postbootscripts with the controller01 node:

```
# lsdef controller01 -i postbootscripts
Object name: controller01
    postbootscripts=otherpkgs
```

Each OpenStack node will be provisioned first within the operating system that is defined by the MIN. Therefore, the Chef server will take over the automation installation process by installing the right cookbooks, as described by the node role assignment. However, how will the Chef server be aware of the OpenStack nodes? We missed a link that connects the chain!

Ideally, the node that is aware of the Chef server should have a Chef client running on it. This means that any node from the OpenStack environment should be authenticated from the Chef server's perspective. We will not do the authentication manually. We will just tell the MIN to install the Chef client on the OpenStack nodes using postboot scripts, as follows:

```
# chdef controller -p postbootscripts=install_chef_client
# chdef compute -p postbootscripts=install_chef_client
# chdef storage -p postbootscripts=install_chef_client
# chdef network  -p postbootscripts=install_chef_client
```

At this stage, we have the following two main concerns that should be taken into account:

- We will need an external network bridge to make Open vSwitch work properly in the network node. We can use the `configbr-ex` script, which is placed in the MIN, to run on boot time in the following way:

  ```
  # chdef network  -p postbootscripts="confignics -script config-ex"
  ```

- For every storage node, we will provision each one by using an Ubuntu image. The reason behind such a choice is the support of the official cookbook, which is stable and works fine for the Ubuntu operating system as well as for Debian. The storage nodes that run `ceph-osd` and `ceph-mon` will be provisioned using an Ubuntu OS image. You may associate it in the storage group node and check it using the following command:

  ```
  # lsdef -i storage -i promethod
  ```

Now, let MIN and the Chef server do the rest. Boot the rest of the nodes by starting first with the controller nodes, network nodes, and the compute nodes and then ending by the storage nodes. The provision process ended by the Chef client installation should be accomplished without errors. For example, the provisioning of the `controller01` node should give the following output:

```
...
controller01: Postscript: install_chef_client exited with code 0
controller01: Running of postscripts has completed.
```

To validate the correctness of your network node's provisioning, you should be able to see the following output for the verbose console:

```
...
network01: Postscript: confignics --script configbr-ex exited with code 0
network01: Running of postscripts has completed.
```

Testing the cloud

Let's test our first production deployment. From the `controller01.packtpub` node, follow these steps:

1. Populate the `keystone` admin keys, as follows:

    ```
    # . /root/keystone
    ```

2. Create a new image in the following way:

    ```
    # glance image-create --copy-from http://download.cirros-
    cloud.net/0.3.1/cirros-0.3.1-x86_64-disk.img --is-public true
    --container-format bare --disk-format qcow2 --name packtpub_cirros
    ```

3. Create an external network, as follows:

    ```
    # neutron net-create external01 --router:external=True
    ```

4. Configure the IP for the external network that was created, as follows:

    ```
    # neutron subnet-create --name external01-subnet01 --disable-dhcp
    --allocation-pool start=94.49.50.250,end=94.49.50.250 external01
    94.49.0.0/16
    ```

5. Create a `packtpub_tenant` tenant, as follows:

    ```
    # keystone tenant-create --name packtpub_tenant
    ```

    ```
    # keystone user-create --name packtpub --tenant packtpub_tenant
    --pass secrete
    ```

6. Create a private network in the following way:

    ```
    # neutron net-create pack_private
    ```

7. Configure the IP for the tenant network created, as follows:

    ```
    # neutron subnet-create --name private01-subnet01 --dns-nameserver
    8.8.8.8 --gateway 94.49.50.1 pack_private 172.16.17.0/24
    ```

8. Create a router in the following way:

    ```
    # neutron router-create external-router
    ```

9. We need to set the external network to the external router. We will accomplish this by using the following code:

    ```
    # neutron router-gateway-set external-router external01
    ```

10. Add the interface to the router for the internal tenant subnet in the following way:

    ```
    # neutron router-interface-add external-router private01-subnet01
    ```

11. Let's create a virtual machine and assign it to a private network for the `packtpub_tenant` tenant, as follows:

```
# nova boot --poll --flavor m1.small --image packtpub_cirros --nic
net-id=7789a969-4327-4287-a422-bbeff3215472 --key-name packtpub_
key  packtpub_vm
```

12. Once the VM is built, we need to test whether the virtual machine for `packtpub_tenant` is able to connect to the Internet. If it is unable to do so, you should check the following file in the network host:

```
# cat /etc/sysconfig/network-scripts/ifcfg-br-ex

DEVICE=br-ex

DEVICETYPE=ovs

TYPE=OVSBridge

ONBOOT=yes
```

13. Restart the network service to take into account the new changes, as follows:

```
# service network restart

# service neutron-openvswitch-agent restart

# service neutron-l3-agent restart
```

Arming the deployment

By now, we have collected almost all the pieces, and we have a running OpenStack environment within a tenant in production. However, the big picture is not complete yet. Note that the first stage of deployment assumes that only one cloud controller works actively to handle the OpenStack API's services, queuing, and database. The current implementation is being conducted to deploy the complete production environment gradually. This means that the remaining manual configuration has to be done to satisfy our requirements. The first setup does not take into account any node clustering or the redundancy of services. This is what we told Chef when we started deploying the entire environment. We should add the last piece which is a highly available cluster environment. Although *Chapter 3, Learning OpenStack Clustering – Cloud Controllers and Computer Nodes*, outlined a simple trick to automate high availability within the cloud controller nodes using cookbooks, it might be more complicated to adjust all the attributes and recipes that were defined in some of them to provide a complete highly available cluster from the beginning of the deployment. Nonetheless, you can always develop and extend the cookbooks that suit your needs, as cited in *Chapter 2, Deploying OpenStack – DevOps and OpenStack Dual Deal*.

For the sake of simplicity, we will follow a gradual procedure by configuring our current setup to provide a highly available OpenStack environment with a load balancing feature. Based on *Chapter 6, OpenStack HA and Failover*, we will perform the following tasks:

- Installing two HAProxy nodes using MIN
- Configuring HAProxy within Keepalived for stateless OpenStack services
- Reconfiguring the cloud controllers to point to the new Virtual IP
- Reconfiguring the stateful services in the cloud controllers for:
  - The MySQL database, by using the Galera-WRESP solution
  - RabbitMQ, by using the queue mirroring technique
- Installing Pacemaker and Corosync to handle the network nodes' resiliency

Bringing HA into action

In *Chapter 6, OpenStack HA and Failover*, we have given details regarding how one can configure a highly available MySQL database and a RabbitMQ cluster. A complete network controller cluster stack has been configured by using Pacemaker and Corosync for L3, DHCP, and the Neutron metadata.

For instance, we will need to spawn both the HAProxy nodes. From the MIN, we can define a new node HAProxy set, as follows:

```
# mkdef haproxy[01-02]    groups=ha,all
```

Add them to /etc/hosts and run makedns, as follows:

```
47.147.50.45    haproxy01    haproxy01.packtpub
47.147.50.46    haproxy02    haproxy02.packtpub
# makedns
```

Both the HAProxy nodes will use the following three interfaces:

- eth0 for the administration network
- eth1 for the external network
- eth2 for the management network

We will tell the MIN about the existing NICs, as follows:

```
# chdef haproxy01 nicips.eth0=47.147.50.45 nicips.eth1=94.49.50.45
nicips.eth2=172.16.50.45
```

```
# chdef haproxy02 nicips.eth0=47.147.50.46 nicips.eth1=94.49.50.46
nicips.eth2=172.16.50.46
```

We will finish creating the HAProxy nodes by setting up postscripts, which will run after the provisioning of the nodes:

```
# chdef haproxy -p postscripts="confignics -s"
1 object definitions have been created or modified.
# chdef haproxy -p postscripts="configgw eth1"
1 object definitions have been created or modified.
```

Check whether both the nodes are configured to boot by using PXE from the BIOS interface. Power on haproxy01 and then, do the same for haproxy02.

Adapting the deployment

You can refer to *Chapter 6, OpenStack HA and Failover*, to install HAProxy and Keepalived in our new machines. Next, the OpenStack API services, queuing systems, and databases nodes have to be routed to the new virtual IP. First, we need to create a virtual IP on the management interface. We choose 172.16.50.47. In HAProxy01, point to /etc/keepalived/keepalived.conf and check the vrrp_instance and virtual_ipaddress sections, as follows:

```
. . . . . . . . . . . . .
vrrp_instance packtpub-os-vip {
    state MASTER
    priority 100
    interface eth2
    virtual_router_id 47
    advert_int 3

    virtual_ipaddress {
        172.16.50.47
    }
```

For the second HAProxy node, the content of the `/etc/keepalived/keepalived.conf` file will look similar to the following code:

```
. . . . . . . . . . . . . . . . .
vrrp_instance packtpub-os-vip {
    state Master
    priority 99
    interface eth2
    virtual_router_id 47
    advert_int 3

    virtual_ipaddress {
        172.16.50.47
    }
```

The next step is to extend the HAProxy configuration files. For each service that requires a redundant load-balancing feature, we add a new stanza to `/etc/haproxy/haproxy.cfg`.

For each service, we will need to specify the virtual IP within the corresponding port of the running service.

The next snippet shows an example of stanzas that were added to the `haproxy.cfg` files on both the HAProxy nodes for the `cinder-api` service and horizon:

```
defaults
. . . . . .
listen cinder_api
bind 172.16.50.47:8776
. . . . .
server controller01 172.16.50.1:8776   check inter 2000 rise 2 fall 5
server controller02 172.16.50.2:8776   check inter 2000 rise 2 fall 5
server controller03 172.16.50.3:8776   check inter 2000 rise 2 fall 5

listen horizon
bind 172.16.50.47:80
```

```
balance   source
....
mode   http
server controller01 172.16.50.1:80 cookie control01 check inter 2000
rise 2 fall 5
server controller02 172.16.50.2:80 cookie control02 check inter 2000
rise 2 fall 5
server controller03 172.16.50.3:80 cookie control03 check inter 2000
rise 2 fall 5
```

It is possible to add other services to the load balancer configuration file by specifying the right port for each one, as follows:

- The binding port for `mysql_wsrep`: 3360
- The binding port for `glance-api`: 9292
- The binding port for `glance-registry`: 9191
- The binding port for `keystone_admin`: 35357
- The binding port for `keystone_public`: 5000
- The binding port for `nova_metadata_api`: 8775
- The binding port for `nova_osapi`: 8774
- The binding port for `novnc`: 6080
- The binding port for `neutron_api`: 9696
- The binding port for `rabbit_cluster`: 5672

You can find a very useful table describing the defaults ports that OpenStack services use by visiting `http://docs.openstack.org/kilo/config-reference/content/firewalls-default-ports.html`.

Make sure that `haproxy` is enabled by default in both the load balancers, as follows:

```
# vim /etc/default/haproxy
ENABLED=1
```

Before starting the `haproxy` and Keepalived services, you can refer to *Chapter 6, OpenStack HA and Failover*, to reconfigure the following files in each cloud controller node:

- `/etc/keystone/keystone.conf`
- `/etc/glance/glance-api.conf`

- `/etc/glance/glance-registry.conf`
- `/etc/cinder/cinder.conf`
- `/etc/cinder/api-paste.ini`
- `/etc/nova/api-paste.ini`

In the network nodes, the `/etc/neutron/neutron.conf` file should be reconfigured to point to the virtual IP.

The same should be done for the compute nodes, which require the `/etc/nova/nova.conf` file to be reconfigured.

After adjusting the virtual IP in the required section of each node configuration file service, you will need to restart the OpenStack services in each cloud controller, compute node, and network node respectively, as follows:

```
# service mysql restart
# service rabbitmq
# service keystone restart
# service glance restart
# service httpd restart
# cd /etc/init.d/; for i in $( ls nova-* ); do sudo service $i restart;
done
# service nova-compute restart
# service neutron-server restart
# service neutron-dhcp-agent restart; service neutron-plugin-openvswitch-
agent restart
```

> For each OpenStack service configuration file, it is easier to refer to the official OpenStack documentation to perform a proper setup within the right directives and sections. For example, you can find a complete list of the available options of `nova.conf` at `http://docs.openstack.org/havana/config-reference/content/list-of-compute-config-options.html`.

You will later need to reload the new configuration in each load balancer node using the following command line:

```
# service haproxy reload
```

Running first tenant

Let's test our setup by creating our first tenant, which is called `tenantA`, and start our first virtual machine in production. The former instance should be accessible from the compute node as well as should be able to reach the Internet.

1. Access the cloud controller and populate the necessary environment variables from the `openrc` file that resides under `root`, as follows:

   ```
   # . /root/openrc
   ```

2. We will need to provision a test image that can be used to create the virtual machine by using Glance. This can be achieved in the following way:

   ```
   # glance image-create --copy-from http://download.cirros-
   cloud.net/0.3.1/cirros-0.3.1-x86_64-disk.img --is-public true
   --container-format bare --disk-format qcow2 --name pack_cirros_img
   ```

   The preceding command yields the following result:

   ```
   +------------------+--------------------------------------+
   | Property         | Value                                |
   +------------------+--------------------------------------+
   | checksum         | None                                 |
   | container_format | bare                                 |
   | created_at       | 2015-03-06T17:54:49                  |
   | deleted          | False                                |
   | deleted_at       | None                                 |
   | disk_format      | qcow2                                |
   | id               | a717e479-f783-4d99-b7da-3533c5c81c93 |
   | is_public        | True                                 |
   | min_disk         | 0                                    |
   | min_ram          | 0                                    |
   | name             | pack_cirros_img                      |
   | owner            | d81ea6cc044741fe949796d1748778ac     |
   | protected        | False                                |
   | size             | 13147648                             |
   | status           | queued                               |
   | updated_at       | 2015-03-06T17:54:49                  |
   | virtual_size     | None                                 |
   +------------------+--------------------------------------+
   ```

3. Add the minimum necessary security group rules, as follows:

   ```
   # nova secgroup-add-rule default icmp -1 -1 0.0.0.0/0
   ```

   ```
   # nova secgroup-add-rule default tcp 1 65535 0.0.0.0/0
   ```

   ```
   # nova secgroup-add-rule default udp 1 65535 0.0.0.0/0
   ```

4. Create an external network from your network node by using the following command:

```
# neutron net-create external01 --router:external=True
```

The preceding command yields the following result:

```
Created a new network:
+---------------------------+--------------------------------------+
| Field                     | Value                                |
+---------------------------+--------------------------------------+
| admin_state_up            | True                                 |
| id                        | 203f453e-3012-49cd-b383-09f4bbed5de8 |
| name                      | external01                           |
| provider:network_type     | vxlan                                |
| provider:physical_network |                                      |
| provider:segmentation_id  | 15                                   |
| router:external           | True                                 |
| shared                    | False                                |
| status                    | ACTIVE                               |
| subnets                   |                                      |
| tenant_id                 | d81ea6cc044741fe949796d1748778ac     |
+---------------------------+--------------------------------------+
```

The following command creates a subnetwork from the external01 external network:

```
#neutron subnet-create --name external01-subnet01 --disable-dhcp
--allocation-pool start= 94.49.0.99,end=94.49.0.200 external01
94.49.0.0/24
```

The following result is obtained on executing the preceding command:

```
Created a new subnet:
+------------------+--------------------------------------------------+
| Field            | Value                                            |
+------------------+--------------------------------------------------+
| allocation_pools | {"start": "94.49.0.99", "end": "94.49.0.200"}    |
| cidr             | 192.168.120.0/24                                 |
| dns_nameservers  |                                                  |
| enable_dhcp      | False                                            |
| gateway_ip       | 94.49.0.1                                        |
| host_routes      |                                                  |
| id               | 8ba96538-553c-4da6-a338-2c662feface8             |
| ip_version       | 4                                                |
| name             | external01-subnet01                              |
| network_id       | 203f453e-3012-49cd-b383-09f4bbed5de8             |
| tenant_id        | d81ea6cc044741fe949796d1748778ac                 |
+------------------+--------------------------------------------------+
```

5. From the `controller01` node, create a tenant named `tenantA` and a user account, `packt_user`, as follows:

```
# keystone tenant-create --name tenantA
```

```
# keystone user-create --name packt_user --tenant tenantA --pass
Pa55W0rd
```

You will need to create and populate its credentials' new file, `openrc_packt`, as follows:

```
export OS_USERNAME= packt_user
export OS_TENANT_NAME= tenantA
export OS_PASSWORD= Pa55W0rd
export OS_AUTH_URL=http:// 172.16.50.47:35357/v2.0/
export PS1='[\u@\h \W(keystone_ packt)]\$ '
```

Now, run the following command:

```
# ./root/openrc_packt
```

6. From the network node, create a private network for the `packt_user` instance user and assign a private IP range for the `192.168.47.0/24` subnet to it in the following way:

```
# neutron net-create private01
```

```
# neutron subnet-create --name private01-subnet01 --dns-nameserver
8.8.8.8 --gateway 192.168.47.1 private01 192.168.47.0/24
```

For the preceding command, we will get the following output:

```
Created a new subnet:
+------------------+------------------------------------------------+
| Field            | Value                                          |
+------------------+------------------------------------------------+
| allocation_pools | {"start": "192.168.47.2", "end": "192.168.47.254"} |
| cidr             | 192.168.47.0/24                                |
| dns_nameservers  | 8.8.8.8                                        |
| enable_dhcp      | True                                           |
| gateway_ip       | 192.168.47.1                                   |
| host_routes      |                                                |
| id               | d7255778-0c98-4afd-bd99-5e96dc5b2377           |
| ip_version       | 4                                              |
| name             | private01-subnet01                             |
| network_id       | 99255c3d-b48b-4ad9-a057-8511bded8af4           |
| tenant_id        | 9d06805835cd49118e951be62b3323c3               |
+------------------+------------------------------------------------+
```

7. Next, we will need to create a router to be able to access other networks. You should set its corresponding gateway, as follows:

```
# neutron router-gateway-set external-router external01
```

Set the gateway for the `external-router` router. Then, add a router interface to the created subnet, as follows:

```
# neutron router-interface-add external-router private01-subnet01
Added interface 79c0958d-6092-4b0c-aecf-3dcca67274dc to router
external-router.
```

8. You can check the networks that were created previously in the router, as follows:

```
# neutron net-list
```

The preceding command gives the following result:

```
+--------------------------------------+------------+--------------------------------------------------------+
| id                                   | name       | subnets                                                |
+--------------------------------------+------------+--------------------------------------------------------+
| 203f453e-3012-49cd-b383-09f4bbed5de8 | external01 | 8ba96538-553c-4da6-a338-2c662feface8                   |
| 99255c3d-b48b-4ad9-a057-8511bded8af4 | private01  | d7255778-0c98-4afd-bd99-5e96dc5b2377 192.168.47.0/24   |
+--------------------------------------+------------+--------------------------------------------------------+
```

9. Now, we can create the first virtual machine by designating the image, flavor, network interface, and name. Remember that we will need to create an authentication key pair first. This can be achieved in the following way:

```
# ssh-keygen -t rsa -b 2048 -N '' -f pack_key
# nova keypair-add --pub-key pack_key.pub tenantA
```

Let's boot the virtual machine, as follows:

```
# nova boot --poll --flavor m1.tiny --image pack_cirros_img --nic
net-id=99255c3d-b48b-4ad9-a057-8511bded8af4 --key-name tenantA
Prod01
```

The preceding command gives the following result:

```
+--------------------------------------+----------------------------------------------------+
| Property                             | Value                                              |
+--------------------------------------+----------------------------------------------------+
| OS-DCF:diskConfig                    | MANUAL                                             |
| OS-EXT-AZ:availability_zone          | nova                                              |
| OS-EXT-STS:power_state               | 0                                                 |
| OS-EXT-STS:task_state                | scheduling                                        |
| OS-EXT-STS:vm_state                  | building                                          |
| OS-SRV-USG:launched_at               | -                                                 |
| OS-SRV-USG:terminated_at             | -                                                 |
| accessIPv4                           |                                                   |
| accessIPv6                           |                                                   |
| adminPass                            | xSBDCcbXN6f2                                       |
| config_drive                         |                                                   |
| created                              | 2015-03-06T18:37:53Z                             |
| flavor                               | m1.tiny (1)                                        |
| hostId                               |                                                   |
| id                                   | 928c2f10-9974-40f0-94e1-deb52bbd00dd             |
| image                                | pack_cirros_img  (a717e479-f783-4d99-b7da-353)   |
| key_name                             | pack_key                                          |
| metadata                             | {}                                                |
| name                                 | Prod01                                            |
| os-extended-volumes:volumes_attached | []                                                |
| progress                             | 0                                                 |
| security_groups                      | default                                           |
| status                               | BUILD                                             |
| tenant_id                            | 9d06805835cd49118e951be62b3323c3                 |
| updated                              | 2015-03-06T18:37:54Z                             |
| user_id                              | 7ac4488d61ca498cb0b485d1acb58e7d                 |
+--------------------------------------+----------------------------------------------------+
Server building... 0% complete
Server building... 100% complete
Finished
```

10. In order to allow the former instance to connect to the external network, we will create a floating IP from the network node, as follows:

```
# neutron floatingip-create external01
# neutron floatingip-list
```

On executing the preceding code, we will get the following result:

```
+--------------------------------------+------------------+---------------------+---------+
| id                                   | fixed_ip_address | floating_ip_address | port_id |
+--------------------------------------+------------------+---------------------+---------+
| 76384bbf-f58c-42a8-9d96-8cd6a72ff256 |                  | 94.49.0.100         |         |
+--------------------------------------+------------------+---------------------+---------+
```

11. A last step that is required is the assigning of the floating IP, that was created, to one of the router ports, which can be accomplished in the following way:

```
# neutron port-list
```

From the previous output list, assign an available floating ip to the router port ID as the following:

```
# neutron floatingip-associate 76384bbf-f58c-42a8-9d96-
8cd6a72ff256 9bbe9442-1864-4b97-a31b-aade48936ffd
Associated floatingip 76384bbf-f58c-42a8-9d96-8cd6a72ff256
```

For the preceding command, we will get the following result:

```
+------------------------------------+------+-------------------+------------------------------------------------------------------------------------+
| id                                 | name | mac_address       | fixed_ips                                                                          |
+------------------------------------+------+-------------------+------------------------------------------------------------------------------------+
| 9bbe9442-1864-4b97-a31b-aade48936ffd |      | fa:16:3e:1b:b7:3c | {"subnet_id": "d7255778-0c98-4afd-bd99-5e96dc5b2377", "ip_address": "192.168.47.2"} |
+------------------------------------+------+-------------------+------------------------------------------------------------------------------------+
```

12. Now, check the new instance details, as follows:

    ```
    # nova list
    ```

    For the preceding command, we will get the following result:

    ```
    +--------------------------------------+--------+--------+------------+-------------+----------------------------------------+
    | ID                                   | Name   | Status | Task State | Power State | Networks                               |
    +--------------------------------------+--------+--------+------------+-------------+----------------------------------------+
    | 928c2f10-9974-40f0-94e1-deb52bbd00dd | Prod01 | ACTIVE | -          | Running     | private01=192.168.47.2, 94.49.0.100    |
    +--------------------------------------+--------+--------+------------+-------------+----------------------------------------+
    ```

You can check out from Horizon the private and public network topology of tenantA, which looks as shown in following screenshot:

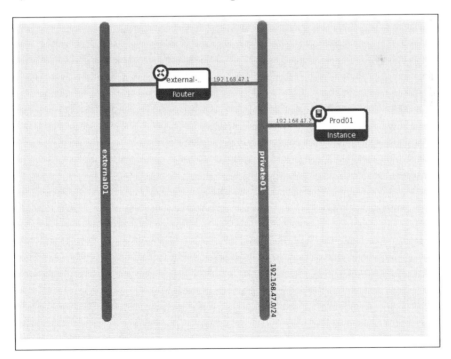

Summary

In this chapter, we delved into our first production day by deploying a complete OpenStack environment, based on the specifications and custom needs that were tailored according to the budget of an organization. This is a sample deployment in which many other layouts can be discussed and implemented as well.

The deployment methodology was adopted to compartmentalize the setup of the overall environment in such a way that the complexity of the production OpenStack cloud installation process was simplified and avoided. At this point, you should know how to smoothly move to production by taking into consideration the various aspects of an organized deployment. Furthermore, you learned how to provide the OpenStack environment from the bare metal level by using tools such as the xCAT tool. This is optional if you started with a medium-sized environment. However, when growing the environment, you should keep in mind that controlling, troubleshooting, and joining new nodes to the cluster might be more *rushing* task.

Note the complexity of the networking feature that was recently integrated within OpenStack – specifically the Neutron project. You may face more challenges when users start creating projects and deploy a virtual environment and multi-tier applications by using the OpenStack private cloud. At this point, you should be able to take care of their application connectivity as if they are running in a real environment, and release the enigma of virtual networking in OpenStack private cloud, which will be the focus of the next chapter.

8
Extending OpenStack – Advanced Networking Features and Deploying Multi-tier Applications

"Man is essentially ignorant, and becomes learned through acquiring knowledge."

–Ibn Khaldun

The previous chapter was a great opportunity to launch a primary OpenStack private cloud in a production environment. Depending on your budget and the hardware solutions available that might better fit your infrastructure, you still have several ways as well as more than one possibility to bring in a fully implemented first draft design in a real production environment. What can be challenging at this stage? Without any doubt, managing networks in OpenStack is still a concern that we cannot ignore. *Chapter 1, Designing OpenStack Cloud Architecture*, detailed a few introductory networking concepts in OpenStack, whereas *Chapter 7, OpenStack Multinode Deployment – Bringing in Production*, exemplified a network implementation using Neutron by extending a previous design in the latter one.

When it comes to actually providing more controlling and administrating networks, you should be aware that understanding the general functionalities in the network software core within Neutron is a must in order to "sail" smoothly in production. On the other hand, it comes to light that not all users will need to build their own virtual environment in your cloud in the same way. In the previous chapter, we saw an example of the Neutron implementation by separating networks by tenants *per tenant routers with private networks*.

In this chapter, we will dive deeper into OpenStack networking in Neutron and discover the following topics:

- Learn Neutron plugins: Linux Bridge and Open vSwitch
- Validate the use case of each plugin

In addition, we will cover more advanced features offered by Neutron. As seen in *Chapter 5, Implementing OpenStack Networking and Security*, with FWaaS and VPNaaS, we will highlight another networking service:

- Learn how to integrate **Load Balancer as a Service (LBaaS)** in OpenStack
- Use LBaaS in a multitier application

The last part of the chapter will explain an amazing orchestrating tool recently added to OpenStack in a nutshell and use it to deploy a multitier application in the load balancing mode using Neutron plugins.

Navigating through Neutron

Prior to Neutron, setting up a network for virtual machines in OpenStack was quite seamless. As was described in *Chapter 1, Designing OpenStack Cloud Architecture*, nova-compute uses the nova-network service to connect instances to an existing network defined by the cloud administrator, where users do not have to bother with the network setup. Also, there was no possibility to do more. With Neutron, new horizons are explored to provide more topologies and advanced network setups that might enrich the user experience and provide more freedom. But first, a slight learning curve might be needed.

Neutron plugins

By virtue of the plugins concept in Neutron, more additional networking features have been introduced in OpenStack, which differ depending on hardware requirements, vendor specs lock-in, scale, or performance. Some of the plugins might use the Linux IP tables and VLANs. Many other plugins are created by third-party vendors that interact with their network devices within Neutron. A variety of neutron plugins can be listed as the following:

- Open vSwitch
- Linux Bridge
- OpenContrail
- IBM SDN VE
- Big Switch Controller
- Nicira Network Virtualization Platform
- Cisco Nexus 1000v

Among the mentioned plugins for Neutron, in this section, we will look at the Linux Bridge and Open vSwitch for OpenStack Neutron. Both plugins are well supported since Havana release and provide a layer two switching infrastructure. You are probably anxious to see how they work separately, so let's dive into them.

 Learn more about the available plugins in Neutron at `http://docs.openstack.org/admin-guide-cloud/content/section_plugin-arch.html`.

Virtual switching infrastructure

Providing layer two connectivity to running instances in your private OpenStack cloud infrastructure requires more advanced virtual/physical switching configuration. You may raise this question: how could an instance in a private tenant "virtual" network connect outside and "ping the world"? Or, is there a way that allows a virtual machine running within tenant B to establish a connection with another one running in a different network within a different tenant C? As you can see, designing complex structures to answer the previous questions is not a simple matter.

Thus, you should understand the two main concepts:

- **Virtual network interfacing**: At instance boot time, a new virtual network interface is created on the compute node (running the hypervisor KVM by default), which is referred as a **tap interface**. The former interface is actually the responsible portal that exposes the virtual instance to the physical network.

 The tap interface should persist after the reboot of the compute node.

- **Virtual network bridging**: Let's tackle this concept as simple thought. A bridge allows two or more layer two networks to create a single network called **aggregate**. Let's virtualize it: a Linux Bridge is a virtual bridge connecting multiple virtual or physical networks' interfaces.

 To connect a physical interface ethX to a bridge, you will need to change its mode to promiscuous; this means that the interface should allow all frames to be processed.

The Linux Bridge plugin

In order to forward traffic between instances and to the virtual switch infrastructure, there is always a necessity to create a bridge, discussed previously, as well as Linux 802.1q kernel modules to ensure connection with the other networks. Eventually, the Linux Bridge plugin implementation will involve the usage of at least three virtual and physical devices, as depicted in the next figure:

- **Tap interface**: TapXX
- **Linux bridge**: **Br**
- **Physical interface(compute node interface)**: ethX

Note that the next network setup illustrates the usage of only one NIC. It is recommended, if possible, that you use two fast NICs per OpenStack server in the production environment and bond them together for high-availability and best performance concerns. By default, Linux offers a bonding module to enable NIC teaming. For each VLAN, a bonded virtual interface should be created. The bonded interface will distribute traffic across the connected NICs using load balancing and failover techniques. NIC bonding is beyond the scope of this book. You can see a detailed NIC bonding setup at `http://docs.oracle.com/cd/E37670_01/E41138/html/ch11s05.html`.

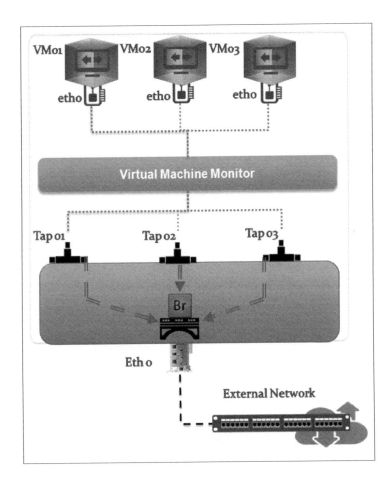

The previous figure shows a Linux Bridge **Br-eth0** that contains a single physical **eth0** interface and three virtual interfaces: **Tap01**, **Tap02**, and **Tap03** corresponding to a network interface within its respective guest instance. Traffic from **eth0** on an instance can be observed on the respective tap interfaces as well as the bridge and the physical interface.

Actually, the previous illustration assumes a simple flat network in which no VLAN tagging may exist. The Ethernet frame trip where all tap interfaces lie in the same layer 2 broadcast domains is quite simple. On the compute node running the network agent, we can check how the bridge looks.

In the case of a more complicated network setup where VLANs exist, the Ethernet frame trip becomes longer with one additional hop. Thus, before reaching the physical interface of the hypervisor host passing through a virtual VLAN interface ethX.ZZ to tag and untag traffic, it will require the following schema:

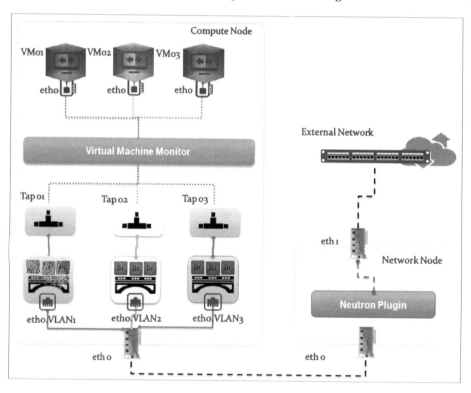

Both **eth0.VLAN1** and **eth0.VLAN2** are bound to the same physical interface, which is **eth0**. Keep in mind that each **eth0.VLAN1** and **eth0.VLAN2** interface tags traffic as **VLAN1** and **VLAN2**, respectively, before dropping it on the **eth0** physical interface. In the other hand, traffic moving toward virtual machines is untagged by each **eth0.VLANX** interface and is forwarded through its respective bridge.

The Open vSwitch plugin

Typically, Open vSwitch is a virtual switch that embodies the emerging concept of **Software Defined Networking (SDN)**. Overall, the former concept aims to treat networks as programs that can be easily deployed and provisioned.

Moreover, what makes it the cat's meow is the ability to integrate a virtual switching environment within a physical one due to many supported features, including:

- 802.1q VLAN tagging
- STP
- OpenFlow and sFlow protocols support
- Tunneling protocol support, including VxLAN, GRE, IPsec, GRE over IPSec, and VXLAN over IPsec
- NIC bonding support LACP

Let's see how Open vSwitch is architected in a simplistic figure:

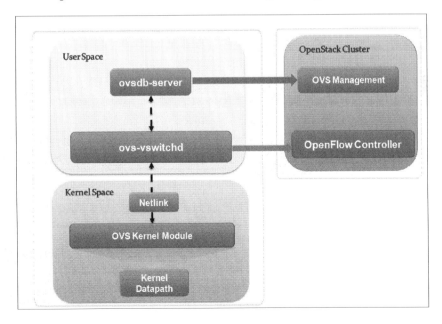

The overall architecture should be straightforward to understand:

- **Open vSwitch daemon (ovs-vswitchd)**: This is essentially a program running within the Linux kernel model in each host, which imposes how the flow would be switched or forwarded

- **Open vSwitch database (ovsdb-server)**: An Open vSwitch database is created in each host running `ovs daemon` to maintain the virtual switch configuration

- **OVS Kernel module**: This is a data path where all packets are forwarded and tunneled or encapsulated and decapsulated

Similar to the Linux Bridge plugin, Open vSwitch relies on the bridge and its kernel modules. What makes the difference are the unique virtual devices that are created in the compute host once you start using the OVS plugin. OVS uses more than one bridge; each one will have a port with the same name as the bridge itself by default. On first glance, we can enumerate bridges used by OVS compared to the Linux Bridge plugin:

- `br-int`: This is the integration bridge with the port called `br-int` by default. Basically, instances, DHCP servers, routers, and switches will be connected to `br-int`. It is imperative to notice that it is not possible to connect the tap devices (the virtual machine network interface) directly to the integration bridge; the reason behind this is the use of iptables rules on tap interfaces whereas Open vSwitch does not support security groups by matter of design. IP tables are applied directly on tap devices. So, what will be the magic link? The solution promotes the usage of simple Linux bridges that connect to the integration bridges in turn. Eventually, tap interfaces will offer a route for filtering to the kernel.

- `br-ex`: This is the physical bridge (the provider bridge another naming fashion) that enables instances to communicate with the physical network on a given interface `ethX` (X is the numbered physical NIC of the host). The `br-ex` bridge can be created and associated within an `ethX` host physical interface, which allows both ingress and egress traffic to the physical network environment.

- `br-tun`: This is a bit confusing if you start forming a picture of how many bridges an Ethernet frame will need to travel from the external network to the virtual machine network interface. To make it simple, we will consider `br-tun` as a form of a physical bridge but for a different purpose. If you use Neutron to create tunnels, a tunnel bridge named `br-tun` will be created to handle and translate VLAN-tagged traffic coming from the integration bridge into GRE or VXLAN tunnels. Flow rules will be installed and applied at this stage.

However, how should `br-int` and `br-tun`, for example, connect? Eventually, integration bridges will connect to either tunnels or physical bridges by means of virtual patch ports. For example, a `patch-tun` patch tunnel port connects an integration bridge to the tunnel one. What about the connection between the integration bridge and the Linux Bridge carrying the tap interface? To answer this question, you can imagine two interconnected switches via trunk; physically, they are connected by means of patch cables. Open vSwitch does the same; each Linux bridge in the virtual environment acquires a virtual interface veth.

 It is imperative that you remember once you implement OVS, every host in your OpenStack environment, including cloud controllers, compute nodes, and network nodes, must have its own integration bridge as well as a physical/tunnel bridge.

Let's resume with the number of virtual type networking devices that are involved when we implement OVS:

- Tap devices
- Linux bridges
- **Virtual Ethernet cable (veth)**
- OVS bridges: `br-int`, `br-ex/br-tun`
- OVS patch ports

Now, let's follow the Ethernet frame traveling from the physical network to a virtual machine interface. We will use a more sophisticated example by showing an implementation involving a GRE network setup in an OpenStack network environment. The next visual representation shows a `compute01.packtpub` compute node connected to a `network01.packtpub` network node. Both nodes are connected by means of the `br-tun` tunnel bridge, as shown in the following figure:

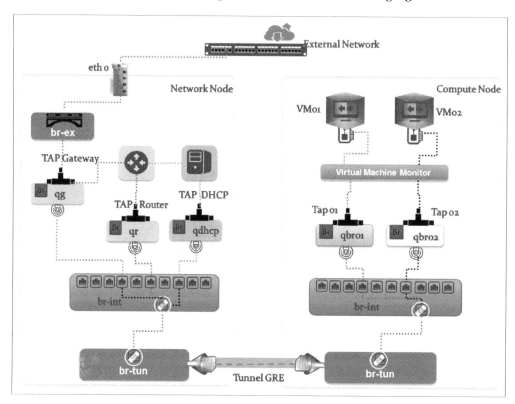

Let's start with the compute node, and check its virtual switch configuration using the next command line:

```
# ovs-vsctl show
Bridge br-int
    Port "qvo6d6ee47e-04"
        tag: 1
        Interface "qvo6d6ee47e-04"
    Port patch-tun
```

```
        Interface patch-tun
            type: patch
            options: {peer=patch-int}
    Port br-int
        Interface br-int
            type: internal
```

Starting from the virtual machine network interface, the Ethernet packet starts its trip from the instance connected to the tap interface device on the compute node `tap6d6ee47e-04`. Then, it drops by the Linux Bridge device attached to it via the `qbr6d6ee47e-04` virtual Ethernet cable. Let's take a closer look and see how packets are processed. Remember that attaching the tap interface to the Linux Bridge instead of the integration bridge is necessary because of the support of firewall rules' compatibility. We should then expect the implication of certain iptables rules at this stage:

```
# iptables -S | grep tap6d6ee47e-04

-A neutron-openvswi-FORWARD -m physdev --physdev-out tap6d6ee47e-04
--physdev-is-bridged -j neutron-openvswi-sg-chain

-A neutron-openvswi-FORWARD -m physdev --physdev-in tap6d6ee47e-04
--physdev-is-bridged -j neutron-openvswi-sg-chain

-A neutron-openvswi-INPUT -m physdev --physdev-in tap6d6ee47e-04
--physdev-is-bridged -j neutron-openvswi-o7c7ae61e-0
```

We can check where our security rules are realized. We see clearly that the **neutron-openvswi-sg-chain** is the security set that controls egress traffic from the virtual machine, which can be seen as the following:

```
-A neutron-openvswi-cc7474ee6-0-m mac ! --mac-source
BA:64:EE:04:50:74 -j DROP

-A neutron-openvswi-cc7474ee6-0-p udp -m udp --sport 68
--dport 67 -j RETURN

-A neutron-openvswi-cc7474ee6-0! -s 172.16.0.5/32 -j DROP

-A neutron-openvswi-cc7474ee6-0-p udp -m udp --sport 67
--dport 68 -j DROP

-A neutron-openvswi-cc7474ee6-0-m state --state INVALID -j DROP
```

On the other hand, ingress traffic toward the instance is controlled by the `neutron-openvswi-icc7474ee6-0` chain, which appears as the following:

```
-A neutron-openvswi-icc7474ee6-0 -m state --state INVALID -j DROP
-A neutron-openvswi-icc7474ee6-0 -m state --state
RELATED,ESTABLISHED -j RETURN
-A neutron-openvswi-icc7474ee6-0 -p icmp -j RETURN
-A neutron-openvswi-icc7474ee6-0 -p tcp -m tcp --dport 22 -j RETURN
-A neutron-openvswi-icc7474ee6-0 -p tcp -m tcp --dport 80 -j RETURN
```

The next transit point of our frame Ethernet is the second interface of the patch cable connected to the Linux Bridge, `qvb6d6ee47e-04`. It next hits the `qvbc7474ee6-05` interface attached to the `br-int` integration bridge, where it performs VLAN tagging/untagging for traffic in both ways. In the next output, you can clearly see that the `br-int` bridge carries VLAN tagged with the 1 ID, whereas its port interface is the `patch-tun` patch port, which connects to the tunnel interface:

```
# ovs-vsctl show
Bridge br-int
    Port "qvo6d6ee47e-04"
        tag: 1
        Interface "qvo6d6ee47e-04"
    Port patch-tun
        Interface patch-tun
            type: patch
            options: {peer=patch-int}
```

Before leaving the compute node, the tunnel bridge implies the tagging of the VLAN traffic and encapsulates it into GRE tunnels. Remember that at the `br-tun` level, flow rules are applied. Basically, flow rules translate VLAN IDs to tunnel IDs. Our second checkpoint will focus on realizing how the flow is applied. The next output command line shows the default flow rules that exist before any instance creation:

```
# ovs-ofctl dump-flows br-tun


NXST_FLOW reply (xid=0x4):
 cookie=0x0, duration=665.284s, table=0, n_packets=4, n_bytes=300,
idle_age=865, priority=1 actions=drop
```

Similar to firewall rules, the default set rules of the tunnel bridge imply the dropping of any traffic.

Let's boot an instance and see what is changed:

```
# ovs-ofctl dump-flows br-tun

NXST_FLOW reply (xid=0x4):

 cookie=0x0, duration=555.543s, table=0, n_packets=2, n_bytes=134,
idle_age=45, priority=3,tun_id=0x2,dl_dst=01:00:00:00:00:00/01:00:00:00:0
0:00
actions=mod_vlan_vid:1,output:1

 cookie=0x0, duration=541.443s, table=0, n_packets=74, n_bytes=8235,
idle_age=13, priority=3,tun_id=0x2,dl_dst=bb:33:e4:ee:b1:12
actions=mod_vlan_vid:1,NORMAL

 cookie=0x0, duration=533.543s, table=0, n_packets=44, n_bytes=12455,
idle_age=44, priority=4,in_port=1,dl_vlan=1
actions=set_tunnel:0x2,NORMAL

 cookie=0x0, duration=987.123s, table=0, n_packets=3, n_bytes=156,
idle_age=431, priority=1 actions=drop
```

What is interesting at this point is the first rule: any traffic on tunnel ID 2 tags our frame Ethernet with VLAN ID 1 and sends out port 1. It is important to know that the VLAN ID 1 is a local VLAN with tag 1 of the integration bridge br-tun. The original VLAN ID—for example, the traffic tagged as VLAN 3—is replaced by local VLAN 1 when the traffic reaches the integration bridge. The rule eventually maps the traffic between VLAN ID 1 used by the integration bridge and the tunnel with ID 2 used by the GRE tunnel. However, how does our Ethernet frame move to the integration bridge while the rule has sent it out to port 1? This might be confusing. Do not despair; it should exist in a way that unveils such ambiguity. To do this, we need to investigate the existence of port 1. Let's see what our ovs command line shows in detail:

```
# ovs-ofctl show br-tun

OFPT_FEATURES_REPLY (xid=0x2): dpid:0000068df4e44a49

n_tables:254, n_buffers:256

capabilities: FLOW_STATS TABLE_STATS PORT_STATS QUEUE_STATS ARP_MATCH_IP

actions: OUTPUT SET_VLAN_VID SET_VLAN_PCP STRIP_VLAN SET_DL_SRC SET_DL_
DST SET_NW_SRC SET_NW_DST SET_NW_TOS SET_TP_SRC SET_TP_DST ENQUEUE

 1(patch-int): addr:34:e3:44:32:ee:f2
     config:     0
```

```
    state:        0
    speed: 0 Mbps now, 0 Mbps max
 2(gre-2): addr:ee:3e:aa:23:92:10
    config:       0
    state:        0
    speed: 0 Mbps now, 0 Mbps max
 LOCAL(br-tun): addr:07:de:ff:44:ba:33
    config:       0
    state:        0
    speed: 0 Mbps now, 0 Mbps max
OFPT_GET_CONFIG_REPLY (xid=0x4): frags=normal miss_send_len=0
```

We can clearly see that the port is designated as a patch interface. Therefore, it will be the next transit point for the Ethernet frame toward the integration bridge. The next rule implies any traffic coming on tunnel 2 within the Ethernet destination `34:e3:44:32:ee:f2` and tags our Ethernet frame with VLAN ID 1 before sending it out to `patch-int`

The next rule implies traffic coming in on port 1 `in_port=1` with VLAN ID 1 `dl_vlan=1` and sets the tunnel ID to 2 (`actions=set_tunnel:0x2`) before sending it out to the GRE tunnel.

Amazing! Then, our frame Ethernet is able to carry on its trip by reaching the network host via the GRE tunnel bridge interface attached to `br-tun`. The next checkpoint will require the implementation of the flow rules at the network node level, which are similar to the ones of `br-tun` in the compute node:

```
# ovs-ofctl dump-flows br-tun

NXST_FLOW reply (xid=0x4):

 cookie=0x0, duration=1239.229s, table=0, n_packets=23, n_bytes=4246,
idle_age=15, priority=3,tun_id=0x2,dl_dst=01:00:00:00:00:00/01:00:00:00:0
0:00
actions=mod_vlan_vid:1,output:1

 cookie=0x0, duration=524.477s, table=0, n_packets=15, n_bytes=3498,
idle_age=10, priority=3,tun_id=0x2,dl_dst=fe:13:2e:45:76:dd
actions=mod_vlan_vid:1,NORMAL

 cookie=0x0, duration=1239.157s, table=0, n_packets=50, n_bytes=4565,
idle_age=148, priority=3,tun_id=0x2,dl_dst=fe:33:fe:ff:ee:3d
actions=mod_vlan_vid:1,NORMAL
```

```
 cookie=0x0, duration=1239.304s, table=0, n_packets=76, n_bytes=9419,
idle_age=10, priority=4,in_port=1,dl_vlan=1
actions=set_tunnel:0x2,NORMAL
 cookie=0x0, duration=1527.016s, table=0, n_packets=12, n_bytes=880,
idle_age=527, priority=1 actions=drop
```

Let's analyze the checkpoints in a nutshell:

- Maps multicast traffic on tunnel ID 2 to VLAN 1

- Matches traffic on the tunnel destined for the DHCP server at `fe:13:2e:45:76:dd`

- Matches traffic on tunnel ID 2 destined for the router at `fe:33:fe:ff:ee:3d`, which is an interface in another network namespace

- Maps outbound traffic on VLAN ID 1 to tunnel ID 2

The existence of two extra rules, as shown, is due to the usage of the DHCP server and the virtual router device in the network node. We can see this in the next output:

```
# ovs-vsctl show
Bridge br-int
    Port patch-tun
        Interface patch-tun
            type: patch
            options: {peer=patch-int}
    Port "tapf32fc99e-47"
        tag: 1
        Interface "tapf32fc99e-47"
    Port br-int
        Interface br-int
        type: internal
    Port "tapcd366e30-54"
        tag: 1
        Interface "tapcd366e30-54"
```

Does this make it more complicated? Well, it might be better to first rekindle the flames and review the namespace concept treated in *Chapter 5*, *Implementing OpenStack Networking and Security*, in a nutshell. Remember that a network namespace is similar to a network container, which groups a certain number of Linux kernel facilities in order to form a complete network stack including iptables rules, routing tables, network interfaces, and so on.

A DHCP service is simply an instance of dnsmasq running in a network namespace. It also includes a router, as cited in the preceding example. Let's check out our network namespace:

```
# ip netns
qdhcp-94245cc2-ed34-0452-4632-47ffe23dee31
qrouter-dd32f23d-ee73-47dd-4582-9923fee20201
```

Here, `qdhcp-*****` is the named DHCP server namespace and `qrouter-****` is the named router namespace.

So, how can we trace our DHCP tap interface in the network node? The best way to do this is by checking the DHCP server's unique address: MAC address. The following command could help us by providing the DHCP namespace:

```
# ip netns exec qdhcp-94245cc2-ed34-0452-4632-47ffe23dee31 ip addr
71: ns-f32fc99e-47: <BROADCAST,MULTICAST,UP,LOWER_UP> mtu 1500 qdisc
pfifo_fast state UP qlen 1000
    link/ether ff:46:ee:07:e3:05 brd ff:ff:ff:ff:ff:ff
    inet 172.16.0.0/24  brd 172.16.0.255 scope global ns-f32fc99e-47
```

We can see that `ns-f32fc99e-47` matches the tap interface derived from the `ovs-ofctl` output received previously, which makes sense. The tap interface can be seen as follows:

```
Port "tapf32fc99e-47"
        tag: 1
        Interface "tapf32fc99e-47"
```

The next checkpoint is the router interface; using the router namespace, we will identify which interface our Ethernet framework will have to transit:

```
# ip netns exec qrouter-dd32f23d-ee73-47dd-4582-9923fee20201 ip addr
66: qg-44de398f-aa: <BROADCAST,MULTICAST,UP,LOWER_UP> mtu 1500 qdisc
pfifo_fast state UP qlen 1000
    link/ether ff:12:e3:5c:22:ac brd ff:ff:ff:ff:ff:ff
```

```
    inet 192.168.47.227/28 brd 192.168.47.239 scope global
qg-44de398f-aa
    inet 192.168.47.228/32 brd 192.168.47.228 scope global
qg-44de398f-aa
......
68: qr-cd366e30-54: <BROADCAST,MULTICAST,UP,LOWER_UP> mtu 1500 qdisc
pfifo_fast state UP qlen 1000
    link/ether ff:46:ee:07:e3:05 brd ff:ff:ff:ff:ff:ff
    inet 172.16.0.1/24 brd 172.16.0.255 scope global qr-cd366e30-54
```

We have two different interfaces:

- `qg-44de398f-aa`: This connects the router to the external gateway assuming that `192.168.47.227/28` is an external network

- `qr-cd366e30-54`: This connects the router to the integration bridge, which can be confirmed from the `ovs-ofctl` output shown previously

Our Ethernet framework is almost connecting to the outside, but before that, we have to tell it which interface it goes from the router. `192.168.47.227/28` is the external network connected to `qg-44de398f-aa` where traffic will flow through the physical bridge `br-ex`:

```
    Bridge br-ex
Port "tapd44de398f-aa"
    Interface "tapd44de398f-aa"
Port br-ex
    Interface br-ex
        type: internal
```

Load Balancer as a Service

The LBaaS extension is an additional feature provided by Neutron. It is possible to add more resiliency to the instances running in the OpenStack environment by balancing traffic to applications running on them. In previous releases of OpenStack, LBaaS was a separate project called **Atlas**, which was a load-balancing solution for OpenStack out of the box. Starting from the Grizzly release, LBaaS is an official extension within the network service and provides even more features within the Havana release. In *Chapter 5, Implementing OpenStack Networking and Security*, we covered some of the security functionalities provided by Neutron, including VPN as a Service and Firewall as a Service; the nirvana of Neutron is not finished yet: we still have to discover Load Balancer as Service.

Work around LBaaS

LBaaS has been fully integrated within OpenStack, starting from the Grizzly release. During this time, the networking service that was formally named **quantum** has taken a new turn to tackle several networking aspects thanks to networking virtualization concepts. Eventually, LBaaS uses drivers to talk to the hardware/software of the load balancer. The first driver uses **HAProxy** by default. Within the Havana release, LBaaS is able to support and talk to many other load balancer vendors. Here's what LBaaS can offer to your private cloud:

- Load balancing traffic between instances
- Health check monitoring based on HTTP and TCP
- Session persistence by forcibly directing client requests to the same node

 Session persistence is frequently used in several web applications. This method forcibly directs client requests to the same node when an application does not share a state between pool members.

- Numerous load balancer algorithms, such as Round Robin, Least connection and Source IP

Basically, we find four new fundamental concepts with LBaaS:

- **Virtual IP or VIP**: This is the IP listening for the incoming connection and used for load balancer failover
- **Pool**: This refers to a set of servers handling identical content
- **Pool member**: This presents one unit from the pool by exposing the IP address of the service and the listening port
- **Health Monitoring**: This refers to two types of check monitoring that can be listed:
    - **Layer 4**: This refer to the test connectivity based on TCP
    - **Layer 7**: This refers to the test member pool connectivity based on HTTP/HTTPS

Integrate LBaaS in the cloud

As was mentioned previously, HAProxy is used as the default load balancer in the Havana release. Let's see how to integrate LBaaS in our private cloud by following the next few instructions,

On the controller node, perform the following steps:

1. We start by installing `haproxy` on the cloud controller node using the following command:

    ```
    # yum install haproxy -y
    ```

2. Check whether the load balancing plugin is listed in the service plugins in `/etc/neutron/neutron.conf`. Depending on the plugins enabled in your `neutron.conf` file, you should at least see the `service_plugins` directive as follows:

    ```
    service_plugins=router,lbaas
    ```

3. In order to make HAProxy work properly, the neutron LBaaS agent needs to talk to a device driver as an interface between the load balancer and the networking service API. You can enable it by editing the following directive:

    ```
    service_provider = LOADBALANCER:Haproxy:neutron.services.
    loadbalancer.drivers.haproxy.plugin_driver.HaproxyOnHostPluginDriv
    er:default
    ```

4. Restart the Neutron server:

    ```
    # service neutron-server restart
    ```

On the network node, perform these steps:

1. Edit the `/etc/neutron/neutron.conf` file to enable LBaaS in Neutron:

    ```
    service_plugins=router,lbaas
    ```

2. Enable the HAProxy device driver in the `service_provider` directive:

    ```
    service_provider = LOADBALANCER:Haproxy:neutron.services.
    loadbalancer.drivers.haproxy.plugin_driver.HaproxyOnHostPluginDriv
    er:default
    ```

3. The LBaaS agent in Neutron needs to be configured to use an interface driver corresponding to a specific networking plugin: either Linux Bridge or Open vSwitch can be chosen. We will go for the Open vSwitch plugin and configure the Neutron LBaaS to use it as follows:

```
# vi /etc/neutron/lbaas_agent.ini
```

4. Enable the Open vSwitch driver by commenting out the following line:

```
interface_driver = neutron.agent.linux.interface.
OVSInterfaceDriver
[haproxy]
user_group = haproxy
```

5. Issue the following commands to start the neutron LBaaS agent and start the Neutron Open vSwitch agent plugin as follows:

```
# service neutron-plugin-openvswitch-agent restart
```

```
# service neutron-lbaas-agent start
```

6. Let's visualize our load balancer management tab in the dashboard by changing the following settings in the `/etc/openstack-dashboard/local_settings` file:

```
OPENSTACK_NEUTRON_NETWORK = {'enable_ lb': True,
```

7. Restart the web server daemon in the cloud controller node:

```
# service httpd restart
```

Here we go; our load balancer service is ready to be used from horizon:

Moreover, Neutron offers a set of commands to fully manage pools, members, virtual IPs, and health monitors. The creation of a load balancer and making it functional is straightforward:

1. Create a pool.
2. Create pool members.
3. Associate the pool members.
4. Create a virtual IP for the pool.
5. Create a health monitor.
6. Associate the health monitor with the pool.

Before bringing a load balancing sample setup into action, we will cover an additional terminology in OpenStack, which can work in tandem with LBaaS.

Stack in OpenStack

As the title promises: here's building stacks in OpenStack! As you may have guessed from the **stack** terminology, this includes any group of connected OpenStack resources, including instances, volumes, virtual routers, firewalls, load balancers and so on, that form a stack. However, how can stacks be created and managed? Starting from the Grizzly release, a new orchestration service named **heat** has been added. Using YAML-based template languages called **Heat Orchestration Template (HOT)**, you will be able to spin up multiple instances, logical networks, and many other cloud services in an automated fashion.

Now you can guess the rest: create stacks from templates.

 If you are familiar with the AWS cloud formation service, heat is fully compatible with AWS templates and provides an API to align the AWS specification using CFN-formatted templates expressed in JSON.

Although the topic of heat might take up a whole chapter, we will rather go for a simple example and build a stack running a load balancer server using the orchestration method. Furthermore, heat will be explained in more detail in the next chapter by joining more servers into the stack and realizing the flexibility of such an orchestration method.

HOT explained

Let's reformulate HOT in a simpler way: define a proper template, and you get a running stack. If you want to have a stack launch three instances connected by a private network and make it load balanced, then the heat engine will expect the definitions for three instances in your template, a network, a subnet, a load balancer, and three network ports. As described previously, HOT has a specific structure based on the YAML syntax. A typical HOT structure would look like the following code:

```
heat_template_version:
description:
parameters:
  param1
    type:
    label:
    description:
    default:
  param2:
    ....
resources:
 resource_name:
    type: OS::*::*
    properties:
      prop1: { get_param: param1}
      prop2: { get_param: param2}
      .......
outputs:
  output1:
    description:
    value: { get_attr: resource_name,attr] }
          ......
```

Let's check out the overall sections of the previous template:

- `heat_template_version`: This specifies the version of the template syntax that is used. Standard versions are 2013-05-23, while new ones labeled 2014-10-16 are introduced with the Juno release and contain a few additions.

- `description`: This includes the description of the template.

- `parameters`: These declare a list of inputs. Each parameter is given a name, type, and description; the default value is optional. Parameters can be any information, such as a specific image or a network ID specified by the user.

- resources: These can be referred to as objects that heat will create or modify as part of its operation. The resources section is where the different components are defined. For example, a resource_name name can be virtual_web with the OS::Nova::Server type, which indicates the type of nova compute instance. It can be forwarded by a list of subproperties that identify which image, flavor, and private network can be used for the virtual_web instance resource.

- outputs: It is possible to export the attributes of a stack after its deployment, defined in this section.

Installing heat

To see how heat can bring charm to your private cloud infrastructure, we will perform these steps to install and run heat on the cloud controller node:

1. Install the required heat packages:

   ```
   yum install openstack-heat-api openstack-heat-api-cfn \
   heat-engine python-heatclient
   ```

2. Log in to the database and create a new heat database and grant privileges to the heat user:

   ```
   # mysql -u root -p
   CREATE DATABASE heat;
   GRANT ALL PRIVILEGES ON heat.* TO 'heat'@'localhost'\
   IDENTIFIED BY 'password';
   GRANT ALL PRIVILEGES ON heat.* TO 'heat'@'%'\
   IDENTIFIED BY 'password';
   ```

3. Source the keystone environment variables for admin access:

   ```
   # source keystonerc_admin
   ```

4. Create a new user for the heat user:

   ```
   # keystone user-create –name heat –pass password
   ```

5. Assign the admin role to the heat user:

   ```
   # keystone user-role-add --user heat --tenant service --role admin
   ```

6. Edit the `/etc/heat/heat.conf` file to configure the database as well as RabbitMQ access:

```
[database]
...
connection = mysql://heat:HEAT_DBPASS@cc01/heat

[DEFAULT]
...
rpc_backend = rabbit
rabbit_host = cc01.packtpub
rabbit_password = RABBIT_PASSWORD
```

7. Specify the identity service endpoint access in the `[keystone_authtoken]` section:

```
[keystone_authtoken]
...
auth_uri = http://cc01.packtpub:5000/v2.0
identity_uri = http://cc01.packtpub:35357
admin_tenant_name = service
admin_user = heat
admin_password = HEAT_PASS
```

8. Populate the `heat` database:

```
# su -s /bin/sh -c "heat-manage db_sync" heat
```

9. Configure the orchestration service for it to be started automatically on boot:

```
# systemctl enable openstack-heat-api.service openstack-heat-api-
cfn.service \
  openstack-heat-engine.service
# systemctl start openstack-heat-api.service openstack-heat-api-
cfn.service \
  openstack-heat-engine.service
```

Heating things up

Building a load-balanced stack using heat is straightforward. The following setup describes the first implementation of a stack running a load balancer within two web servers instances that share a virtual IP. It is important to note that instances will run in a private network called `private_network`. For the sake of simplicity, we will not configure the template to reach the external or public network; we will leave that to the next chapter.

For instance, we will need to prepare a proper structure for our template. Heat templates are modular; you can call other templates for a defined library to be used as HOT objects and launch them based on the default or defined parameters. The way to perform the **nesting** of templates alleviates the complexity of coding the stack. In addition, it proves the simplicity of treating your stack as independent resources rather than introducing multiple changes every time you plan to update them, which is error-prone.

The structure of our file stack is as follows:

```
----stackers
        |--------- web_lb.yaml
        |--------- Lib
                        |---------- env.yaml
```

Let's see the components:

- `web_lb.yaml`: This file contains the main load-balanced web server stack definition.

- `Lib/env.yaml`: This contains global definitions that are imported from templates before parsing them. For example, it can contain only one basic resource section definition as follows:

  ```
  resource_registry:
    packtpub::lb_server: lb_server.yaml
  ```

  Let's understand the terms in this code:

  - `resource_registry`: This is the mapping section of the resource type to the path of the nested template `lb_server.yaml`.

  - `Lib`: This is the prefix name to indicate the usage of nested templates. We will need it later for nested template directory.

  - `packtpub`: This is the definition of a customized namespace.

For the instance, we will need only `web_lb.yaml` file to run our first load balanced stack whereas we keep the file's tree of the for later. The next `web_lb.yaml` file should create a stack with the following details:

- Two instances running `httpd`
- A virtual IP shared between both web servers

- Instances will start being deployed and attached in a private network:

```
heat_template_version: 2013-05-23
description: Load balanced web servers
parameters:
  image:
    type: string
    label: Image name or ID
    description: Image to be used for compute instance
    default: fedora20_box
  flavor:
    type: string
    label: Flavor
    description: Type of instance (flavor) to be used
    default: m1.small
  key:
    type: string
    label: Key name
    description: Name of key-pair for compute instance
    default: my_key
  private_network:
    type: string
    label: Private network name or ID
    description: Network to attach instance to.
    default: private
  subnet_id:
    type: string
    description: subnet on which the load balancer will be located
    default: 9a4d4443-37f0-4680-8efa-7495b52fd8c5
  cluster_size:
    type: number
    description: Number of servers in the cluster
    default: 2
  pool_id:
    type: string
    description: Pool to contact
  external_network_id:
    type: string
    description: UUID of a Neutron external network
  default: 2d4b050b-2cfa-41ac-9b9a-d4ffd5dc3784
resources:
  web_cluster:
  type: OS::Heat::ResourceGroup
  properties:
    count: {get_param: cluster_size}
    resource_def:
      type: OS::Nova::Server
      properties:
```

```
              flavor: {get_param: flavor}
              image: {get_param: image}
              key_name: {get_param: key}
              networks: [{network: {get_param: network} }]
              user_data_format: RAW
              user_data:
                str_replace:
                  template: |
                    #!/bin/bash -v
                    yum -y install httpd
                    systemctl enable httpd.service
                    systemctl start httpd.service
                    setsebool -P httpd_can_network_connect_db=1
                    systemctl restart httpd.service
        member:
          type: OS::Neutron::PoolMember
          properties:
            pool_id: {get_param: pool_id}
            address: {get_attr: [web_cluster, first_address]}
            protocol_port: 80

        pool:
          type: OS::Neutron::Pool
          properties:
            name: pool.vip
            protocol: HTTP
            subnet_id: {get_param: subnet_id}
            lb_method: ROUND_ROBIN
            vip:
              protocol_port: 80
        lb:
          type: OS::Neutron::LoadBalancer
          properties:
            protocol_port: 80
            pool_id: {get_resource: pool }
            members: {get_resource: web_cluster}

        lb_floating:
          type: OS::Neutron::FloatingIP
          properties:
            floating_network_id: {get_param: external_network_id}
            port_id: {get_attr: [pool, vip, port_id]}
    outputs:
      instance_ip:
        description: IP address of the instance
        value: { get_attr: [web_cluster, first_address] }
```

Let's build the `lb_stacker` stack using the following command:

```
# heat stack-create lb_stacker -f web_lb.yaml
```

This command gives the following result:

```
+-----------------------------------------+------------+-------------------+-----------------------+
| id                                      | stack_name | stack_status      | creation_time         |
+-----------------------------------------+------------+-------------------+-----------------------+
| 1e4930ee-50d8-4873-bba3-12aecd1c9234    | lb_stacker | CREATE_IN_PROGRESS | 2015-05-25T04:36:10Z |
+-----------------------------------------+------------+-------------------+-----------------------+
```

Parameter values can be also specified via heat command line. For example, the following command line creates the same heat stack without going through default values of parameters in the template file:

```
# heat stack-create lb_stacker -f web_lb.yaml  -P subnet_
id=9a4d4443-37f0-4680-8efa-7495b52fd8c5 -P key="my_key"
-P flavor=m1.small -P image=14614d95-d9c5-43ef-9dfd-
25eb526850d5 -P external_network_id=2d4b050b-2cfa-41ac-
9b9a-d4ffd5dc3784 -P network=private
```

We can further check out the creation of a virtual IP for the load balancing settings:

```
# neutron lb-vip-list
```

This command gives the following output:

```
+-----------------------------------------+----------+-----------+----------+---------------+--------+
| id                                      | name     | address   | protocol | admin_state_up | status |
+-----------------------------------------+----------+-----------+----------+---------------+--------+
| 6c69c288-66f0-4ef8-b75c-35b3a999c189    | pool.vip | 10.0.0.8  | HTTP     | True          | ACTIVE |
+-----------------------------------------+----------+-----------+----------+---------------+--------+
```

From horizon, we can check whether a new member has been newly added to the load balancer pool:

The installation of the apache web server (httpd) will be processed by cloud-init. It might be useful to monitor the process of the instance deployment and service installation by going checking in the Log section of every instance from horizon as the following:

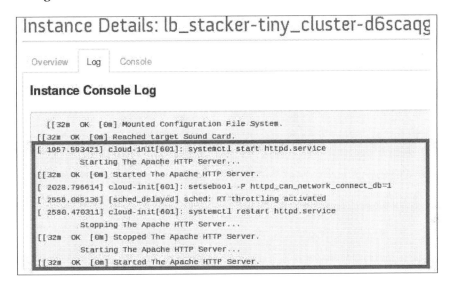

When the installation of both instances is accomplished successfully, we intend to test the access to the web server default page using the VIP. Basically, we should associate a floating IP to the VIP shown previously. We can pick up a non assigned floating IP from the neutron `floatingip-list` and associate it to the VIP as the following:

```
# neutron lb-vip-show pool.vip | grep port_id
```

```
| port_id           | d4e94b15-dae6-4ccd-bd0d-ca45a6322295 |
```

```
# neutron floatingip-list
```

```
+--------------------------------------+----------------+---------------------+--------------------------------------+
| id                                   | fixed_ip_address | floating_ip_address | port_id                              |
+--------------------------------------+----------------+---------------------+--------------------------------------+
| 15e329aa-2821-457a-8622-1c85df5e1b59 |                | 192.168.59.248      |                                      |
| c84b4dd7-4d75-4caa-9179-c4c56ea7c404 | 10.0.0.14      | 192.168.59.249      | ee51f346-7844-4a0c-ad55-be625c81b883 |
| d7105201-6d1d-41d0-9998-812b31653fa8 | 10.0.0.15      | 192.168.59.246      | f66771ab-56a1-4afb-be6c-879bc9af1b73 |
+--------------------------------------+----------------+---------------------+--------------------------------------+
```

```
# neutron floatongip-associate 15e329aa-2821-457a-8622-1c85df5e1b59
d4e9b15-dae6-bd0d-ca45a6322295
```

id	fixed_ip_address	floating_ip_address	port_id
15e329aa-2821-457a-8622-1c85df5e1b59	10.0.0.8	192.168.59.246	d4e94b15-dae6-4ccd-bd0d-ca45a6322295

Now we can verify the access to the default web page of apache using the VIP:

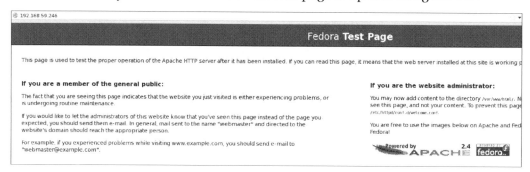

Summary

This chapter covered a few topics on Neutron plugins in OpenStack. Open vSwitch and Linux Bridge have proven to be flexible and a great solution to manage networks for instances in the OpenStack private cloud. You should understand that Open vSwitch has played a big part in this chapter due to its multiple features as compared to the Linux Bridge plugin. You also learned about the difference between them and how you can control traffic ingress and egress in your virtual machines environment by means of flow rules. We were guided through the discovery of a third service, which can be linked to VPNaaS and FWaaS, covered in *Chapter 5, Implementing OpenStack Networking and Security*, which is LBaaS. Today, tenants in OpenStack are able to scale their application and balance traffic to pools. The usage of LBaaS from the dashboard is straightforward. It was a good opportunity to build a first LBaaS setup by means of an advent orchestration service called heat. You may realize the modularity of such an orchestration engine and imagine how you can build a larger stack in no time. Although this chapter introduced LBaaS, which might be great to scale instances for tenants, you still need to monitor them and investigate how to bring in a more transparent solution to watch your OpenStack private cloud performance.

The next chapter will introduce monitoring topics such as Ceilometer, Zabbix, and stack health check monitoring and continue to extend our stack example based on heat with more details.

9
Monitoring OpenStack – Ceilometer and Zabbix

"Tomorrow is often the busiest day of the week."

–Spanish Proverb

OpenStack is intended to run like a charm, from private clouds to large and public clouds. So far, you have learned about the modular architecture of OpenStack and should be aware of how it is growing within several incubating projects, which make it an amazing cloud set: a real cloud. But unfortunately, concentrating on building and extending your infrastructure might jeopardize the stability of your cloud environment. The rule of thumb prioritizes a good strategy on how to keep your cloud under control; in other words, keeping a close eye on every piece of the OpenStack cloud. Running a large and complex infrastructure will need the best effort management that comes in tandem with a well-maintained monitoring strategy. As you will learn in this chapter, a new telemetry module in OpenStack called **Ceilometer** provides a dedicated monitoring solution for your instances, as well as alerting and triggering events capabilities. In this chapter, you will learn the following:

- Ceilometer concepts and integration in OpenStack
- How to install Ceilometer in the cloud controller node

The next part will guide you through an extension of HOT, defined in *Chapter 8, Extending OpenStack – Advanced Networking Features and Deploying Multi-tier Applications*, and learn to:

- Integrate heat within the Ceilometer service from the architectural level
- Extend the heat template to support metering and alarming
- Create a first alarming event in Ceilometer

On the other hand, you will see the varying the ways in which monitoring the OpenStack environment is a sort of necessity when we intend to implement more complicated monitoring features. By the end of this chapter, you will have learned the following:

- Integrating an external monitoring system in your production environment
- Installing Zabbix Server and its agents
- Discovering a flexible way to monitor your OpenStack nodes in no time
- Starting to monitoring your first node using Zabbix server and getting your first alert

Telemetry in OpenStack – Ceilometer

The telemetry module has been fully integrated since the launch of OpenStack's Grizzly release. The project named Ceilometer provides an expandable monitoring and metering platform for OpenStack.

> The Ceilometer naming concept originally comes from **light device technology** to detect and measure the height of the cloud generally used in a plane metering system.

Ceilometer definition

Ceilometer was originally intended (due the Folsom release) to collect usage data and transform it into billable items so that the cloud operator would be able to create the customer's invoice.

The Ceilometer project has been intensively developed and has enlarged its features to cover more measurement purposes for other needs in OpenStack. The primary targets of Ceilometer can be seen as follows:

- Customer billing
- System infrastructure monitoring
- System infrastructure alerting

Ceilometer glossary

It might be crucial to provide a basic understanding of the Ceilometer terminology before we take a closer look at its overall architecture within OpenStack's core integration:

- **Resource**: The Ceilometer resource can be any OpenStack entity that is being metered, such as instance, volume, and so on.

- **Meters**: A meter is a measurement tracked for a resource. It can also be called a *counter*. Meters simply convert a particular resource usage to a human-readable value, such as CPU utilization per instance or overall bandwidth consumption in a particular host. Meters are defined as string values that have a unit of measurement and can be categorized essentially in three types:

  - **Cumulative**: This increases over a period of time

  - **Gauge**: The value is updated only when a change occurs in the current gauge or duration

  - **Delta**: This changes over a period of time when the previous value is updated

- **Samples**: Each meter is associated with a data sample compelling its attributes.

- **Agent**: This is a software service that runs on the OpenStack infrastructure and measures the usage and sends the results to a **collector**.

- **Pipelines**: Ideally, a given metric data gathered by agents is pushed to the **transformer** for it to be manipulated and visualized via pipelines before delivering it to the **publisher** and being emitted to the collector afterwards.

- **Alarms**: These define a trigger that is launched once a certain threshold is attained. It has been newly implemented within Ceilometer, starting from the Havana release, and has well-supported functionality by the OpenStack community.

- **Statistics**: Similar to any other monitoring tool, collecting a set of values in certain laps of time and applying a defined function might construct a statistical overview of a given metric. We find five functions in Ceilometer to perform different kinds of preliminary calculations, and they are as follows:

  - avg: This is the average value in the specified laps of time

  - sum: This is the sum of all the values in the specified laps of time

○ `min`: This is the minimum value registered in the specified laps of time

○ `max`: This is the maximum value registered in the specified laps of time

○ `count`: This gives the number or values registered in the specified laps of time

The Ceilometer architecture

Putting the Ceilometer architecture under the micro scope might clarify how such a telemetry module has been integrated in OpenStack. The following bullets highlight a general overview of the Ceilometer components evaluated within the Grizzly release:

- The **API server (ceilometer-api)**: This is a standard API that provides access to the Ceilometer database via a REST API to access the metering data.

- The **compute agent (ceilometer-agent-compute)**: The main role of a compute agent is to gather statistics mainly from instances running in the compute node and poll them to the message queue.

 Note that every compute node must run an agent.

- The **central agent (ceilometer-agent-central)**: Unlike the compute agent, a central agent specifically polls statistics of resources other than instances.

 Note that a central agent can run in a central management server, such as the cloud controller node.

- The **collector (ceilometer-collector)**: This monitors the message queues and takes care of the notification messages processed in the queue by the agent. Any notification message will be translated to a metering message before pushing it back to the appropriate message queue. Therefore, the new metering message will be written and saved in the data store.

- The **data store**: This is a sample database to store the collected data for telemetry. Databases such as MongoDB and SQLs compatible with SQLAlchemy are supported. Due to write concurrency from different collectors from the API server, MongoDB is mostly used in Ceilometer, which is capable of handling concurrent read/write operations.

For our sanity, let's take a step back and first analyze the agents that manipulate gathered data by using the pipeline mechanism:

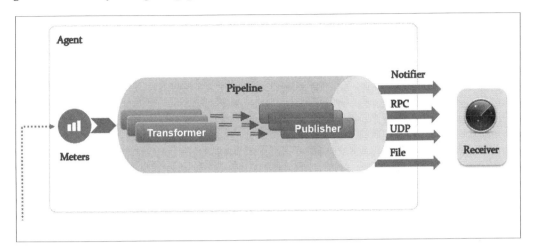

Eventually, agents periodically send requests for sample objects, which reflect a certain meter. Every sample request will be forwarded to the pipeline.

> You may note that the compute agent will poll meters for instances via the hypervisor, whereas the central agent polls statistics of other resources, such as Nova, Cinder, and others.

Once passed to the pipeline, meters can be manipulated by several transformer types:

- **Accumulator**: This accumulates multivalues and sends them in a batch
- **Aggregator**: This aggregates multivalues into a single one
- **Arithmetic**: This includes arithmetic functions to compute the percentage
- **Rate of change**: This identifies trends by deriving another meter from the previous data
- **Unit conversion**: This gives the type of unit conversion to be used

Once manipulated and transformed, a meter might follow its path via one of the multiple publisher types:

- **Notifier**: This is the meter data pushed over reliable AMQP messaging
- **rpc**: This is the synchronous RPC meter data publisher
- **udp**: This is the meter data sent over UDP
- **file**: This is the meter data sent into a file

An overall of the Ceilometer architecture can be seen as the following:

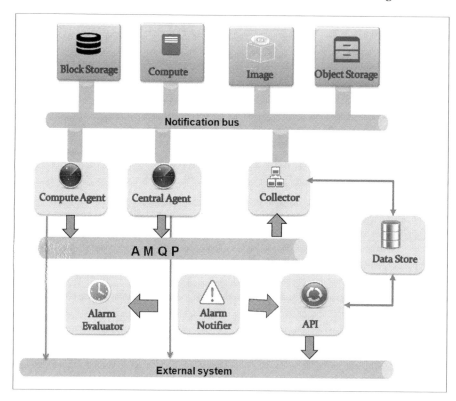

Now, it is time for the bigger picture. As you might have noticed in the previous section, the metric data has been manipulated and is ready to be grabbed by the collector. To do this, notifications will be sent via the **AMQP** system message bus, as well as other external APIs, which the collector forwards to the store to be saved. So, now that we have the monitoring information saved in the database, how can an alarm be triggered and fire a notification event? Eventually, an `alarm-evaluator` service checks the store periodically via the API server by determining whether a certain condition is satisfied for a certain meter; then, it can be declared to the `alarm-notifier` service in the case of a match and then it can start to shout.

The Ceilometer installation

The next steps show how to install Ceilometer in our existing environment. We will begin by configuring our controller node, cc01.packtpub:

1. Install the core components described previously:

   ```
   # yum install openstack-ceilometer-api openstack-ceilometer-
   collector openstack-ceilometer-central python-ceilometerclient
   ```

2. Install MongoDB, which Ceilometer needs for the backend database:

   ```
   # yum --enablerepo=epel -y install mongodb-server mongodb
   ```

3. Start the MongoDB server and make it autostart on machine boot:

   ```
   # service mongod start
   ```
   ```
   # chkonfig mongod on
   ```

4. Ensure that MongoDB binds to the management IP address of our cloud controller in the /etc/mongodb.conf file:

   ```
   bind_ip = 172.16.50.1
   ```

   > By default, MongoDB creates a file of 1 GB to journal in the /var/lib/mongodb/journal directory. Optionally, you can reduce the size of the journaling space allocation, asserting a directive in /etc/mongodb.conf file:smallfiles = true. In order for the changes to take effect, follow your modification by restarting the mongodb service:
   >
   > ```
   > # service mongodb stop
   > # rm /var/lib/mongodb/journal/prealloc.*
   > # service mongodb start
   > ```

5. Create a database for Ceilometer:

   ```
   #   mongo --host 172.16.50.1 --eval '
   db = db.getSiblingDB("ceilometer");
   db.createUser({user: "ceilometer",
   pwd: "ceilometer_password",
   roles: [ "readWrite", "dbAdmin" ]})'
   ```

After getting a successful configuration issued, you should see the output as follows:

```
MongoDB shell version: 2.6.5

connecting to: 172.16.50.1:27017/test

Successfully added user: { "user" : "ceilometer", "roles" : [
"readWrite", "dbAdmin" ] }
```

> For the sake of simplicity, MongoDB has been installed in the controller node within one running database instance. Remember that we have created a Single Point Of Failure within the Ceilometer database, which might need a mongodb cluster among other cloud controller nodes. Deploying Ceilometer with the MongoDB shared cluster is out of the scope of this book.

6. Point the Ceilometer service to use the created database:

```
# openstack-config --set /etc/ceilometer/ceilometer.conf \
    database connection mongodb://ceilometer: ceilometer_password @
cc01:27017/ceilometer
```

7. For a secure connection between the Ceilometer service and its agents running in other nodes in our OpenStack environment, define a secret key that can be generated by using OpenSSL. We will need to install the rest of the agents in compute nodes later:

```
# ADMIN_TOKEN=$(openssl rand -hex 10)
```

8. Store the token generated in the Ceilometer configuration file:

```
# openstack-config --set /etc/ceilometer/ceilometer.conf\
publisher_rpc metering_secret $ADMIN_TOKEN
```

9. Like any other newly added service, we will always tell Keystone to authenticate against it. To do this, we create a new `ceilometer` user, which will have the role of `admin`:

```
# keystone user-create --name=ceilometer --pass=ceil_pass\
--email=ceilometer@example.com

# keystone user-role-add --user=ceilometer --tenant=service\
--role=admin
```

10. Register the Ceilometer service with the Keystone identity service by specifying its correspondent endpoint as follows:

```
# keystone service-create --name=ceilometer --type=metering \
  --description="Ceilometer Telemetry Service"
# keystone endpoint-create \
  --service-id $(keystone service-list | awk '/ metering / {print
$2}') \
  --publicurl http://cc01:8777 \
  --internalurl http://cc01:8777 \
  --adminurl http://cc01:8777 \
```

11. Edit the `/etc/ceilometer/ceilometer.conf` file and change the right directives in each section of the file as follows:

Change the following database connection information for MongoDB:

```
connection= mongodb://ceilometer: ceilometer_password @cc01:27017/
ceilometer
```

Change the following in the RabbitMQ section:

```
rabbit_host=172.16.50.1
rabbit_port=5672
rabbit_password=RABBIT_PASS
rpc_backend=rabbit
Authentication info for Ceilometer:
  [service_credentials]
os_username=ceilometer
os_password=service_password
os_tenant_name=service
os_auth_url=http:// 172.16.50.1:35357/v2.0
Connection info for Keystone
[keystone_authtoken]
auth_host=172.16.50.1
auth_port=35357
auth_protocol=http
auth_uri=http://172.16.50.1:5000/v2.0
admin_user=ceilometer
admin_password=service_password
admin_tenant_name=service
```

Change the shared secret key among the nodes participating in the telemetry service:

```
[publisher]
metering_secret=ceilo_secret
```

12. Finally, restart Ceilometer services, as follows:

```
# service ceilometer-agent-central ceilometer-agent-notification\
ceilometer-api ceilometer-collector ceilometer-alarm-evaluator\
ceilometer-alarm-notifier restart
```

The next stage will basically tell our compute nodes to run a set of agents to communicate via the API service to collect metrics' data and send them back to the database, where it will be stored and visualized. Remember that it is imperative that you install a Ceilometer agent in each compute node.

 StackForge cookbooks' repository provides a stable *Telemetry cookbook* for Chef, which can be found at https://github.com/stackforge/ cookbook-openstack-telemetry. It is advisable that you automate the installation of the Ceilometer agent in the rest of your OpenStack environment if you intend to include glance, network, and object storage to be metered as well. A simple update of the right settings has to be done in the default attribute file of the Telemetry cookbook before executing the Chef client.

To install a Ceilometer agent in each compute node, perform the following steps:

1. Install the Ceilometer agent on the first compute node, cn01.packtpub:

   ```
   # yum install openstack-ceilometer-compute
   ```

2. Edit the /etc/nova/nova.conf file to enable the Ceilometer notification drivers in the default section:

   ```
   notification_driver = nova.openstack.common.notifier.rpc_notifier
   notification_driver = ceilometer.compute.nova_notifier
   instance_usage_audit = True
   instance_usage_audit_period = hour
   notify_on_state_change = vm_and_task_state
   ```

3. Keep updating the following sections in the `/etc/ceilometer/ceilometer.conf` file. Add the same `$ADMIN_TOKEN` shared secret key generated in our cloud controller node:

```
[publisher_rpc]
metering_secret= 47583f5423df27685ced
```

Configure RabbitMQ access:

```
[DEFAULT]
rabbit_host = cc01
rabbit_password = $RABBIT_PASS
```

Add identity service credentials:

```
[keystone_authtoken]
auth_host = cc01
auth_port = 35357
auth_protocol = http
admin_tenant_name = service
admin_user = ceilometer
admin_password = service_password
```

Add service credentials:

```
[service_credentials]
os_auth_url = http://cc01.packtpub:5000/v2.0
os_username = ceilometer
os_tenant_name = service
os_password = service_password
```

For troubleshooting purposes, we will need to configure the log directory by commenting out the `log_dir` directive:

```
[DEFAULT]
log_dir = /var/log/ceilometer
```

4. Restart `ceilometer-agent` and `nova-compute`:

```
# service ceilometer-agent-compute nova-compute restart
```

Let's check our telemetry service installation by logging in through the **Admin** account to the **System Info** section in Horizon. You can see the Ceilometer service enabled and running in the controller node:

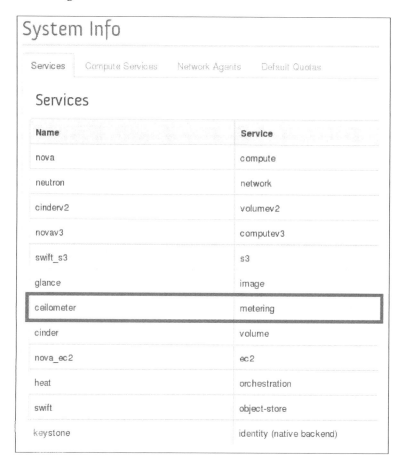

Name	Service
nova	compute
neutron	network
cinderv2	volumev2
novav3	computev3
swift_s3	s3
glance	image
ceilometer	metering
cinder	volume
nova_ec2	ec2
heat	orchestration
swift	object-store
keystone	identity (native backend)

Prior to the OpenStack Grizzly release, Ceilometer is capable of only monitoring virtual machines belonging to tenants. Latter releases incubate an extension of Ceilometer to monitor physical devices.

Ceilometer and heat

Remember that in *Chapter 8, Extending OpenStack – Advanced Networking Features and Deploying Multi-tier Applications*, we had promised to continue with heat. Well, at first glance, it might be difficult to find a face of commonality between the metering infrastructure Ceilometer and the cloud application orchestration heat.

Before extending the latter example, we will shine a bright spotlight on understanding how heat is architected. Essentially, heat has a few major components, as follows:

- `heat-api`: This is a native OpenStack HTTPd RESTful API. It mainly processes API calls by sending them to the heat engine via an advanced message queuing protocol.

- `heat-api-cfn`: This is a `CloudFormation` API service that's compatible with heat. It forwards API requests to the heat engine via an advanced messaging queue protocol.

- `Heat Engine`: This is the main part of the orchestration service where templates are processed and launched.

 Note that the heat engine is able to provide autoscaling and high-availability functionalities implemented in its core.

- `Heat CLI tools`: The heat tool client CLI communicates with `heat-api`.

- `heat-api-cloudwatch`: This is an additional API that is essentially responsible for monitoring stacks and orchestration services when the AWS CloudFormation service is used.

 Note that all these components could be installed on the cloud controller, whereas heat uses a backend database to maintain the state information.

Autoscaling

Since the big move of Ceilometer within the Havana release and it starting to perform alarmingly for OpenStack, billing aside, it has been performed as an event trigger to the heat API to autoscale systems using the alarms. For example, alarms can be created based on instance CPU usage to perform trigger actions based on the threshold match. The actions triggered might vary by spinning up new virtual machines (upscale) or terminating old virtual machines (downscale), as shown in the next figure:

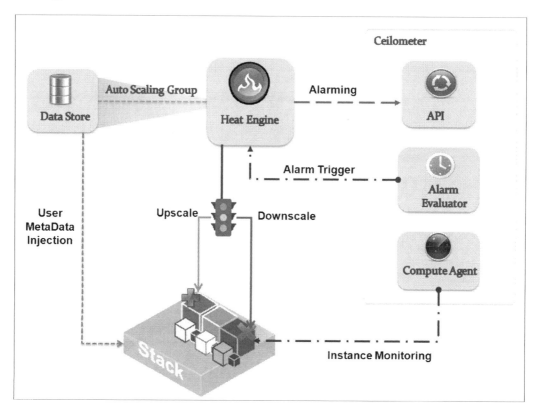

Extending HOT for alarming

Our first template, web_lb.yaml, exemplified in *Chapter 8, Extending OpenStack – Advanced Networking Features and Deploying Multi-tier Applications*, provides a sample web server cluster with a load balancer but does not provide an autoscaling feature, as we did not define any alarm policy. To meet autoscaling requirements, we will need to add two new types of resource:

- `OS::Ceilometer::Alarm`: This triggers an alarm based on the threshold value defined in the metric parameter
- `OS::Heat::ScalingPolicy`: This manages scaling defined in the `OS::Heat::AutoScalingGroup` resource

The new file structure of our stack is as the following:

```
----stackers
        |--------- web_lb.yaml
        |--------- Lib
                    |---------- env.yaml
                    |---------- lb_server.yaml
```

You can notice that we have added a new `lb_server.yaml` file. This is a template definition for a load balancer server. The file is imported from the GitHub repository and serves as the library file for our stack. It can be found at `https://github.com/openstack/heat-templates/blob/master/hot/lb_server.yaml`. The `Lib/env.yaml` file will contain the following resource section:

```
resource_registry:
    lamp_stack::lb_server: lb_server.yaml
```

Note that the *lamp_stack* field defines a customized namespace which will be referred in the core of the new template. Additionally, we will try to install a **LAMP** stack running wordpress. Before adding in our main template the scale policies and alarming for Ceilometer, we will need first to adjust our resources by adding a new server to run the **wordpress** database as the following:

```
parameters:
  database_name:
    type: string
    description: Name of the wordpress DB
    default: wordpress
  database_user:
    type: string
    description: Name of the wordpress user
    default: wordpress
```

Then we need to create new resource for the database. The next snippet will install a new **mariadb** database instance. Keep in mind that you will need to specify the username and the password on heat command line. Optionally, it is possible to mention them in the template:

```
resources:
  database_password:
    type: OS::Heat::RandomString
  database_root_password:
    type: OS::Heat::RandomString
  db:
    type: OS::Nova::Server
    properties:
      flavor: {get_param: flavor}
      image: {get_param: image}
      key_name: {get_param: key}
      networks: [{network: {get_param: network} }]
      user_data_format: RAW
      user_data:
        str_replace:
          template: |
            #!/bin/bash -v
            yum -y install mariadb mariadb-server
            systemctl enable mariadb.service
            systemctl start mariadb.service
            mysqladmin -u root password $db_rootpassword
            cat << EOF | mysql -u root --password=$db_rootpassword
            CREATE DATABASE $db_name;
            GRANT ALL PRIVILEGES ON $db_name.* TO "$db_user"@"%"
            IDENTIFIED BY "$db_password";
            FLUSH PRIVILEGES;
            EXIT
            EOF
          params:
            $db_rootpassword: {get_attr: [database_root_password,
            value]}
            $db_name: {get_param: database_name}
            $db_user: {get_param: database_user}
            $db_password: {get_attr: [database_password, value]}
```

The last important check of the new resource template will require to replace the resources section named `web_cluster` by `lamp_scale` resource specified in the `env.yaml` file as follows:

```
lamp_scale:
    type: OS::Heat::AutoScalingGroup
    properties:
      min_size: 3
      max_size: 3
      resource:
        type: Lib::lamp_scale::lb_server.yaml
        properties:
          flavor: {get_param: flavor}
          image: {get_param: image}
          key_name: {get_param: key}
          network: {get_param: network}
          pool_id: {get_resource: pool}
          metadata: {"metering.stack": {get_param: "OS::stack_id"}}
          user_data:
            str_replace:
              template: |
                #!/bin/bash -v
                yum -y install httpd wordpress
                systemctl enable httpd.service
                systemctl start httpd.service
                setsebool -P httpd_can_network_connect_db=1

                sed -i "/Deny from All/d" /etc/httpd/conf.d/
                wordpress.conf
                sed -i "s/Require local/Require all granted/"
                /etc/httpd/conf.d/wordpress.conf
                sed -i s/database_name_here/$db_name/
                /etc/wordpress/wp-config.php
                sed -i s/username_here/$db_user/
                /etc/wordpress/wp-config.php
                sed -i s/password_here/$db_password/
                /etc/wordpress/wp-config.php
                sed -i s/localhost/$db_host/
                /etc/wordpress/wp-config.php

                systemctl restart httpd.service
              params:
                $db_name: {get_param: database_name}
                $db_user: {get_param: database_user}
                $db_password: {get_attr: [database_password, value]}
                $db_host: {get_attr: [db, first_address]}
```

You may notice the line on bold type `Lib::lamp_scale::lb_server.yaml` which will create a load balancer instance based on the nested template in Lib directory.

Now, it is time to monitor our LAMP stack by updating our **Heat Orchestration Template (HOT)** `web_lb.yaml`. This can be done by adding the following section at the end of the `resources` section:

```
. . .
web_server_scaleup_policy:
    type: OS::Heat::ScalingPolicy
    properties:
      adjustment_type: change_in_capacity
      auto_scaling_group_id: {get_resource: lamp_scale }
      cooldown: 60
      scaling_adjustment: 1

  web_server_scaledown_policy:
    type: OS::Heat::ScalingPolicy
    properties:
      adjustment_type: change_in_capacity
      auto_scaling_group_id: {get_resource: lamp_scale }
      cooldown: 60
      scaling_adjustment: -1
. . .
```

Eventually, we define two scaling policies to spin up and destroy a web server node referred to the `web_server_scaleup_policy` and `web_server_scaledown_policy` policies, respectively. Most importantly, you must realize the `auto_scaling_group_id` property, which has to point to the `AutoScalingGroup` resource instance, `lamp_scale`. Thus, the heat engine might be aware which pool resource is to be scaled from after getting notified by Ceilometer.

Let's arm our Ceilometer alarm by adding the next section to our HOT:

```
....
cpu_alarm_high:
    type: OS::Ceilometer::Alarm
    properties:
      description: Scale-up if the average CPU > 75% for 30 seconds
      meter_name: cpu_util
      statistic: avg
      period: 30
      evaluation_periods: 1
      threshold: 75
```

```
          alarm_actions:
            - {get_attr: [web_server_scaleup_policy, alarm_url]}
          matching_metadata: {'metadata.user_metadata.stack':
            {get_param: "OS::stack_id"}}
          comparison_operator: gt

    cpu_alarm_low:
      type: OS::Ceilometer::Alarm
      properties:
        description: Scale-down if the average CPU < 5% for 5 minutes
        meter_name: cpu_util
        statistic: avg
        period: 300
        evaluation_periods: 1
        threshold: 5
        alarm_actions:
          - {get_attr: [web_server_scaledown_policy, alarm_url]}
        matching_metadata: {'metadata.user_metadata.stack':
          {get_param: "OS::stack_id"}}
        comparison_operator: lt
....
```

The previous sections declare two alarms: cpu_usage_high and cpu_usage_low. Analyzing them brings the following properties derived from the Ceilometer alarm resource under the microscope:

- Description: This is a simple description of the action that should be taken.

- meter_name: This is a predefined metric watched by the alarm in Ceilometer.

- statistic: This is the evaluated statistical value of the metric: average, max, min, count, and sum.

- period: This is the watching period of the evaluated metric in seconds.

- evaluation_periods: This defines how many periods keep watching the metric.

- threshold: This defines the value to trigger the alarm against.

- alarm_actions: This is the action taken after changing the state to alarm. The trigger uses an alarm URL to launch the action Webhooks.

- `matching_metadata`: Every meter corresponds to a predefined resource metadata within the `key=value` form . To run the action, the resource metadata should match, such as verifying the right stack ID.

- `comparaison_operator`: This is the comparison operator to compare the value of the threshold and statistic values in question. Different operators can be used as follows:

  - `ge: > =`

  - `gt: >`

  - `eq: =`

  - `ne: <>`

  - `lt: <`

  - `le: <=`

Finally, we will need to keep an eye on our load balancer health monitors as well. This might be crucial if you intend to ensure the availability of an application running in your stack. Simply put, we will add a new `OS::Neutron::HealthMonitor` resource type named `monitor` to the following code:

```
...
monitor:
    type: OS::Neutron::HealthMonitor
    properties:
      type: TCP
      delay: 5
      max_retries: 5
      timeout: 5
...
```

You can clearly see that we have told heat to deploy health check monitoring using Neutron based on TCP. A timeout of 5 seconds has been defined before changing the connection to the next member in the pool. Five permissible connection failures are defined in `max_retries` before transiting the member status to `INACTIVE`. Finally, a `delay` value of 5 seconds determines the minimum time of the regular connection of a member in the pool.

Let's update our stack by using the following command:

```
# heat stack-update lb_stacker -f web_lb.yaml  -e Lib/env.yaml
```

Note that this time we have mentioned in the command line the environment file to pinpoint to the nested template of `lb_server` using –e argument.

From the **Stack** section in Horizon, an amazing connection diagram is created, which visualizes all the dependency of all the resources defined in the heat template, as shown in the next illustration:

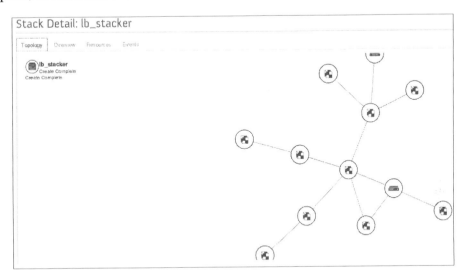

The previous graph shows the state of each resource deployed in the LAMP stack.

On the other hand, we should check the new alarms created by issuing the following command in our cloud controller node:

```
# ceilometer alarm-list
```

This command yields the following output:

```
+----------------------------------------+------------------------------------------+-------------------+---------+------------+---------------------------------+------------------+
| Alarm ID                               | Name                                     | State             | Enabled | Continuous | Alarm condition                 | Time constraints |
+----------------------------------------+------------------------------------------+-------------------+---------+------------+---------------------------------+------------------+
| 847f5259-0bd6-4b31-9af2-0da4c7671c8f   | lb_stacker-cpu_alarm_high-bjpny2a64onj   | insufficient data | True    | False      | cpu_util > 50.0 during 1 x 60s  | None             |
| 8ad30ac0-4712-45b8-84ef-44f263896095   | lb_stacker-cpu_alarm_low-51jn4s6dp7on    | insufficient data | True    | False      | cpu_util < 15.0 during 1 x 600s | None             |
+----------------------------------------+------------------------------------------+-------------------+---------+------------+---------------------------------+------------------+
```

Accidently, Ceilometer reports the alarm state as **insufficient data** in the **State** column from the previous output. Eventually, `/etc/ceilometer/ceilometer.conf` points a default value or the `evaluation_interval` value to 60 seconds. The latter value must be greater or equal to the source interval defined in the `/etc/ceilometer/pipeline.yaml` configuration file in each compute node. It is the responsibility of the alarm evaluator to find recent data that might need an evaluation period superior to the one defined in the pipeline set in the compute node.

Ceilometer offers a number of commands that can be used to create and manage alarms, metric thresholds, events, resources, and statistics.

 A complete description of the telemetry client command line can be found at http://docs.openstack.org/cli-reference/content/ceilometerclient_commands.html.

By keeping the default value of the evaluation_interval in /etc/ceilometer/ceilometer.conf, it might be needed to wait some time to change the alarm state from **insufficient data** state to **OK** or **alarm** state. The new stack is composed of 3 servers including web server and database. To test the autoscaling feature within Ceilometer, we can create a CPU spike of the first web server instance by running the following command line:

```
[fedora@lb-xj3f-5f6nxkmt64pv-ngbjv7v2fpm3-server-5355mfznt571 ~]$ dd if=/
dev/zero of=/dev/null &
```

 dd is a perfect tool to benchmark which can be invoked to test the write speed of disk. Additionally, it is a good alternative to stress the CPU on any GNU/Linux system without the need to install any additional software. From CPU perspective, results might not be very accurate, a very specific tool named 'stress' can be installed in any Linux distributions. A simple example can be stressing 4 cores for 2 minutes described in the following command line:

```
# stress --cpu 4 --timeout 120
```

We can check again the alarm status by issuing the previous command line:

```
# ceilometer alarm-list
```

This command yields the following output:

State	Enabled	Continuous	Alarm condition
alarm	True	False	cpu_util > 50.0 during 1 x 60s
ok	True	False	cpu_util < 15.0 during 1 x 600s

Here we go! It looks like our telemetry service started already to shout and triggers an alarm. You should notice that the **scaleup** policy is fired up by launching a new server in the stack.

Let's grab a statistical overview of our CPU usage defined in our `cpu_util` HOT:

```
# ceilometer statistics -m cpu_util
```

This command yields the following output:

Period	Period Start	Period End	Max	Min	Avg	Sum	Count	Duration	Duration Start	Duration End
0	2015-03-12T14:36:02	2015-03-12T14:36:02	38.22909699	7.15833333333	24.8135914798	4962.71829597	200	493465.0	2015-03-12T14:36:02	2015-03-18T07:40:27

> Note that you should access to the web server instance firstly to run the dd command line. List any available floating ip and associate it to the instance. You can use simply **neutron floatingip-associate** or **nova add-floating-ip** command line.

Arming OpenStack monitoring

There are several ways to keep an eye on and watch what is going on in your OpenStack private cloud. We have already hacked Ceilometer as an official monitoring service well integrated into OpenStack. It might be a very fruitful solution to facilitate customer billing as well. You have noticed already how Ceilometer can even watch customer instances that we have deployed in a sample example via HOT. Although the former telemetry module is expanding its metrics to cover the image, block and object storage, and network service, it might be necessary to bring in your more mature infrastructure monitoring tools for additional alerting. Zabbix is one of the greatest tools that keeps an eye on our OpenStack environment.

Zabbix in action

You have most probably used and installed one or many monitoring tools in your infrastructure. Nagios, Munin, and StatsD are also good candidates to fulfill the monitoring position in our system. Feel free to bring any of the monitoring tools that you might feel more familiar with. In the next section, we will use the Zabbix server.

Placing Zabbix

We will be configuring Zabbix on a separate server that has access to all OpenStack servers. In addition, we will need Internet access to download the required package for the Zabbix server installation.

Our new monitoring server will eventually join:

- Administrative networks
- External networks

 If you intend to get e-mail notifications using Zabbix, you may need to ensure external network access to the Zabbix server in order to contact the SMTP server if you are running an external one.

Installing the Zabbix server

The next steps assume the installation of a Zabbix server in a dedicated server running in the OpenStack environment. We must install it as follows:

1. Configure and enable the CentOS repository to update the operating system and download the Zabbix server package dependency. CentOS version is 6.5, whereas the Zabbix server version is 2.2, which can be installed by using the repository configuration management as follows (http://repo.zabbix. com/zabbix/2.2/rhel/6/x86_64/zabbix-release-2.2-1.el6.noarch. rpm):

   ```
   # rpm -ivh
   ```

2. Install Zabbix packages: Zabbix server, MySQL database, and web frontend:

   ```
   # yum install zabbix-server-mysql zabbix-web-mysql
   ```

3. Create the Zabbix database:

   ```
   # mysql -uroot
   mysql> create database zabbix character set utf8 collate utf8_bin;
   mysql> grant all privileges on zabbix.* to zabbix@localhost
   identified by 'zabbix';
   mysql> exit
   ```

4. Configure database settings in `/etc/zabbix/zabbix_server.conf`:

   ```
   # nano /etc/zabbix/zabbix_server.conf
   DBHost=localhost
   DBName=zabbix
   DBUser=zabbix
   DBPassword=Zabbix
   ```

5. Disable SELinux on your CentOS box:

   ```
   # setenforce 0
   # nano /etc/sysconfig/selinux
   SELINUX=disabled
   ```

6. Start the Zabbix server:

   ```
   # service zabbix-server start
   ```

7. Configure PHP for the Zabbix frontend:

   ```
   # nano /etc/httpd/conf.d/zabbix.conf
   php_value max_execution_time 300
   php_value memory_limit 512M
   php_value post_max_size 16M
   php_value upload_max_filesize 2M
   php_value max_input_time 250
   php_value date.timezone Europe/Amsterdam
   ```

8. Finally, restart the Apache server:

   ```
   # service httpd restart
   ```

If everything went well without any errors, you will be able to access the Zabbix frontend from your favorite browser by following `http://zabbix_host_ip_address/zabbix`. By default, the username and password are `Admin` and `zabbix`, respectively.

Configuring the Zabbix agent on OpenStack nodes

Now that you have a Zabbix installation that is properly completed, you will want to actually start monitoring your OpenStack nodes. We will go straightforward without delving into the details of the Zabbix architecture and data flow, which is out of the scope of this book. However, if you are not familiar with Zabbix's monitoring concepts, you should understand what exactly you need to configure for a proper monitoring process. Zabbix handles metrics such as Ceilometer and they are defined as items. They are highly customized with a multitude of features. To collect and process data items to the Zabbix server, we will need a particular probe to grab these items. Zabbix, in fact, defines several ways to do this, but we will only concentrate on two of them:

- **Passive agent**: The server periodically asks the agent to get the desired measurement and report it back
- **Active agent**: The agent asks the server about the kind of monitoring data it should send them back

Now, you can see the difference between both modes; more flexibility of the monitoring period within the active agents. From a configuration standpoint, we will proceed by installing the Zabbix agent in each OpenStack node, starting with the first cloud controller node, as follows:

1. Depending on your CentOS version, install the Zabbix agent by using the repository configuration management:

   ```
   # rpm -Uvh (http://repo.zabbix.com/zabbix/2.2/rhel/6/x86_64/
   zabbix-release-2.2-1.el6.noarch.rpm)
   # yum install zabbix zabbix-agent
   ```

2. Update the Zabbix agent configuration file to be able to connect to the Zabbix server for the active mode in /etc/zabbix/zabbix_agentd.conf:

   ```
   ...
   Server = 47.147.0.225
   Hostname = cc01.packtpub
   ```

3. Allow port access for the Zabbix agent:

   ```
   # iptables -D INPUT -p tcp -m tcp --dport 10050 -j ACCEPT
   ```

4. Restart the Zabbix agent:

   ```
   # /etc/init.d/zabbix-agent restart
   ```

Watching OpenStack

Now, we have a basic monitoring setup in our OpenStack infrastructure. Therefore, we should proceed by collecting some monitored data. But first, we need to define items. Most probably, we intend to measure several metrics in our production machines. One of the most powerful features in Zabbix is the usage of templates. We are deploying a large environment with thousands of objects, including items, hosts, graphs, and triggers. It might even become impossible to manually check and configure each of them. Furthermore, it would be cumbersome to loop over your OpenStack nodes and add the same items in a repetitive fashion. The template facility in Zabbix can solve this complexity. What we need to do is just define a collection of items and triggers and apply them to all hosts from one template. Let's start with the basic monitoring of our OpenStack Linux boxes. The Zabbix website offers amazing templates, which can be found at `https://www.zabbix.com/wiki/templates/start`. Let's pick up one and see how to start a flexible monitoring experience within Zabbix in OpenStack.

Since we are running Linux boxes within the CentOS operating system, we can eventually make it easier by just grabbing, as a starting example, a Zabbix template for the Linux operating system monitoring from `https://www.zabbix.com/wiki/_media/contrib/linux.xml`.

Going through the template we have just added, you may notice a predefined list of triggers. Without any doubt, Zabbix also takes care of checking the conditions and alarms of your OpenStack infrastructure. Ceilometer is able to do this within instances. The exclusiveness within triggers in Zabbix comes from their high flexibility. You can upload the template using the Zabbix frontend by pointing to the configuration template and create template. Then, you can choose to import it from your own local drive. Once successfully uploaded, you should see it in the template list and you can associate to it a certain number of hosts or a group. To validate your upload, you can check the collection of items, triggers, and graphs in the template section, as illustrated in the next screenshot:

Template OS Linux: Available memory	Triggers (1)	vm.memory.size[available]	60	?	365
Template OS Linux: Checksum of /etc/passwd	Triggers (1)	vfs.file.cksum[/etc/passwd]	3600	?	365
Template OS Linux: Context switches per second		system.cpu.switches	60	?	365
Template OS Linux: CPU softirq time		system.cpu.util[,softirq]	60	?	365
Template OS Linux: CPU steal time		system.cpu.util[,steal]	60	?	365
Template OS Linux: CPU system time		system.cpu.util[,system]	60	?	365
Template OS Linux: CPU user time		system.cpu.util[,user]	60	?	365

Let's define our monitored host, `cc01.packtpub`, in the Zabbix frontend. Navigate to **Configuration | Hosts** and click on the **create host** button. We will need to fill in the following fields, as shown in the next screenshot:

Next, we can create a trigger and stress our CPU to start overheating. For example, a few simple command lines can do the job, as follows:

```
# dd if=/dev/zero of=/dev/null  &
# dd if=/dev/zero of=/dev/null  &
# dd if=/dev/zero of=/dev/null  &
```

Eventually, the Linux OS template defines a trigger that fires up once the host CPU activity reaches 3.5 after a period of 5 minutes. In the following section, we can observe that the trigger starts shouting:

Summary

In this chapter, we barely scratched the surface of what is possible once you begin to configure the telemetry module in your existing OpenStack environment. You should also notice the awesomeness of heat by supporting Ceilometer resources and note that they work in tandem to manage instance scalability in a given stack. You should also keep in mind that Ceilometer is under heavy development and is extended to cover more metrics and monitoring facilities for image, block storage, object storage, and compute and network services. Although we did not cover them at all once, you should learn how metrics are implemented and measured. More advanced monitoring features are now available via Ceilometer resources, which might dictate an integration of an external monitoring tool, such as the Zabbix server. Relying on alarms in Ceilometer and Zabbix triggers, for example, might help you have a better understanding of your OpenStack environment and give you more control over what alerts or alarms you should receive.

An OpenStack service might be down, the cluster node could suddenly be stopped, or the API might be not reachable; you already have alerts generated and you can directly see what happened but still know how it happened and how to get to the root cause of the errors. Answers to these questions can be found in the next chapter, in which you will explore the utility of log files in OpenStack and the wealth of information that we might get from them for a fast and straightforward troubleshooting task.

10
Keeping Track for Logs – Centralizing Logs with Logstash

"Somewhere, something incredible is waiting to be known."

–Carl Sagan

You may have realized the importance of a complete suite of monitoring solutions for your private OpenStack Cloud environment. *Chapter 9, Monitoring OpenStack – Ceilometer and Zabbix*, demonstrated a mixed approach by adopting an inbox telemetry solution named *Ceilometer*, which works in tandem with an external monitoring solution such as *Zabbix* for a more advanced monitoring strategy in order to store detailed information of what is happening in the Cloud. On the other hand, we have mainly focused on the first part of the equation, namely the exposing of alerts and warnings. The second part of the equation involves reacting to the issues. Troubleshooting a complex suite of software such as OpenStack might not be an easy task for system administrators. The issues can be resolved by relying on the logs that help you track down the root cause of errors. Furthermore, if you attempt to upgrade the OpenStack packages, it can result in pressing fire on the new bugs that are not fixed yet. Diving into the logs is a great way of encountering them. While logging is a standard practice for the system administrators to trace system errors, identifying the exact issue quickly and efficiently is highly required to minimize the downtime. Although the existence of many free and commercial logging tools is able to serve the complex IT infrastructure logging strategy, it is vital to learn how to deal with logs of information in OpenStack and bring them into a highly customized logging system solution.

This chapter draws back the curtain on logging in OpenStack and discusses the following topics:

- Where the OpenStack logs reside
- Adjusting the logging options with the OpenStack service
- Centralizing the tones of the OpenStack log files in a logging system named Logstash
- Integrating the Logstash server in the OpenStack private cloud
- Using Logstash to serve logs of the OpenStack services

Tackling logging

Tackling logging is a painful but crucial process. This is what many system administrators and developers claim when they start debugging an error by consulting a huge log file. Depending on the system that you are trying to fix, cutting down on the troubleshooting time is valid if you do not know where the OpenStack logs are stored and how they are organized.

Demystifying logs in OpenStack

Most probably, you have installed a version of OpenStack that was released prior to the Grizzly or Havana releases. You might be tempted to start looking for logs in the default location in the Linux system, `/var/log`. Eventually, their locations may vary depending on how you deployed OpenStack. Since you deployed your first OpenStack infrastructure using Chef, you can check or modify the location of the logs by service in each attribute file that corresponds to its respective OpenStack service. For example, you can have a look at the Chef **openstack-compute** cookbook that was used in *Chapter 2, Deploying OpenStack DevOps and OpenStack Dual Deal*. In the `attributes` directory, the `default.rb` filename describes all the default settings of your nova service installation, including the directory location of the nova log files. For example, the next line from the recipe code dictates the default location of the nova log files that are to be created in `/var/log/nova`:

```
default['openstack']['compute']['log_dir'] = '/var/log/nova'
```

 If you have tried to install OpenStack using DevStack from `https://git.openstack.org/openstack-dev/devstack`, you will need to activate the `logging` option in the `localrc` file once it is installed.

The log's location

Most of the standard services in the Linux/Unix systems write their logs under the `/var/log` directory in the subdirectories. A node that runs any OpenStack service stores its log files under the `/var/log/` directory. The following table depicts, in a nutshell, where the logs reside by default:

Service name	Log location
Compute	`/var/log/nova`
Image	`/var/log/glance`
Identity	`/var/log/keystone`
Dashboard	`/var/log/apache2/` `/var/log/httpd/`
Block storage	`/var/log/cinder/`
Object storage	`/var/log/swift/` `/var/log/syslog/`
Console	`/var/lib/nova/instances/instance-ID/`
Network	`/var/log/neutron/`
Metering	`/var/log/ceilometer/`
Orchestration	`/var/log/heat/`

 Note that Horizon merges its log files depending on the Apache convention names.

If you are using Fedora's distribution, log files will reside under `/var/log/httpd`. An operating system based on the Ubuntu or Debian distribution supports the `apache2` naming. By default, you will find the log files under `/var/log/apache2`. In addition, the compute nodes generally merge the log files for the VM boot up messages that reside in the `console.log` file. Every instance within its ID will generate the same file in a different subdirectory: `/var/lib/nova/instances/instance-ID`.

 Ceph is not a native OpenStack service. Since it operates and is well-integrated in the OpenStack private Cloud setup, you can find all the Ceph log files regardless of how OSD and the monitors have been distributed in the numerous nodes under `/var/log/ceph`.

Adjusting logs in OpenStack

It is possible to adjust the logging level in OpenStack for each running service. If you get an alert or a message from your monitoring system telling you that one of the services has encountered a problem, you can always refer to your logs by using a different logging method. For example, if you would like to troubleshoot a compute service, it is best practice to refer to its configuration file, `/etc/nova/nova.conf`, and increase the debug level by changing its default value from `False` to `True`, as follows:

```
debug=True
```

Once you finish fixing the issue, it will be necessary to disable the debug directive by changing `True` to `False`. Doing so will protect your node from being overloaded with a huge amount of debug messages, which might not be necessary when your nodes are running without any issues.

Two eyes are better than one eye

OpenStack produces tons of log files in a real production environment. It becomes harder for a Cloud operating team to analyze and parse them by extracting data in each file using a few combinations of tail, grep, and perl tools. The more hosts you build, the more logs you have to manage. Moving forward a few paces should be accompanied by a serious trace keeper. To overcome such challenges, the log environment must become centralized. A good way to accomplish this is by starting flowing logs in a dedicated **rsyslog** server. You may put so much data that your log server may start craving for a larger storage capacity. Furthermore, archiving the former data will not be handy when you need to extract information for a particular context. Additionally, correlating the logs' data that has a different format (taking into consideration the RabbitMQ and MySQL logs) with the generated event might even be impossible. So, what we need at this point is a set of quality requirement points for a good OpenStack logging experience. These points are as follows:

- A better way to parse logs
- A more meaningful log searching process
- Indexing the processed log data
- An elegant exposure of logs

Emerging as the spearhead of the free logging open source project called **Logstash**, let's take a moment and see how it is useful to log a task for the OpenStack production environment.

Logstash under the hood

The Logstash server receives any types of logs. The server processes and filters them based on some predefined filters. A source of input is supported by Logstash, such as TCP, UDP, files, Syslog, and so on. What you need to do is just push the logs to the Logstash server. This process is also known as *shipping*. Once collected, Logstash helps you query any stored event and sort logs the way you wish. A basic understanding of the Logstash architecture will be very helpful for a successful OpenStack logging mission. Logstash eventually does not work alone. The following illustration depicts the major components of the logging platform:

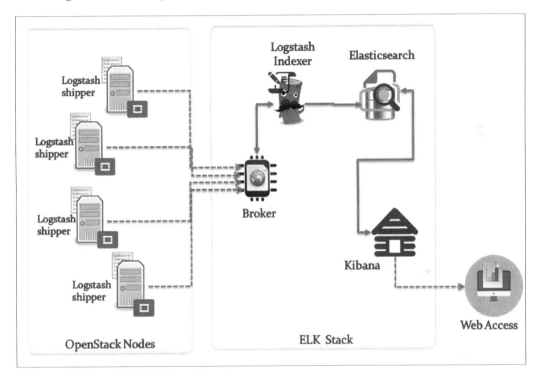

In the preceding figure, the various components involved are as follows:

- **The Logstash shipper**: This transfers the logs and events to Logstash

 A Logstash shipper can be any host that runs a Logstash agent or forwarder, which sends the log files to the Logstash server.

- **The Broker**: This keeps receiving the events' logs from the Logstash shippers

 Generally, Logstash uses Redis to act as a broker to hold the data received by an agent running in the Logstash shipper.

- **The Logstash Indexer**: This indexes the events within the Logstash server
- **Elasticsearch**: This is a powerful search and analytics engine for text data
- **Kibana**: This is a graphical user interface that is used to visualize and search log data

The previous figure depicts a simplistic overview of the Logstash architecture, which is sometimes called the **ELK** stack, as an abbreviation of **Elasticsearch, Logstash, Kibana**; the log event that was started by sending the collected logs by the Logstash agent to the central logging server. At this stage, where the Logstash server is running, the broker (Redis) buffers the formerly collected logs, which will be indexed next by the Logstash indexer. Now, it comes the role of the Elasticsearch engine to store the former log events and provide a full-text index so that the logs become searchable. The final stage of the log event ends up executing the log queries at the Logstash dashboard or Kibana.

 It is possible to run each component independently for scalability reasons.

The Logstash workflow

Getting up to speed for Logstash involves getting to grips with the basic configuration parameterization. Basically, we will come across three main sections in any given Logstash configuration file. These sections are as follows:

- **The input**: This defines how the events are generated and get into Logstash
- **The filters**: This defines the way the events are manipulated and customized
- **The output**: This defines how the events can be sent from Logstash to the external system

The following code serves as an example of a Logstash configuration file:

```
input {
    stdin { }
    ...
}
```

```
filter {
    ...
}
output {
    stdout {
    .....
}
```

The input and output blocks define an event respectively from the STDIN and to the STDOUT standards streams in the I/O of the terminal. In Logstash, the events that enter via the input that was modified in the filter and end up via the output form a pipeline.

Placing the Logstash server

Now, we will configure the Logstash server on a separate server that has access to all the OpenStack servers.

Our new monitoring server will join eventually:

- The administrative network
- The external network

Let's discover the different players that need to be installed in our logging server in order to ensure a successful installation:

- **Redis**: This will be installed as a broker for Logstash. It ameliorates the logging environment by acting as a cache buffer for the log events.
- **Java**: Both Elasticsearch and Logstash require Java. The latest Java version is recommended, while using OpenJDK is also an alternative to the Java installation.
- **Elasticsearch**: This is a powerful indexing and search engine for events that are shipped to the Logstash.
- **Logstash**: This defines the central log server that processes the incoming logs.
- **Kibana**: This is a powerful web interface that is used to query the log events. It is highly customizable with several visualization capabilities.
- **Nginx**: The Kibana web interface will need a reverse proxy that can be accessed externally. For this purpose, we will use nginx.

Installing the Logstash server

The next installation snippet will guide you through the package-based installation of the following Logstash components on a CentOS operation system:

- Logstash 1.4.2
- Elasticsearch 1.4.0
- Kibana 4.0
- Java 8
- Nginx
- Redis

We intend to gather a substantial volume of log files for the OpenStack environment. It is essential to plan for the consumption of resources that is expected in the future as your private Cloud keeps growing gradually. Thus, a minimum set of specs will be required for the Logstash server. The requirements are as follows:

- **Processor**: 64-bit x86
- **Memory**: 8 GB RAM
- **Disk space**: 500 GB
- **Network**: Two 1 Gbps **Network Interface Cards (NICs)**

> Running CentOS with the default configuration might prevent the new services from running due to the SELinux and iptables restrictions. Be sure that SELinux is running at least in the permissive mode or is disabled and update the iptables so that the packets can be forwarded to the Logstash server.

Let's get started with the setting up of the central log management server:

1. Download and install Java 8 from the Oracle website (http://download.oracle.com/otn-pub/java/jdk/8u40-b25/jre-8u40-linux-x64.tar.gz), as follows:

```
# wget --no-cookies --no-check-certificate --header "Cookie:
gpw_e24=http%3A%2F%2Fwww.oracle.com%2F; oraclelicense=accept-
securebackup-cookie"

# tar xvf jre-8*.tar.gz
```

2. Add a symbolic link in the `/usr/bin` directory to the `java` command, as follows:

```
# alternatives --install /usr/bin/java java /jre1.8*/bin/java 1
```

3. Install Elasticsearch, which first requires setting up the repository file, `/etc/yum.repos.d/elasticsearch.repo`, as follows:

```
# nano /etc/yum.repos.d/elasticsearch.repo
[elasticsearch]
name=Elasticsearch
baseurl=http://packages.elasticsearch.org/elasticsearch/1.4/centos
gpgcheck=1
gpgkey=http://packages.elasticsearch.org/GPG-KEY-elasticsearch
enabled=1
```

4. Then, install Elasticsearch by using the `yum` command line, as follows:

```
# yum install elasticsearch -y
```

5. Download and install Kibana version 4 (`https://download.elasticsearch.org/kibana/kibana/kibana-4.0.1-linux-x64.tar.gz`), as follows:

```
# wget https://download.elasticsearch.org/kibana/kibana/kibana-4.0.1-linux-x64.tar.gz
# tar xvf kibana-4.0.1-linux-x64.tar.gz
```

Relocate the kibana-4.0.1 directory under `/usr/share/kibana`.

```
# mv kibana-4.0.1 /usr/share/kibana
```

6. Reconfigure Kibana to pinpoint the location of Elasticsearch. For this, you can use the FQDN of your Logstash server, as follows:

```
# nano /usr/share/kibana/config.js
...
elasticsearch: "http://logstash.packtpub:9200"
...
```

 Add the FQDN to the `/etc/hosts` file, hostname, and its external IP for name service resolution.

7. Next, make sure that your system is up to date. Then, we can install nginx and Redis using the `yum` command line, as follows:

```
# yum clean all
# yum update -y
# yum install nginx redis -y
```

8. Now, we need to configure nginx to run Kibana. First, be sure that the following excerpt in `/etc/nginx/nginx.conf` is commented out:

```
...
include /etc/nginx/conf.d/*.conf;
...
```

9. Create a new nginx server block for Kibana in a new file, as follows:

```
# nano /etc/nginx/conf.d/kibana.conf
server {
  listen                *:80 ;

  server_name           logstash.packtpub;
  access_log            /var/log/nginx/kibana.log;

  location / {
    root   /usr/share/kibana;
    index  index.html  index.htm;
proxy_pass   http://localhost:5601/;
proxy_next_upstream error timeout invalid_header http_500 http_502
http_503 http_504;
proxy_set_header          Host             $host;
proxy_set_header          X-Real-IP        $remote_addr;
        proxy_set_header          X-Forwarded-For $proxy_add_x_
forwarded_for;
  }
}
```

10. Update the `/etc/redis/redis.conf` file to point to the appropriate IP address of the Logstash server so that it can listen on an external interface to receive events, as follows:

```
# nano /etc/redis.conf
...
# bind 127.0.0.1
 bind   47.147.50.240
...
```

11. Let's install Logstash by creating a new yum repository file, as follows:

```
# nano /etc/yum.repos.d/logstash.repo
[logstash]
name=Logstash
baseurl=http://packages.elasticsearch.org/logstash/1.4/centos
gpgcheck=1
gpgkey=http://packages.elasticsearch.org/GPG-KEY-elasticsearch
enabled=1
```

12. Install Logstash using the yum command line, as follows:

```
# yum install logstash -y
```

13. Start the ELK stack services and configure them to run on boot:

```
# service elasticsearch start
# service nginx start
# service redis start
# service logstash start
# cd /usr/share/kibana/bin; . /kibana
```

 Note that at the time of writing this book, Kibana 4 is the newest version of Kibana.

Kibana 4 includes a lot of changes and improvements as compared to the previous version, Kibana 3. As a site plugin, you can easily run Kibana by navigating to its /bin directory and running the kibana shell script, as shown in the last command line. Optionally, you can create a start up init script under /etc/init.d/ for Kibana.

 You can use the following init script at GitHub https://github.com/Xaway/script/blob/master/init_kibana.

Be sure to change the Kibana directory line to point to the right path in your directory tree, as follows:

```
# chkconfig -level 2345 elasticsearch on
# chkconfig -level 2345 redis on
# chkconfig -level 2345 nginx on
# chkconfig -level 2345 logstash on
```

By default, the Kibana web interface uses the `5601` port. We can access the graphical user interface via FQDN or the IP of the Logstash server following the URL `http://logstash.packtpub/:`

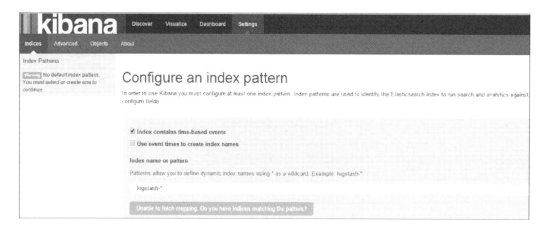

Configuring Logstash

At this point, the ELK stack is up and running. We need to tell the Logstash server how to handle the upcoming events. To do so, we need to create a Logstash configuration file under `/etc/logstash`. Let's call it `openstash.conf`. We will edit and explain the file block by block for better understanding, as follows:

```
# nano /etc/logstash/openstash.conf
```

```
input {
  redis {
    host => "47.147.50.240"
    type => "redis-input"
    data_type => "list"
    key => "logstash"
  }
}
```

```
output {
 elasticsearch { host => "logstash.packtpub" }
}
```

The input block defines the Redis plugin to listen to events on the `47.147.50.240` host interface. The broker will listen for the incoming Logstash events and pass them to the `logstash` list. Therefore, the received events will be labeled with the `redis-input` type. The output block defines another plugin named `elasticsearch`, which sends the events from Logstash to Elasticsearch, which will be saved and transformed for searching. We have specified the `host` option to announce the name of the Elasticsearch node to the Logstash server.

Logstash at your beck and call

The Logstash server is up and running and is now waiting to receive events. We need somebody to send the events. Shipping logs to the central monitoring server can be done in the following different ways:

- You can use the Logstash agent that is installed in each host to generate logs and ship them to the Logstash server.

- You can also use syslog by activating the `syslog` plugin in the Logstash configuration file.

 Rsyslog, syslog-ng, and syslogd are the three typical syslog daemons that are supported in many Linux distributions and which are used to send log messages to the Logstash server.

- The Logstash forwarder (*Lumberjack*), a very lightweight client, can be used to send messages to Logstash. In addition, it includes better security features that are based on SSL encryption, unlike the previous message transports.

We will go for the third option. Every node in the OpenStack environment needs a Logstash forwarder installed and configured to connect to the Logstash server. Let's make it happen and install it on the OpenStack Cloud controller node with the `47.147.50.1` IP address. The generated log traffic will be secure. Thus, the first step in configuring the forwarder is to generate a self-signed certificate and a key pair, as follows:

1. Add the Logstash server's IP address to the SAN (`subjectAltName`) directive of the SSL certificate, as follows:

```
# nano /etc/pki/tls/openssl.cnf

...

[ v3_ca ]

subjectAltName = IP : 47.147.50.240

...
```

2. Generate the SSL certificate and private key. Feel free to create a new directory to store your files, as follows:

```
# mkdir certs
# openssl req -config /etc/pki/tls/openssl.cnf -x509 -days 3650
-batch -nodes -newkey rsa:2048 -keyout certs/server.key -out
certs/server.crt
```

3. Now, let's update the Logstash configuration file by adding a new section in the input block to specify the Logstash forwarder plugin named Lumberjack, as follows:

```
input {
...
lumberjack {
  port => 6782
  ssl_certificate => "/certs/server.crt"
  ssl_key => "/certs/server.key"
  type => "lumberjack"
    }
```

The Lumberjack input defines the listening port on the 6782 TCP port, which will use the SSL certificate and the private key that we created previously.

4. Restart the Logstash service in the following way so that the new changes will take effect:

```
# service logstash restart
```

5. Let's move to our first OpenStack node to install the Logstash forwarder. We will start with our first Cloud controller. We will begin by creating a new yum repository for the Logstash forwarder, as follows:

```
# nano /etc/yum.repos.d/Logstash-forwarder.repo

[logstash-forwarder]
name=logstash-forwarder repository
baseurl=http://packages.elasticsearch.org/logstashforwarder/centos
gpgcheck=1
gpgkey=http://packages.elasticsearch.org/GPG-KEY-elasticsearch
enabled=1
```

6. Install the Logstash forwarder package by using the yum command line:

```
# yum install logstash-forwarder -y
```

7. To authenticate against the Logstash server, we need to copy the SSL certificate to the new Logstash client. You can use the `scp` command to copy the certificate. We will create a `certs` directory in the Cloud controller node to copy over the file, as follows:

```
# mkdir certs
# scp packtpub@47.147.50.1:/home/packtpub/certs/server.crt  certs/
```

8. The Logstash forwarder is configured with a JSON-based configuration file. Let's create a new `logstash-forwarder.conf` file in the following way so that we can start shipping logs to the server:

```
# nano /etc/logstash-forwarder.conf
{
    "network": {
    "servers": [ "47.147.50.240:6782" ],
    "ssl ca": "/certs/logstash-forwarder.crt",
    "timeout": 15
    }
}
```

The `network` section defines the Logstash server IP and uses the SSL certificate that we copied earlier.

9. The previous step constructs the minimum configuration requirements to connect to the Logstash server. We should tell our forwarder which files we need to ship to our server. Let's start by shipping a nova-api log file under `/var/log/nova/api.log`. We will add more log files later. To do so, we need to create a new `files` section in the `logstash-forwarder.conf` file to specify the path of the log files, as follows:

```
{
    "network": {
    "servers": ["47.147.50.240:6782"],
    "ssl ca": "/etc/logstash/logstash-forwarder.crt",
    "timeout": 15
     },
    "files": [
    {
        "paths": [ "/var/log/nova/api.log"],
        "fields": { "type": "openstack", "component":"nova" }
    }
    ]
}
```

A very interesting point in the last configuration snippet is the additional component option in the `fields` line. Each log file is a JSON object that contains some standard fields, such as the timestamp and filename. The additional field will help us tag each message. We can easily browse logs and show only the interesting messages from the Kibana interface within a specific tag. For example, we can classify the logs that come from the OpenStack nodes into two different types: system and OpenStack logs. The second type can also be refined to support the other subtypes that are tagged by the component option, such as nova, glance, keystone, cinder, ceph, and so on.

10. Test the connection to the server. We can use the `-config` option to test the configuration file in the debug level. It is very useful for troubleshooting further. Let's see how this works. On the Cloud controller node, run the following command after restarting the `logstash-forwarder` service, and do not forget to adjust the settings according to your needs:

```
# service Logstash-forwarder restart
# /opt/logstash-forwarder/bin/logstash-forwarder -config /etc/
logstash-forwarder.conf
...
2015/04/11 16:54:22.991945        --- options -------
2015/04/11 16:54:22.992827        config-arg:        /etc/
logstash-forwarder.conf
2015/04/11 16:54:22.992874        idle-timeout:      5s
2015/04/11 16:54:22.992893        spool-size:        1024
...
        2015/04/11 16:54:22.995550 Waiting for 2 prospectors to
initialise
2015/04/11 16:54:22.995985 Launching harvester on new file: /var/
log/nova/api.log
2015/04/11 16:54:23.186545 All prospectors initialised with 0
states to persist
2015/04/11 16:54:23.193737 harvest: "/var/log/nova/api.log"
(offset snapshot:0)
2015/04/11 16:54:24.260040 Setting trusted CA from file: /certs/
server.crt
        2015/04/11 16:54:24.277672 Connecting to
[47.147.50.240]:6782 (47.147.50.240)
2015/04/11 16:54:25.207739 Failure connecting to 47.147.50.240:
dial tcp 47.147.50.240:6782: connection refused
```

```
2015/04/11 16:54:25.208219 Connecting to [47.147.50.240]:6782
(47.147.50.240)
2015/04/11 16:54:26.208403 Failure connecting to 47.147.50.240:
dial tcp 47.147.50.240:6782: connection refused
2015/04/11 16:54:26.208865 Connecting to [47.147.50.240]:6782
(47.147.50.240)
2015/04/11 16:54:27.827370 Connected to 47.147.50.240
```

Note that it might take a while to connect to the server. The initial connection attempts might be refused. Once the Logstash server becomes aware of the client, the new connection will be established. On the other hand, if the Logstash server is not initialized, the connection refused loop will continue until you start the server.

Filtering the OpenStack logs

We will not be able to parse or browse any log files in the graphical user interface. We have only prepared and established a connection between the client and the server. We will need to update the Logstash configuration file on the Logstash server to define a way of manipulating the files that are shipped by the forwarder. The format of the file logs is not standard. Sending logs as one blob of data will not be useful. Therefore, we want a way to identify their type and drill down into the events to extract their values. The heart of the Logstash contribution in the log files' management is **filtering**.

In our case, we have different log files that were generated either by the Linux system or other services, most importantly the OpenStack ones.

 Note that the syslog messages are useful as well since they track down the internal system messages of the base operating system that runs the OpenStack node.

However, the most interesting aspect is how we can classify our logs by type in the first place. The following code snippet depicts a new `filter` section in the central Logstash configuration file:

```
input {
. . .
    }
filter{
  if [type] == "openstack" {
    grok {
      patterns_dir => "/opt/logstash/patterns/"
```

```
        match=>[ "message","%{TIMESTAMP_ISO8601:timestamp}
%{NUMBER:response} %{AUDITLOGLEVEL:level} %{NOTSPACE:module} \
[%{GREEDYDATA:program}\] %{GREEDYDATA:content}"]
      }
multiline {
      negate => false
      pattern => "^%{TIMESTAMP_ISO8601}%{SPACE}%{NUMBER}?%{SPACE}?TRA
CE"
      what => "previous"
      stream_identity => "%{host}.%{filename}"
   }
   date {
      type   =>   "openstack"
      match => [ "timestamp", "yyyy-MM-dd HH:mm:ss.SSS" ]
   }
  }
}

output {
 ...
}
```

Let's take a closer look at the new filter plugin section, grok. The grok filter parses text and with the help of its patterns, processes and structures it in an elegant way.

> We will not go much deeper into this context, but it might be very useful to check the official Logstash website, http://logstash. net/docs/1.1.8/filters/grok, for extra filtering functionalities and more than 120 patterns that can be used.

The grok section defines the following options:

- patterns_dir: By default, Logstash comes with a few patterns, which can be found under /opt/logstash/patterns. Keep in mind that patterns are packaged regular expressions that are needed by the filter to parse the text and forward any match within the regular expression.

- match: The match option is the *workhorse* of filtering events. It defines any matching of the grok expression within the log file format.

Of course, if you intend to run the Logstash service with the new filter plugin, it will throw an error that shows that the matched pattern is not supported. To be more precise, the AUDITLOGLEVEL tag is not defined and Logstash will need to know how its pattern should be. Thus, we will need to create a new AUDITLOGLEVEL file under /opt/logstash/patterns/ and add the following regular expression package content:

```
AUDITLOGLEVEL([C|c]ritical|CRITICAL[A|a]udit|AUDIT|[D|d]
ebug|DEBUG|[N|n]otice|NOTICE|[I|i]nfo|INFO|[W|w]
arn?(?:ing)?|WARN?(?:ING)?|[E|e]rr?(?:or)?|ERR?(?:OR)?|[C|c]rit?(?:ica
l)?|CRIT?(?:ICAL)?|[F|f]atal|FATAL|[S|s]evere|SEVERE)
```

> Moreover, if you intend to create more patterns and test them, you can use http://grokdebug.herokuapp.com/.

The online grok syntax checker is very useful if you wish to verify the correctness of the customized patterns. You can validate the default patterns within the conjunction of the custom ones and test by pasting an event line from the log file that is being considered. The custom OpenStack grok filter pattern was tested first via the grok debug application and added later to the Logstash configuration file.

The next multiline block is very useful when we intend to combine disparate events into a single event. Let's grab the following events from the ceilometer api log file:

```
2015-04-07 20:51:42.833 2691 CRITICAL ceilometer [-]
ConnectionFailure: could not connect to 47.147.50.1:27017: [Errno 101]
ENETUNREACH
2015-04-07 20:51:42.833 2691 TRACE ceilometer Traceback (most recent
call last):
2015-04-07 20:51:42.833 2691 TRACE ceilometer   File "/usr/bin/
ceilometer-api", line 10, in <module>
2015-04-07 20:51:42.833 2691 TRACE ceilometer     sys.exit(api())
2015-04-07 20:51:42.833 2691 TRACE ceilometer   File "/usr/lib/
python2.6/site-packages/ceilometer/cli.py", line 96, in api
```

The previous output shows a number of Python exception stack traces. Ceilometer was not able to find the IP address of the Cloud controller to connect to and so it threw an exception from its native Python code. Now imagine a situation where we keep the default `grok` filter. Logstash will parse each line as a separate event. We won't be able to identify which line belongs to which exception. Moreover, such information about the exceptions treated in each line might hide the root cause of its generator. For example, we will need to point firstly at the first line `CRITICAL ceilometer [-] ConnectionFailure: could not connect`. Then, the exception in the first line that matches the same date will appear in our dashboard. In this way, you will be able to trace the event and its exception separately.

We can resume the multiline options in the following:

- `negate`: The value of this is false by default. Any message matching the pattern will not be considered a match by the multiline filter and vice versa when it is set to true.

- `pattern`: Any regular expression indicating that the fields of a certain event constitute multiple lines of logs.

- `what`: If the line matches the regular expressions defined in the pattern, the Logstash will merge the current event either with the previous or the next line. In the case of our Python stack traces, we want to merge the event with the one prior to it.

- `stream_identity`: Imagine a scenario where the Logstash forwarder has been restarted and needs to reconnect. In this case, Logstash will create a new TCP connection for the same stream. In this case, we will need to identify which stream belongs to which event by the `%{host}` host. Also, we are asking Logstash to differentiate the events coming from multiple files in the same file input, `%{filename}`.

The last filter, `date`, is the simplest plugin. Its main task is to parse dates and use them as a Logstash timestamp. We would like to use the `yyyy-MM-dd HH:mm:ss.SSS` date format to parse the timestamps of the OpenStack log files. An example of this date format is `2015-04-07 20:51:42.833`.

We can see the date filter with a type of `openstack` that was specified to ensure that it only matches the OpenStack events.

The Logstash configuration file is continued in the next figure. You may note that the filters are independent and the log file is being manipulated sequentially, starting with the first `grok` filter when the filter matches the `openstack` type. Therefore, it is manipulated by the multiline filter, and it ends up with the final filtering process by stamping the date of Logstash using the date filter.

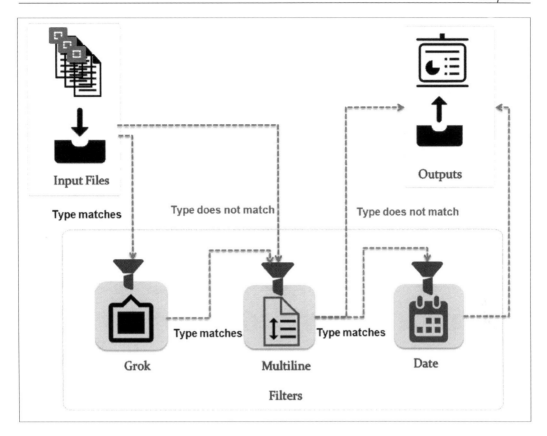

The main Logstash configuration file is ready. A final step requires us to tell every node in our OpenStack environment to start shipping its logs to the Logstash server. We will show a simple example in which the log files are shipped from the Cloud controller for the compute, image, block storage, and telemetry services. The new `files` section of the Logstash forwarder will look like the following code:

```
...
"files": [
{
        "paths": [ "/var/log/nova/*.log"],
        "fields": { "type": "openstack", "component":"nova" }
},
{
        "paths": [ "/var/log/glance/*.log"],
        "fields": { "type": "openstack", "component":"glance" }
},
{
```

```
            "paths": [ "/var/log/cinder/*.log"],
            "fields": { "type": "openstack", "component":"cinder" }
    },
    {

            "paths": [ "/var/log/ceilometer/*.log"],
            "fields": { "type": "openstack", "component":"ceilometer" }
    }
]
```

Visualizing the OpenStack logs

Once the Logstash forwarder and the central server are configured and restarted, we can start browsing the Kibana interface. Make sure that the Logstash forwarder has successfully run and started processing events to the central logging server, as follows:

```
2015/04/12 00:43:30.445923 Registrar: processing 638 events
```

Amazing! Now it is time for Kibana. The first web page will ask you to define an index pattern so that you will be able to run searches against it. We can use the default Logstash value, logstash-*, in the index field. Then, select the default time field, @timestamp, from the drop-down menu, as shown in the following screenshot:

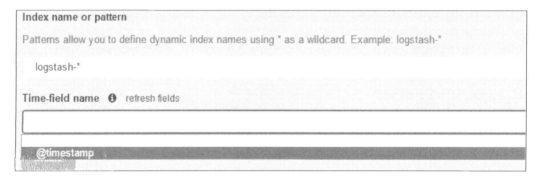

Now, we have defined an index that we can rely on when searching for data in our logs. Let's jump to the **Discover** link in the upper toolbar of the Kibana interface. Generally, no data is displayed. It might take a while. By default, the log data will be refreshed after every 15 minutes. On the other hand, you can specify a certain interval to process data, as follows:

Once you see the data flooding into the **Log View** section and counted by the date histogram, start browsing the OpenStack logs using the **Search Bar** under the main navigation menu. For example, we can type a search keyword, such as `cinder`. The search query will give results that show only the events within the `cinder` string from all the collected files. Most importantly, we can see how useful the `multiline` filter is by going through a `cinder` exception trace, as shown in the following screenshot:

```
t message    Q Q  2015-04-12 20:51:42.833 2691 CRITICAL ceilometer [-] ConnectionFailure: could not connect to 192.168.120.250:27017: [Errno 101] ENETU
                  NREACH
                  2015-04-12 20:51:42.833 2691 TRACE ceilometer Traceback (most recent call last):
                  2015-03-27 20:11:57.889 8919 TRACE ceilometer   File "/usr/lib/python2.6/site-packages/ceilometer/api/app.py", line 126, in build_ser
                  ver
                  2015-04-12 20:51:42.833 2691 TRACE ceilometer   File "/usr/bin/ceilometer-api", line 10, in <module>
                  2015-04-12 20:51:42.833 2691 TRACE ceilometer     sys.exit(api())
                  2015-03-27 20:11:57.889 8919 TRACE ceilometer     root = VersionSelectorApplication()
                  2015-04-12 20:51:42.833 2691 TRACE ceilometer   File "/usr/lib/python2.6/site-packages/ceilometer/cli.py", line 96, in api
                  2015-03-27 20:11:57.889 8919 TRACE ceilometer   File "/usr/lib/python2.6/site-packages/ceilometer/api/app.py", line 102, in __init__
                  2015-04-12 20:51:42.833 2691 TRACE ceilometer     srv = app.build_server()
                  2015-04-12 20:51:42.833 2691 TRACE ceilometer   File "/usr/lib/python2.6/site-packages/ceilometer/api/app.py", line 126, in build_ser
```

We find visualizing data more interesting then parsing through individual lines. For example, vertical bars or pie charts provide a better analysis of the overall picture of the behavior of certain services in a certain amount of time. For example, we can visualize different IP addresses by using certain services in a given period of time or compare the logging status between the OpenStack services, which reflects how they are being consumed or used. The next example will look at a simple statistical overview of events that were generated in a period of half a day between the compute, image, telemetry, and block storage services.

Using the search bar, we will start browsing the event that matches the query, as follows:

```
type: "openstack" AND component: "glance"
```

The preceding command gives the following result:

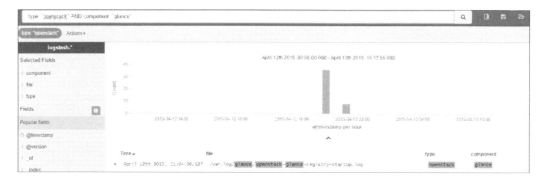

Next, save the query result from the right side of the search bar where the **Save** button is. We can name it Glance_OS-04132015.

To create the visualization, click on the **Visualize** menu item and select the **pie charts** type. The search source is Glance_OS-04132015, which was created previously by us. First, select the **Split Slices** bucket. Click on the **Aggregation** drop-down list and select **Significant Terms**. Then, click on the **Field** drop-down list and select **component.raw**. Finally, click on the **Size** field and press *Enter*. Now, click on the **Apply** button, and you should see something that looks like the following screenshot:

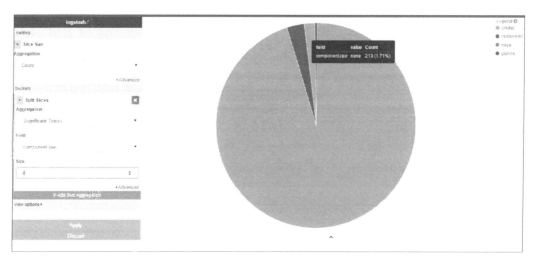

Summary

In this chapter, we covered the process of logging information in OpenStack. You should give importance to how the log files are treated. The troubleshooting tasks rely primarily on the logs' content. A major part of this chapter talks about how one can centralize the OpenStack log files using a Logstash server. Also, it shows a few examples of how one can filter specific log information and present it in an elegant way using Kibana. This forces you to be precise and requires you to take a lot of care during the troubleshooting task. Regarding the increasing load on your OpenStack private Cloud, logs can be huge, and searching for the right information will not be easy. You should appreciate how Logstash makes life easier for the OpenStack logs, with its overwhelming features and filtering capabilities.

Based on the logging and monitoring results, you can conclude that some pieces of the OpenStack environment may face performance degradation and may need to be tuned. Thus, some advanced settings should be adjusted to keep your private Cloud responsive to a heavy workload. This aspect will be covered in the next chapter.

11
Tuning OpenStack Performance – Advanced Configuration

"Millions saw the apple fall, Newton was the only one who asked why?"

–Bernard M. Baruch

Understanding OpenStack to know how it works is great, but that's not enough. The previous chapters guided you through several topics about deploying your first OpenStack infrastructure. Now you may intend to expose your environment and let users start creating and managing virtual resources in your private OpenStack cloud, and you are most probably self-confident that you have a monitoring process that keeps watching what is happening in the cloud and works in tandem with a logging system, helping you troubleshoot if an error occurs. It sounds amazing! But when it actually comes to troubleshooting issues related to performance degradation, you will most probably ask your team: *why didn't we expect that?* It was so fast that the server was suddenly overloaded and could not handle any new requests to launch virtual machines. This can be one out of dozens of questions that you may ask when you face surprises. From the user's perspective, a cloud environment should always respond to their requests. Whatever they demand from your resources, the cloud has to say, "Here it is!" Basically, to become more efficient as the user population grows, it might be crucial to know your limits in advance; then you can go beyond and improve. A practical way is to measure your OpenStack cloud by simply generating workloads and watching what happens.

On the other hand, you will sooner or later have to proof your **service-level agreement (SLA)**. This can be done in different ways. We will choose the easiest one: benchmarking our OpenStack environment. Our private cloud is a vast ecosystem, where each component of our OpenStack system has the potential to become a bottleneck if it is not chosen carefully. The database and the message queuing system are ones of the most critical components in OpenStack. In the following, final pages of this book, you will learn these topics:

- How to improve the database's performance in OpenStack
- What memcached is and how it helps to empower the database in OpenStack
- How to detect possible bottlenecks in the queuing message in OpenStack
- How to benchmark OpenStack at scale
- What Rally is and how it can help boost your OpenStack infrastructure's performance
- How to formulate assumptions based on test benchmarking and resolve performance issues

Pushing the limits of the database

One of the most critical parts of OpenStack is the database. Usually, MySQL is used when there is no special configuration to prepare specifically for OpenStack to run smoothly and satisfy its multiple services. On the other hand, it becomes pretty tough to maintain your MySQL databases when your cloud keeps growing. Database inconsistency constitutes one of the biggest challenges when running OpenStack in production. For example, it could happen that you have disassociated a network from an instance but the status in the database has not been changed. Nova claims that the network is associated within the instance, while Neutron claims the opposite. In this case, you will have to edit the database manually and change the state in the database. In rare cases, manual intervention can be error-prone. Generally, it is much more difficult to keep consistency when other changes are being performed in a given database table. All of this points to another database challenge—concurrency. For example, Nova keeps relying on a wrong status of a terminated instance that expects to deassociate the floating IP. At the same time, a new instance is being created, but it is not able to associate a floating IP (it is an extreme case when only one floating IP remains). Again, manual intervention can resolve the issue.

However, you will need to enter many MySQL queries, and this might lead to another inconsistent state where you accidently remove a table entry, using a wrong instance ID for example. We will consider that manual correction of an OpenStack database can be left as a last resort. On the other hand, we first keep track of how to avoid such cases but taking care of our OpenStack databases. Of course, as your infrastructure grows, the risk of inconsistency in your data might increase. With a large number of tables for every OpenStack service, it might be a good idea to plan in advance for preventive actions that can save your production day.

Eventually, you should guarantee completion of the query in a shorter period of time from the database level. In other words, reduce the response time of database statements for a given workload. Several factors come into play if you aim to improve your OpenStack database's performance. Typically, there are these ways:

- Learn the OpenStack core software and start measuring performance when you get expertise in the internal system calls and database queries
- Keep improving the hardware capabilities and the configuration that is running in the databases

In our case, the second approach might be more convenient for the first OpenStack production cycle. For example, your database administrator can decide how the hardware should be configured to avoid any unexpected bottleneck in your environment. We have seen in *Chapter 6, OpenStack HA and Failover*, a few examples focusing on the use case of database architecture to reach a certain level of high availability and scalability. These concepts are vast and need deeper hacks and expertise to adjust to your needs. Eventually, from the alerts sent by your monitoring system, you can decide what kind of improvement should be done at the hardware level. For example, watching the CPU of your master database increasing slightly everyday during 2 weeks could be graded to a critical issue after a longer period. There are high chances that the CPU will be saturated when a huge amount of MySQL data in a short period of time fits in the memory and needs to be processed. I/O saturation is also considered a primary cause of bottlenecks affecting the performance of your MySQL database. This happens when your OpenStack environment generates much more data than you can fit in the memory.

Deciding the resources outfit

Investing in the input/output subsystem's performance might be the best option when you consider that you still have to add memory to fit your data. The nature of physical disks has a great influence on their capability to perform a certain number of operations. For example, it might be a good option to use in **Solid State Devices (SSDs)** for database nodes. Depending on the type of database query, starting to play on the input/output wait factor can be very beneficial by improving the access time and transfer data speed. As we have stated previously, SSDs have evolved recently to forth many improvements to storage design. They are known as Flash storage devices and perform pretty well by:

- Improving read and write operations
- Handling high operations rate concurrency well

Once the data is fitted into the memory, you should ensure that your memory-disk ratio is proper. On the other hand, such a goal cannot be achieved if you do not take into consideration the following challenge: avoid disk input/output. Increasing memory per MySQL node does not necessarily mean that you are improving the performance of your OpenStack databases. It still needs to find a good match to balance the memory and your disk's characteristics, such as size and speed.

Caching for OpenStack

Planning for the best outfit of hardware configuration to boost your OpenStack database's performance is strongly recommended. Even if you are not able to afford the right hardware specifications to handle the workload, you still have more options. You can shine brightly on an inexpensive solution that might come in the second place to tackle your MySQL database workload — **caching**. This technique might be very powerful to handle high-load applications.

Caching might happen at every step along the way, from the servers to the browsers of end users. In our case, Horizon, as an application level from the end user's perspective, can benefit from caching by minimizing any unresponsive status when passing queries all the way to the database. Moreover, caching might be very suitable to move a long queue of database queries entirely outside of the database server. In such cases, you are better off looking at an external caching solution, such as **memcached**.

It can be used by OpenStack components to cache data. Then your database will appreciate it!

In a nutshell, memcached is a high-performance and distributed memory object caching system. By exposing a memory server, your OpenStack database servers can benefit from a caching layer for Horizon to store OpenStack services data. One important thing to be taken into consideration is that memcached does not store data. Once a memcached instance restarts, the data will be lost.

 memcached uses the least recently used cache. The oldest data will be replaced with new data when its memory capacity limit is reached.

You can run memcached in any type of configuration, unless you prefer to choose a dedicated server to run it. It can also run in a memcached cluster architecture, or even in multiple instances in the same server. A typical memcached setup requires only the usage hardware with less CPU specifications in contrast to database requirements. What you need is a set of instances providing memory. The next illustration depicts how memcached is used in a proposed OpenStack setup:

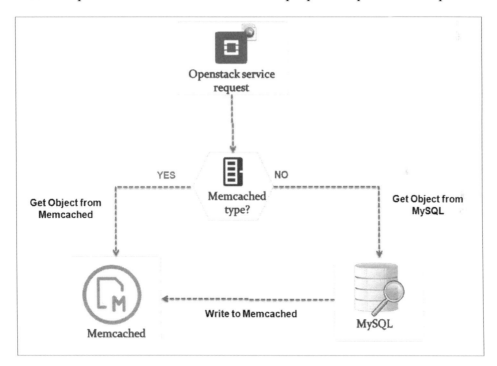

This workflow diagram exposes a write-through caching mechanism by getting data that is stored in memcached while it performs a read to the MySQL database.

Memcached in OpenStack

We will discuss in this section an example of a performance problem that might appear frequently, especially in an expanded OpenStack production environment. Basically, every service in OpenStack asks for a token while trying to execute a command or to perform a specific task. A basic scenario could be the creation of a new instance. Several API requests are generated from different services:

- Horizon to Nova
- Nova to Glance to retrieve an image
- Nova to Cinder to attach a volume
- Nova to Neutron to assign network ports, bring up firewall rules, and so on

Such processes include internal token checks' validity by Keystone. The former Keystone process will have to check its records lying in the database at every request. Now imagine thousands of API requests being performed and forwarded by token checks at every call. This can affect your OpenStack's performance, since Keystone spends lots of CPU cycles to fetch tokens from large database tables. Furthermore, it can reach a point at which Keystone hangs and is not able to handle new incoming authorization requests. The end result is a long delay in lookup through the database table caused by expired tokens. So, this is what we can conclude from this scenario:

- Keystone keeps eating CPU
- Keystone's data layer becomes inconsistent

At the first glance, you may think of introducing a CPU upgrade. This can be useful unless you want to spend more time and money. On the other hand, do you think expired tokens are still useful? Continuously expanding tables might generate unwanted database behavior at some workload, since it keeps running inefficient queries. Let's see how memcached can be part of a complementary solution to this problem. We make it simple: we tell Keystone to stop saving our tokens in the database and find our memcached layer. Keystone will save all its token records in a memcached server. This is also beneficial for speeding up authentication. The next section will show you how to install a memcached instance and integrate it with your OpenStack environment.

Integrating memcached

As mentioned previously, it is up to you to decide whether to offer dedicated servers for memcached instances or not. The following example assumes a simple installation of memcached on cloud controller nodes running the Keystone service. So, do not forget to adjust your settings when installing memcached, including the IP addresses of cloud controllers:

1. Install memcached on your first cloud controller, as follows:

   ```
   # yum install -y memcached python-memcache
   ```

    If you have installed OpenStack using other automated tools, check whether memcached was installed and configured in /etc/keystone/keystone.conf. If the driver directive in the token section looks like keystone.token.backends.memcache. Token, you can skip the next two steps.

2. Ensure that memcached starts automatically on system boot time:

   ```
   # chkconfig memcached on
   ```

    If you intend to set up a new memcached node, be sure that the time zone of the operating system is set properly by changing the ZONE parameter in your /etc/sysconfig/clock file. This is very important to verify because memcached determines the expiration date for Keystone according to **Coordinated Universal Time (UTC)**.

3. You can check the current statistics of your memcached instance like this:

   ```
   #  memcached-tool 127.0.0.1:11211 stats
   ```

4. Optionally, you can adjust the cache size by editing the /etc/sysconfig/memcached file as follows:

   ```
   # nano /etc/sysconfig/memcached
   CACHESIZE=2048
   ```

5. Restart your memcached service:

   ```
   # service memcached restart
   ```

6. Adjust the Keystone configuration file to use the memcached driver as shown here:

```
# nano /etc/keystone/keystone.conf
[token]
driver = keystone.token.backends.memcache.Token
...
[cache]
enabled = True
config_prefix = cache.keystone
expiration_time = 300
backend = dogpile.cache.memcached
backend_argument = url:localhost:11211
use_key_mangler = True
debug_cache_backend = False
```

7. Restart the Keystone service:

```
# service keystone restart
```

8. Keystone should start connecting to the memcached instance that is running in our snippet example in the same machine. We can check the connection establishment within the `11211` default port used by memcached:

```
# lsof -i :11211
```

This command gives the following result:

```
COMMAND      PID      USER    FD   TYPE   DEVICE SIZE/OFF NODE NAME
memcached 30172 memcached   26u   IPv4 25088862      0t0  TCP *:memcache (LISTEN)
memcached 30172 memcached   27u   IPv4 25088864      0t0  UDP *:memcache
memcached 30172 memcached   28u   IPv4 53276131      0t0  TCP localhost:memcache->localhost:35610 (ESTABLISHED)
memcached 30172 memcached  126u   IPv4 53266723      0t0  TCP localhost:memcache->localhost:35333 (ESTABLISHED)
keystone- 31509  keystone   12u   IPv4 53276128      0t0  TCP localhost:35610->localhost:memcache (ESTABLISHED)
keystone- 31509  keystone  168u   IPv4 53266720      0t0  TCP localhost:35333->localhost:memcache (ESTABLISHED)
```

9. We can dynamically check every second the `get_hits` value increasing using the `watch` command line, as follows:

```
# watch -d -n 1 'memcached-tool 127.0.0.1:11211 stats'
```

This command yields the following result:

```
Every 1.0s: memcached-tool 127.0.0.1:1

#127.0.0.1:11211    Field          Value
           accepting_conns             1
                 auth_cmds             0
               auth_errors             0
                     bytes        695422
                bytes_read        785559
             bytes_written       1454945
                cas_badval             0
                  cas_hits             0
                cas_misses             0
                 cmd_flush             0
                   cmd_get           282
                   cmd_set           239
               conn_yields             0
     connection_structures            29
          curr_connections             7
                curr_items            80
                 decr_hits             0
               decr_misses             0
               delete_hits            88
             delete_misses             0
                 evictions             0
                  get_hits           165
                get_misses           117
                 incr_hits             0
               incr_misses             0
            limit_maxbytes    4294967296
        listen_disabled_num            0
                       pid          8349
             pointer_size            64
             rusage_system      0.341948
               rusage_user      0.015997
                   threads             4
                      time    1429872008
         total_connections           142
               total_items           209
                    uptime           888
                   version         1.4.4
```

Nova services can also get benefits from the usage of memcached. In each compute and controller node, you will need to specify in each `nova.conf` file where memcached is running. It is important to bring under the scope how memcached can scale out easily. The deployment of a large OpenStack environment will require a scalable memcached setup if a single instance is not able to handle the current workload. For this purpose, you can use HAProxy to make use of multiple memcached instances in the `tcp` mode. The next snippet describes how HAProxy should be configured for a proper, scalable memcached setup.

We assume in this setup the configuration elaborated in *Chapter 6, OpenStack HA and Failover*, for an HAProxy node. We will just add a new stanza at the end of both the /etc/haproxy/haproxy.cfg files, and restart both the HAProxy nodes, as follows:

```
. . .
listen memcached-cluster 192.168.47.47:11211
        balance roundrobin
        maxconn 10000
     mode tcp
        server cc01 192.168.47.100:11211 check inter 5s rise 2 fall 3
        server cc02 192.168.47.101:11211 check inter 5s rise 2 fall 3
        server cc03 192.168.47.102:11211 check inter 5s rise 2 fall 3
haproxy01# service haproxy reload
haproxy02# service haproxy reload
```

We will need to tell Nova services that we already have multiple memcached instances running in three different cloud controller nodes. When cc01 becomes unavailable, cc02 takes over, and so on. We set the following directive in each controller and compute node in the /etc/nova/nova.conf file:

```
. . .
memcached_servers = cc01:11211,cc02:11211,cc03:11211
. . .
```

Memcached can also be beneficial for our dashboard. We can tell Horizon to use memcached for the Web for **Django** web caching. It just needs to point to the virtual IP, considering a scalable cloud controller setup. The dashboard includes the CACHES settings, which we need to edit/add. On your cloud controller nodes, edit the /etc/openstack-dashboard/local_settings.py file like this:

```
. . .
CACHES = {
    'default': {
        'BACKEND' : 'django.core.cache.backends.memcached.
MemcachedCache',
        'LOCATION' : '192.168.47.47:11211',
    }
}
. . .
```

We can add the next stanza to each HAProxy instance to boost a scalable Django dashboard, which is now using a scalable memcached setup:

```
...
listen horizon 192.168.47.47:80
        balance roundrobin
        maxconn 10000
      mode tcp
        server cc01 192.168.47.100:80 cookie cc01 check inter 5s rise
2 fall 3
        server cc02 192.168.47.101:80 cookie cc02 check inter 5s rise
2 fall 3
        server cc03 192.168.47.102:80 cookie cc03 check inter 5s rise
2 fall 3
```

We finish our new, empowering caching setup with some scalability extension by reloading the newest configuration in each HAProxy node:

```
haproxy01# service haproxy reload
haproxy02# service haproxy reload
```

Stressing RabbitMQ

We have classified in *Chapter 1, Designing OpenStack Cloud Architecture*, the database and queuing message system as very critical components in the OpenStack environment. If you have already found different ways to boost your database and ensured that is performing well, you will need on the other hand to measure the RabbitMQ capacity so you can identify any bottleneck at an early stage. Although we have clustered our message queuing system, we should take into account that if one of the nodes in the cluster becomes down or unreachable, the remaining one can face a sudden heavy workload which may lead to a bottleneck. Then what? All the OpenStack services will not be able to talk to RabbitMQ and the entire cluster stops working. Basically, when adding new compute nodes simultaneously to the controller node, RabbitMQ will need to create more processes and threads to be able to manage the new compute services and join them to talk to other running OpenStack services. Default RabbitMQ parameters such as **Socket Descriptors** and **File Descriptors** can be limited factors when the system scales. It is possible to check these parameters by issuing the command line on your RabbitMQ node:

```
# rabbitmqctl status
```

This will generate few lines including the instance version and a detailed description of the memory and disk status reserved for RabbitMQ. At the end of the command line output, we can focus on the file descriptors section as the following:

```
{file_descriptors,[{total_limit,924},
                   {total_used,91},
                   {sockets_limit,829},
                   {sockets_used,89}]},
```

By default, the previous illustration shows that RabbitMQ was installed by limiting the maximum number of file descriptors to 924 and maximum number of sockets to 829. Eventually, the real number of `total_limit` is 1024. By default, RabbitMQ omits 100 for any `ulimit` assigned to its processes. It is obvious that the `total_used` and `sockets_used` values did not reach respectively the `total_limit` and `sockets_limit` values which indicates that our OpenStack environment is in a safe zone. However, bringing more compute nodes to the cluster will require more file and socket descriptors and both values will increase. Moreover, with more additional load on each compute node that runs hundreds of VMs each might increase the total number of sockets and file descriptors drastically. Thus, it might maximize the risk of a possible bottleneck. In this case, RabbitMQ can behave very strangely: For example, creating a new instance from Horizon can hang in infinite **scheduling** state. However, the RabbitMQ service keeps running but the OpenStack cannot communicate with it due to lack of file and socket descriptors. With this thought in mind, the performance limits of the RabbitMQ system should be known as early as possible. This will bring its performance to its optimization limits and get ready to respond unexpected issues. To work around such serious issue, it is possible to edit the default security limits in the Linux box as the following:

1. Create a new file in /etc/security/limits.d/ named rabbitmq.conf with the following content:

   ```
   # OpenStack: RabbitMQ
   # Increase maximum number of open fi to 4096 for RabbitMQ

   #<domain>    <type>    <item>    <value>
   rabbitmq     soft      nofile    4096
   ```

   We have adjusted the number of file descriptors to 4096.

2. Check if the new setting is accepted:

   ```
   # su - rabbitmq -s /bin/sh -c 'ulimit -n'
   4096
   ```

3. A simple restart of the rabbitmq-server service will be enough to detect the new settings.

```
# service rabbitmq-server restart
```

It will take some time to clean the RabbitMQ cache and start rabbitmq-server service.

4. Now, we can see the new updated ulimit values by running the following command line:

```
# rabbitmqctl status | grep -A 4 file_descriptors
```

```
{file_descriptors,[{total_limit,3996},
                   {total_used,57},
                   {sockets_limit,3594},
                   {sockets_used,55}]},
```

Note that by default, the RabbitMQ omits 100 from the new adjusted 4096 value as discussed previously.

It is possible to apply the new changes without restarting the RabbitMQ service. This can be needed to avoid the reestablishment of all connections of the OpenStack services which are trying to reach the RabbitMQ service. To do so, you will need to figure out all the RabbitMQ processes by running:

```
# ps auxw | grep ^rabbit | cut -d' ' -f 3
```

Then, for each **PID** listed in the **ps** command line, you will need to increase its ulimit value by taking into account to subtract 100 from the new ulimit value. For example to increase the default ulimit value 1024 for the RabbitMQ user with PID 2231 to 4096, you can run the following command lines:

```
# echo -n "Max open files=1024:4096" > /proc/2231/limits
# rabbitmqctl eval 'file_handle_cache:set_limit(3996)'
```

Performing stress tests on the RabbitMQ cluster will make sure how many compute nodes can a controller node handle. On the other hand, it not advised to adjust the security limits to **unlimited**. This can be a real problem when the RabbitMQ reaches a huge number of file and socket descriptors while other services compete as well to create new descriptors. This case is very special when the RabbitMQ cluster is designed to run in the controller nodes and not in a dedicated cluster.

Benchmarking OpenStack at scale

You still have one last step left to accomplish the production day mission. As the title of this book promises, we will ensure that our design and deployment are done well by testing our OpenStack scalability.

In other words, we will make sure that our private cloud keeps functioning as it faces a huge amount of workload or sudden sizing changes of resources. We keep our smiley users' faces. How we can do that? We will benchmark our OpenStack environment.

Bear in mind that benchmarking OpenStack is not an option, but it's highly demanded. This is when you can rate both your design and deployment:

- Determine what sort of improvements should be made from the hardware or software perspective
- Rate our OpenStack private cloud by analyzing how other cloud providers achieve a high performance level
- Improve our OpenStack performance environment based on the collected information from the benchmarking results

Generally, benchmarking a computer application is a slightly complicated task that needs a specific test environment with complex hands-on lab installation. Set up the test environment to mimic a real workload, picking up the right tool and decide to execute several scenarios might be a time-consuming phase. Moreover, the results cannot be accurate if you mistakenly choose the wrong benchmark test. Do we need to build or develop the right benchmarking tools for OpenStack? The answer is, *no!* If you want to set aside a part of your budget and time, then the answer is a slight "Yes!" Most probably, you have noticed over the course of this book that OpenStack is very modular, with multiple extensions and features. Incubated projects make OpenStack unique. Even in benchmarking art, specifically for OpenStack, we have Rally.

Rally in a nutshell

Rally is simply a benchmarking tool designed to tell you more about how your OpenStack infrastructure performs under a workload at scale. Originally, the OpenStack's official test suite was **Tempest**. It is built on many Python testing frameworks. Tempest basically accommodates several test scenarios against OpenStack service endpoints by executing API calls, and ends up with response verification and validation from the endpoints.

You can read more about Tempest and execute individual tests cited on GitHub at `https://github.com/openstack/tempest`.

Tempest is used by the OpenStack community for the continuous integration process, which is covered in *Chapter 2, Deploying OpenStack – DevOps and OpenStack Dual Deal*. Eventually, it might be useful to report and publish relevant results based on Tempest execution, which helps identify what should be changed or improved in OpenStack code. It might also be useful if you intend to adopt any system configuration tool, such as Chef or Puppet, to deploy and manage your OpenStack infrastructure, which will help you zero in on what should be fixed from the OpenStack code base in the first stage and reflect high-level changes in the second stage to your cookbooks for example.

Using the power of Tempest is very fruitful with respect to testing your OpenStack cluster environment. However, it might become more complicated and time-consuming by diving into inline Python code to start testing. Moreover, the results should be collected and easily deduced. To overcome such challenges, Rally might be a perfect solution. You should know that Rally is *not* an alternative to Tempest. However, it is a performance and benchmarking framework that installs, configures, and uses Tempest tests during the benchmarking process.

Eventually, Rally expands the Tempest use cases to:

- Verify and validate OpenStack deployment at scale
- Run with more flexibility tests in more than one OpenStack cloud site
- Compare benchmarking results by reposing on the historical data residing in Rally's database
- Execute more realistic test workloads within multiple simulated tenants and active users

Meeting OpenStack SLA

Service uptime is what your cloud user is concerned about. Most probably, the SLA in the cloud still somehow silent on some points most importantly the variation of the cloud performance level during a certain period of time. With this thought in mind, performance awareness should be taken into consideration as early as possible where comes SLA into play to act for both parties (the cloud provider and the end user) as a road map for possible changes in the OpenStack cloud service. Running your OpenStack in production is not the end of the journey—we have just begun the fun!

The next aim is to agree on the desired service level for your cloud end user and take realistic measurement results. Bear in mind that an SLA is something not to be ignored. In some sense, end users would rather be informed about the cloud limits and expectations. In other words, you should represent the workload performance metrics. Issues such as frequency of failures, mean time between failures, and mean time to recover are some of the indicators that can be stated in an SLA for the OpenStack cloud infrastructure. Submitting credible performance benchmarks might help you, as a provider, appear as a more trustworthy party, while giving more confidence to the consumer cloud service. A growing cloud infrastructure will be accompanied by working on SLA improvement. In order to consistently put the headlines of our OpenStack SLA, we will use Rally.

Installing Rally

We will install Rally on a separate server that has access to all OpenStack servers. The Rally node will eventually join the following OpenStack networks:

- Administrative network
- External network

The next installation snippet will guide you through a package-based installation of Rally on a CentOS operation system, with minimum hardware and software requirements as follows:

- **Processor**: 64-bit x86
- **Memory**: 2 GB RAM
- **Disk space**: 100 GB
- **Network**: Two 1 Gbps **Network Interface Cards (NICs)**
- Python 2.6 or a higher version

Let's get some hands-on experience and install Rally:

1. Download Rally from the GitHub repository and run the `install_rally.sh` installation script as follows:

   ```
   # git clone https://github.com/stackforge/rally.git
   # cd rally && sudo ./install_rally.sh
   ```

2. Register your OpenStack environment with Rally. This can be done via the `openrc` local environment variables, for example. You can copy it from your cloud controller to the Rally server and source it as follows:

   ```
   # scp packtpub@cc01:/openrc .
   # source openrc admin admin
   ```

The next command will register your OpenStack cloud with Rally based on the environment variables:

```
# rally deployment create  --name existing--fromenv
```

A sample `deployment create` output may look as follows:

```
+------------------------------------------+------------------------------+----------+-------------------+--------+
| uuid                                     | created_at                   | name     | status            | active |
+------------------------------------------+------------------------------+----------+-------------------+--------+
| dcd3bdef-06f9-4101-89ee-2db779f0c912     | 2015-04-21 19:39:35.311337   | existing | deploy->finished  |        |
+------------------------------------------+------------------------------+----------+-------------------+--------+
Using deployment: dcd3bdef-06f9-4101-89ee-2db779f0c912
~/.rally/openrc was updated
```

3. Verify the availability of your OpenStack deployment by means of the `deployment check` command:

    ```
    # rally deployment check
    ```

    This command yields the following output:

    ```
    keystone endpoints are valid and following services are available:
    +-------------+-----------------+-------------+
    | services    | type            | status      |
    +-------------+-----------------+-------------+
    | ceilometer  | metering        | Available   |
    | cinder      | volume          | Available   |
    | cinderv2    | volumev2        | Available   |
    | glance      | image           | Available   |
    | heat        | orchestration   | Available   |
    | keystone    | identity        | Available   |
    | neutron     | network         | Available   |
    | nova        | compute         | Available   |
    | nova_ec2    | ec2             | Available   |
    | novav3      | computev3       | Available   |
    | swift       | object-store    | Available   |
    | swift_s3    | s3              | Available   |
    +-------------+-----------------+-------------+
    ```

The preceding output shows a proper Rally setup by listing the status of the running services from an OpenStack environment.

> If the `deployment check` command throws the
> **Authentication Issue: wrong keystone credentials specified
> in your endpoint properties. (HTTP 401)** error message,
> you will have to update your registration credentials in your
> `openrc` file by including the right credentials.

Rally in action

Now that we have a Rally server installed and properly configured to talk to the OpenStack APIs, it's time for cloud benchmarking. By default, you may find numerous benchmarking scenarios under /rally/sample/tasks/scenarios for all OpenStack services, including incubated projects such as **murano**, **sahara**, and others. We will concentrate on benchmarking our existing and running OpenStack services. Before starting our first benchmark test, it might be great to shine the spotlight on how Rally works. Scenarios in Rally are performed based on tasks. A task might include a set of running benchmarks against your OpenStack cloud written in sample JSON or YAML file formats. The former file generally has the following structure:

```
---
    ScenarioClass.scenario_method:
-
        args:
...
        runner:
            ...
        context
            ...
        sla:
            ...
```

Let's understand this structure:

- ScenarioClass.scenario_method: This defines the name of the benchmark scenario.

- args: Every method corresponding to a specific class scenario can be customized by passing parameters before launching the benchmark.

- runners: This defines the workload frequency type and the order of the benchmarking scenarios. The runners stanza can support different types, as follows:
    - constant: Running the scenario for a fixed number of times. For example, a scenario can be run 10 times in the total test period.
    - constant_for_duration: Running the scenario for a fixed number of times up to a certain point in time.
    - periodic: Define a certain period of time (intervals) to run two consecutive benchmark scenarios.
    - serial: Running the scenario for a fixed number of times in a single benchmark thread.

- `context`: This defines the environment type in which our benchmark scenario (or scenarios) can run. Usually, the concept of context defines how many tenants and active users will be associated with a given OpenStack project. It can also specify the quota per tenant/user for certain granted roles.

- `sla`: This is very useful for identifying the overall scenario average success rate of the benchmark.

For those hoping to find a convenient benchmarking scenario that will reveal more significant results from your current OpenStack deployment, you'll have to keep looking for a real use case that is more specific for cloud operators. For example, Rally can help developers to easily run synthetic workloads, such as VM provisioning and destroy, for a limited period of time.

However, the case of cloud operators seems more complicated. Such results generated from workloads are more high-level results, but allow you to identify bottlenecks in the cloud. Let's see a real-world example: companies have several applications that need to be deployed in different usage patterns. If we have multiple concurrent instances application for QA/dev, they will be deployed in a different version of that application on the cloud several times a day. Consider a use case of a large deployment where there is a set number of teams running a bunch of standard stack applications, and each application contains a lot of VMs that need to be deployed a certain number of times a day. Such workload requirements might be translated into OpenStack terms as follows: we have M number of users provisioning N number of virtual machines within a specific flavor T times in a certain period of time and in a concurrent way.

As we know, OpenStack is not just a monolithic structure. It is a distributed system, with different daemons and services talking to each other. If we decompose a use case of provisioning of an instance to the primitives, it will be amazing to understand where we spend most of the time during the virtual machine provisioning phase. As soon as we get the baseline, our main goal is to provide some historical data, for example, running the same benchmark several times by changing a certain number of parameters, in each runtime, in the database configuration, or by enabling glance caching.

Scenario example 1

Our first shining example is to mimic a simple real workflow that consists of creating an image using Glance and booting an instance from it. The next scenario is based on the `GlanceImages` class running a method named `create_image_and_boot_instances`:

```
---
  GlanceImages.create_image_and_boot_instances:
    -
      args:
        image_location: "http://download.cirros-
          cloud.net/0.3.1/cirros-0.3.1-x86_64-disk.img"
        container_format: "bare"
        disk_format: "qcow2"
        flavor:
            name: "m1.nano"
        number_instances: 2
      runner:
        type: "constant"
        times: 10
        concurrency: 2
      context:
        users:
          tenants: 3
          users_per_tenant: 5
```

How does this work? We intend to run three tenants. Each tenant has five users, so in all, we will have 15 temporary users trying to create the Glance image by downloading a `cirros` image within an OpenStack flavor **nano**. Be sure that the **nano** flavor exists, otherwise Rally will throw an error message because of the missing flavor name, as was defined in its task file. The benchmark will run 10 times in total. At any time, only two users will be running the scenario workflow simultaneously.

To run the benchmark, you can use the following command:

```
# rally task start create-image-and-boot-instances.yaml
```

You can check the validity of the task inputs via the Rally task command output:

```
- - - - - - - - - - - - - - - - - - - - - - - - - - - - - - - - - - - - - - - - - - - - - - - - - - - -
 Preparing input task
- - - - - - - - - - - - - - - - - - - - - - - - - - - - - - - - - - - - - - - - - - - - - - - - - - - -

Input task is:
- - -
  GlanceImages.create_image_and_boot_instances:
      -
      args:
        image_location: "http://download.cirros-cloud.net/0.3.1/cirros-0.3.1-x86_64-disk.img"
        container_format: "bare"
        disk_format: "qcow2"
        flavor:
             name: "m1.nano"
        number_instances: 2
      runner:
        type: "constant"
        times: 10
        concurrency: 2
      context:
        users:
           tenants: 3
           users_per_tenant: 5

- - - - - - - - - - - - - - - - - - - - - - - - - - - - - - - - - - - - - - - - - - - - - - - - - - - -
 Task  6909ee21-d6d7-4dbb-a299-0db9a916f2a1: started
- - - - - - - - - - - - - - - - - - - - - - - - - - - - - - - - - - - - - - - - - - - - - - - - - - - -

Benchmarking... This can take a while...
```

Such kinds of scenarios might take some time to complete. It might be interesting to monitor the task process in two ways. First, the task status can be checked by opening a new terminal in your Rally server and running this command:

```
# rally task status
```

This gives the following output:

```
- - - - - - - - - - - - - - - - - - - - - - - - - - - - - - - - - - - - - - - - - - - - - - - - - - - -
Task 6909ee21-d6d7-4dbb-a299-0db9a916f2a1: running
```

The second way is to keep an eye on your monitoring server and check the resource activity on both cloud controller and your compute node. This is very useful for checking any bottleneck that may occur in advance. Then you can formulate your results' analysis as early as possible. For example, a quick look at the `top` command on the compute node depicts the following sorted resource consumption per process:

```
PID USER      PR  NI  VIRT  RES  SHR S %CPU %MEM    TIME+  COMMAND
3972 qemu      20   0  466m  23m 5812 R 50.2  0.8   0:07.22 qemu-kvm
3961 qemu      20   0  466m  25m 5812 R 49.9  0.9   0:06.85 qemu-kvm
3425 qemu      20   0 1016m 110m 2904 R 26.9  3.8   0:29.88 qemu-kvm
3431 qemu      20   0  954m 112m 2888 R 26.6  3.9   0:30.34 qemu-kvm
1413 qemu      20   0 1337m  30m 2332 S 22.3  1.1   1:15.08 qemu-kvm
1626 qemu      20   0 1086m  29m 2340 R 22.3  1.0   1:38.10 qemu-kvm
2663 qemu      20   0  760m  29m 2344 S 22.3  1.0   1:18.74 qemu-kvm
5566 qemu      20   0 1531m  16m 1900 R 22.3  0.6  3990:48 qemu-kvm
2313 qemu      20   0 1538m  27m 2356 S 21.6  0.9   1:11.18 qemu-kvm
2322 qemu      20   0 1600m  27m 2332 R 21.6  0.9   1:13.28 qemu-kvm
2669 qemu      20   0 1274m  32m 2356 S 21.6  1.1   1:17.17 qemu-kvm
1632 qemu      20   0 2535m  75m 2380 S 21.3  2.6   0:56.68 qemu-kvm
1416 qemu      20   0 1603m  26m 2280 R 20.9  0.9   1:57.59 qemu-kvm
```

We can see clearly that **qemu-kvm** is the most frequent computing resources consumer, which might be understandable. On the other hand, if such a process keeps hanging on our process list, it will be interesting to take a closer look from the logging perspective and check the Nova and Glance log files. We can first check what is going on in our instance deployment process from Horizon:

Unfortunately, a few instances have failed to boot, as illustrated previously. The fact is that Rally kept sending the workload, trying all different iterations, which we were not able to check it from the Rally task process. Instead of waiting longer for Rally to finish the execution, we can abort the task execution and adjust our scenario to make the cluster capable of handling such a workload. The previous screenshot shows the **No valid host was found** error message. The root cause of this issue is that the compute host selected by the nova-scheduler does not have enough free resources to host more virtual machines. As you may know, nova-scheduler is responsible for determining which physical host the instance should launch on. In some cases, instances need to be evacuated from compute nodes when they fail due to a hardware malfunction. The default scheduler will not pick up the next host, and you will have to declare the evacuation process explicitly using the `nova evacuate` command line. This is can be valid assumption when your monitoring server declares a serious hardware problem on your compute node.

Scheduling in OpenStack is a very interesting topic for performance boosting, which is beyond the scope of this book. To learn more about scheduling in OpenStack, check out `http://docs.`
`openstack.org/havana/config-reference/content/`
`section_compute-scheduler.html`.

For the sake of simplicity, we will free a few RAM and CPU resources on a specific host by dismissing unused virtual machines, and let the scheduler filter it and launch our instances from the benchmark task. More physical resources can be optionally patched to the physical host. At least, you have a first impression about your hardware capacity.

Let's run our task again by keeping an eye on the monitoring server:

```
# rally task start create-image-and-boot-instances.yaml
```

After a while, we can see some results:

```
+----------------------+-----------+-----------+-----------+----------------+----------------+---------+-------+
| action               | min (sec) | avg (sec) | max (sec) | 90 percentile  | 95 percentile  | success | count |
+----------------------+-----------+-----------+-----------+----------------+----------------+---------+-------+
| glance.create_image  | 7.799     | 13.369    | 23.956    | 23.024         | 23.49          | 100.0%  | 10    |
| nova.boot_servers    | 96.466    | 196.482   | 261.603   | 260.501        | 261.052        | 100.0%  | 10    |
| total                | 119.387   | 209.852   | 272.95    | 271.119        | 272.034        | 100.0%  | 10    |
+----------------------+-----------+-----------+-----------+----------------+----------------+---------+-------+
Load duration: 1073.03213596
Full duration: 1138.09469104
```

We have conducted a benchmark test with a **100%** success rate. We now have golden information about our physical hardware capabilities. To make our results more elegant to analyze further, Rally gives the hand to generate plots and graphs in HTML format, using the following Rally powerful command:

```
# rally task report 473e3499-545a-dd32-1238-197821dafe470 - -output
inst_report.html
```

The 473e3499-545a-dd32-1238-197821dafe470 value refers to the task ID generated by Rally when executing the `rally task start` command line. The benchmark results can be illustrated as the following:

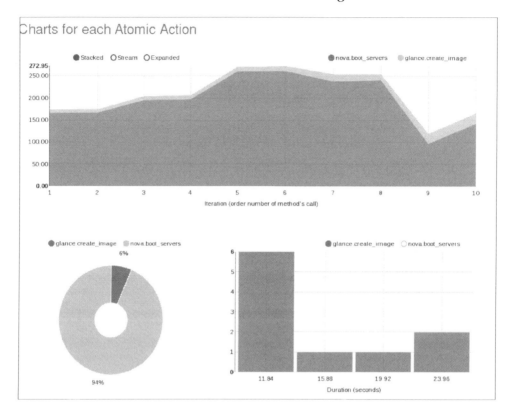

The graphs are pretty useful and help derive under-the-hood results during the image and boot instance among the different iterations. We can clearly see, for example, where the workflow takes longer time, which is the Nova boot phase in our case. When the workload becomes error-prone, it might be useful to conduct a granular analysis of every phase based on your logging output information.

This example might be very useful to identify how many VMs a single compute node can handle. Of course, you will not stick to a single Rally configuration. A good stress performance practice is to vary the different parameters during the Rally benchmarking exercise as the following:

- Increase the number of tenants;
- Increase the number of users per tenant;
- Increase the number of active users;
- Use different flavors with different compute pools

A practical way of performance analysis is simply generating the load for each configuration test and watching how resources are being consumed for each compute node. Therefore, it might be clear to identify the limitation of the compute nodes capability based on different indicators: Number of Active VMs, Number of VMs in Error state and number of VMs failed to service. Using monitoring tools such as Zabbix or Linux tools such as **'vmstat'** help reach a successful performance measurement. From different observed results, it is possible to conclude several points of interest as the following:

- Maximum number of VMs of a certain flavor per compute node
- Maximum number of VMs with a mixed number of flavors per compute node
- Maximum number of VMs in all compute nodes
- Max/Min/Avg provisioning time required for each VM per compute node
- Maximum number of provisioned VMs with a certain over-commit value

Additionally, this kind of benchmarking exercise validates the first decisions made for different hardware specifications discussed in *Chapter 1, Designing OpenStack Cloud Architecture*. Based on the new observations, you might be tempted to adjust your hardware settings and the OpenStack configurations such as:

- Change the over-commit ratio for RAM/CPU per compute node;
- Use a different or a custom scheduler for better resources provisioning;
- Limit the number of provisioned VM for a given flavor;
- Limit the number of tenants per controller node with a fixed number of users

Most importantly, these are not all the possible adjustments. As you start benchmarking your OpenStack computing infrastructure, several performance use cases can be brought under the hood and become more aware of its limits, then you go beyond.

Scenario example 2

Our second shining example will be Keystone authentication based on a Rally scenario named KeystoneBasic.authenticate. Let's create a new file named keystone_pp.yaml.

The content of the file task looks as follows:

```
Authenticate.keystone:
    -
    runner:
      type: "rps"
      times: 600
      rps: 20
    context:
      users:
        tenants: 5
        users_per_tenant: 10
    sla:
      max_avg_duration: 5
```

How does this work? We intend to create, in all, 5 tenants. Each tenant will have 10 users who will authenticate 600 times against Keystone. The rps (that is, **request per second**) option defines 20 authentications per second, which means executing one authentication every 0.05 seconds. The sla section defines the following condition: if the maximum average duration of an authentication takes longer than 5 seconds, the task will be aborted.

 Running similar scenarios with several authentication requests running simultaneously is a very useful use case for testing DDoS attack use cases against your Keystone service.

Let's run the previous benchmark using the Rally command line, as follows:

```
# rally task start --abort-on-sla-failure keystone_pp.yaml
```

Note that, this time, we add a new option to our command — abort-on-sla-failure. This is a very useful argument if you are running such a benchmark scenario in a real OpenStack production environment. Rally generates a heavy workload, which might cause performance troubles to the existing cloud. Thus, we tell Rally to stop the load at a certain moment when the sla conditions are met.

The output of our executed task is as follows:

```
+--------+-----------+-----------+-----------+---------------+---------------+---------+-------+
| action | min (sec) | avg (sec) | max (sec) | 90 percentile | 95 percentile | success | count |
+--------+-----------+-----------+-----------+---------------+---------------+---------+-------+
| total  | 0.623     | 51.195    | 80.672    | 74.937        | 76.615        | 96.1%   | 560   |
+--------+-----------+-----------+-----------+---------------+---------------+---------+-------+
Load duration: 84.9917628765
Full duration: 103.821238041
```

The Rally benchmark results show that Rally performed **560** authentication requests instead of 600, while the average time was high compared to what was mentioned in our `sla` section.

To dive into more details, we generate the HTML report by running this command:

```
# rally task report  3e734a11-d52e-42ad-ab33-400ca1d797cd - -out
keystone_report01.html
```

It generates the following result:

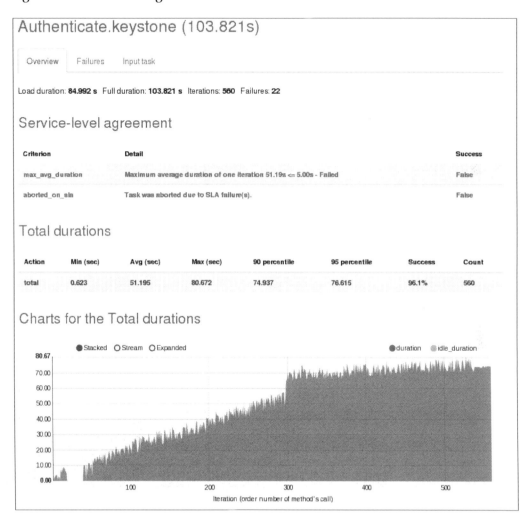

We can observe from the chart the end of load generation when the duration of authentication request reaches 80 seconds. Without sufficient success criteria, Rally has stopped generating load of the attempts to authenticate. We can see in detail the reasons for failure from the HTML report. Go to the **Failures** section, as shown in the following screenshot:

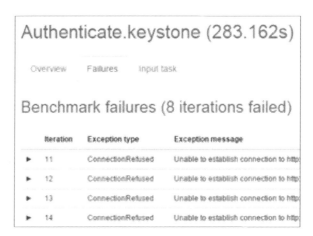

We can adjust our success criteria parameters a bit in the next iteration to perform a more realistic scenario. For example, we can modify our `sla` section to become like this:

```
...
sla:
    max_avg_duration: 5
    max_seconds_per_iteration: 50
    failure_rate:
     max: 1
```

The new `sla` section defines three conditions:

- `max_avg_duration`: If the maximum average duration of an authentication takes longer than 5 seconds, the task will be aborted

- `max_seconds_per_iteration`: If the maximum duration of an authentication request takes longer than 50 seconds, the task will be aborted

- `failure_rate: max`: More than one failed authentication will abort the task

Rerun the task:

```
# rally task start --abort-on-sla-failure keystone_pp.yaml
```

Let's check out our charts again by generating a new report with a different name so that we can compare the difference in results with the previous iteration:

```
# rally task report  43e26392-dd23-3e33-be12-0024736fdc239- -out
keystone_report02.html
```

Here's the result:

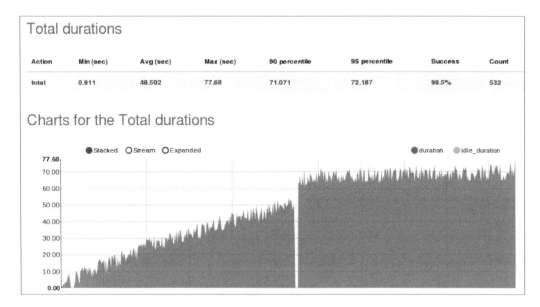

According to the last graph, the load stopped at **532** iterations. Most probably, at the first 50-second period, the authentication requests realized about 275 iterations, followed by a silent time when no authentication was processed. The last 20 seconds kept generating the authentication load gradually. It might be interesting to take a closer look at the logs in the **Failure** section:

▶	272	AuthorizationFailure	Authorization Failed: An unexpected error prevented the server from fulfilling your request. (HTTP 500)
▶	273	AuthorizationFailure	Authorization Failed: An unexpected error prevented the server from fulfilling your request. (HTTP 500)
▶	274	AuthorizationFailure	Authorization Failed: An unexpected error prevented the server from fulfilling your request. (HTTP 500)
▶	275	AuthorizationFailure	Authorization Failed: An unexpected error prevented the server from fulfilling your request. (HTTP 500)

The **AuthenticationFailure** exception might not be very useful for surrounding the root cause of bad requests. Thus, we can check out what was happening from our monitoring server or our Keystone files. A very interesting line can explain part of the problem:

```
OS error :TRACE keystone.common.wsgi OSError: [Errno 24] Too many open files
```

Basically, once Rally finished running the benchmark, the cloud controller under test kept the tenants created by Rally active. We can check this by using the following command on our cloud controller node:

```
# keystone tenant-list
```

It yields the following result:

```
+----------------------------------+----------------------------------------------------------+---------+
|                id                |                           name                           | enabled |
+----------------------------------+----------------------------------------------------------+---------+
| 287df4ce5da548ca80398646eef51b7b |                          admin                           |  True   |
| c4569307e3974482a9bb254b844d2aa6 | ctx_rally_31f8445d-2d17-4660-b22d-54d6060a9dd4_tenant_0  |  True   |
| 71b811883c0941149577ec6d218e4ac5 | ctx_rally_31f8445d-2d17-4660-b22d-54d6060a9dd4_tenant_1  |  True   |
| 9a1ac9bc183f477aa9b5b8d6cf86c88c | ctx_rally_31f8445d-2d17-4660-b22d-54d6060a9dd4_tenant_2  |  True   |
| df747866f73d4afb9e54dc579ff1e975 | ctx_rally_31f8445d-2d17-4660-b22d-54d6060a9dd4_tenant_3  |  True   |
| df3948c2380145cf890c414851207c3a | ctx_rally_31f8445d-2d17-4660-b22d-54d6060a9dd4_tenant_4  |  True   |
| 0fd4aa2c150d434d88f0ba8de9bc75b8 | ctx_rally_39501331-e98b-451b-b152-f5b315fbdb5e_tenant_0  |  True   |
| 9e2140be993c46ccb4ca47d08e8f2058 | ctx_rally_39501331-e98b-451b-b152-f5b315fbdb5e_tenant_1  |  True   |
| d8a26bfbe79a4c72b0421825b757546d | ctx_rally_39501331-e98b-451b-b152-f5b315fbdb5e_tenant_2  |  True   |
| 58989e9f1d464b3aa7be00a969958c9c |                         services                         |  True   |
+----------------------------------+----------------------------------------------------------+---------+
```

Each tenant has 10 users, which makes it impossible to satisfy new coming connections. For instance, our cloud controller should be in idle state, except for connections handled for the admin and the default tenant service. However, you can check the remaining connections listening on port 35357 using the following command:

```
# lsof -a -i 35357 | wc -l
```

Thus, the problem can be escalated to the operation system level itself, which might be undersized in terms of file descriptors that can be opened. On the other hand, it can be seen as a software bug. In our case, Rally kept sending requests by keystoneclient to the cloud controller. Each request initiated by the client will create a session which does not get closed and kept open for reuse. The problem apparently relies on the opened socket for each session; they never get closed, neither by the server nor by the client. The end result is reaching the limit of the opened file of the cloud controller. A preliminary workaround for this problem can be simply increasing the files descriptor's limits on the CentOS box of the cloud controller.

Then, we will have to look at the following system parameters:

```
# cat /proc/sys/fs/file-max
75000
# cat /proc/sys/net/core/somaxconn
1024
# ulimit -Sn
1024
# ulimit -Hn
4096
```

We simply adjust the aforementioned parameters by increasing the `ulimit`, `file-max`, and `somaxconn` values, as follows:

```
# sysctl -w net.core.somaxconn=150000
# sysctl -w fs.file-max=100000
```

Add the following lines to the `/etc/security/limits.conf` file:

```
*               soft    nofile          65535
*               hard    nofile          65535
```

To free the unused Keystone connections and reconstruct a clean Keystone benchmark, the Keystone service should be restarted. After running the authentication scenario several times, we can clearly see an improvement in the SLA success rate, which has increased to **99.1%**, as shown in this screenshot:

Service-level agreement

Criterion	Detail	Success
max_seconds_per_iteration	Maximum seconds per iteration 72.02s <= 10.00s - Failed	False
failure_rate	Failure rate criteria 0.00% <= 0.93% <= 1.00% - Passed	True
max_avg_duration	Maximum average duration of one iteration 47.55s <= 50.00s - Passed	True
aborted_on_sla	Task was aborted due to SLA failure(s).	False

Total durations

Action	Min (sec)	Avg (sec)	Max (sec)	90 percentile	95 percentile	Success	Count
total	1.117	47.547	72.019	68.69	69.87	99.1%	536

Summary

Our journey of mastering the OpenStack cloud system has come to an end. In the course of this book, you learned how to plan and design the general OpenStack architecture, deploy and manage your cloud using automation tools, such as Chef (covering more incubated projects for storage), as well as decide and use a network in OpenStack. You were also informed about several design patterns for clustering, high availability, and scalability in OpenStack. Your OpenStack production day was accompanied by an exploration of ways to monitor and collect logging data for faster troubleshooting tasks. You should notice how rich and welcoming such a cloud platform is for new cloud-based open source solutions.

In this chapter, we highlighted real-world scenarios for performance enhancement in OpenStack database, queuing message system and OpenStack services. Now you should also be able to use Rally and perform scenario benchmarking based on more advanced workflows. You may have noticed how Rally can be fruitful for an OpenStack cloud operator by detecting performance issues as quickly as possible. This is useful for considering new approaches and deciding what sort of hardware should be used or improved, how to refine your deployment design, and how to create better infrastructure code. You should focus on proving that your OpenStack cloud can scale enough to handle a massive workload, which might be your next stage for a new OpenStack journey.

With this book, we hope that you have refreshed your knowledge and have discovered what is newly introduced in OpenStack. Before ending this book, you should be confident that you are ready to take a step further and be one of hundreds of organizations which are enjoying such amazing cloud computing adventure led by OpenStack where the journey of knowledge never ends.

Index

Symbols

HA level
L1 173

A

account server, Swift 106
AMQP system message bus 280
apache web server (httpd)
 installing 273
Application Programming
 Interface (API) 78
architecture, Ceilometer
 about 278
 API server (ceilometer-api) 278
 central agent (ceilometer-agent-central) 278
 collector (ceilometer-collector) 278
 compute agent
  (ceilometer-agent-compute) 278
 data store 278
architecture, Swift
 about 105
 account server 106
 container server 106
 object server 106
 Swift proxy server 106
args 348
asymmetric clustering 75
Atlas 261

B

back up
 with backup-manager 100
benchmarking
 OpenStack 344

Berksfile 60
Berkshelf 60
block live migration 174
Broker 310

C

caching 334
CAP
 about 121
 availability 121
 consistency 121
 partition tolerance 121
 URL, for theorem 121
Ceilometer
 about 275, 276
 and heat 287
 architecture 278
 autoscaling 288
 definition 276
 glossary 277
 Heat Orchestration Template (HOT),
  extending for alarming 288-295
 installation 281-286
Ceilometer alarm resource, properties
 alarm_actions 293
 comparaison_operator 294
 Description 293
 evaluation_periods 293
 matching_metadata 294
 meter_name 293
 period 293
 statistic 293
 threshold 293

Ceph
  about 25, 127
  architecture 128
  CRUSH maps 129
  deploying 132-137
  images, storing 138, 139
  in OpenStack 131
  Object Storage Devices (OSDs) 128
  Placement groups (PGs) 129
  pool 129
Certification Based Replication (CBR) 184
cfgmgr 225
cfgmgtroles 225
cfgserver 225
chains, iptables
  about 144
  FORWARD chain 144
  INPUT chain 144
  OUTPUT chain 144
  POSTROUTING chain 144
  PREROUTING chain 144
Chef
  about 52
  attribute files 53
  cookbook 52
  node 53
  prerequisites 53, 54
  recipe 52
  role 53
  server installation 54, 55
  workstation installation 56-58
Chef server preinstallation 226
Cinder
  about 6, 7, 118-124
  features 6
  use case 119, 125-127
Cinder support matrix
  URL 122
cloud
  LBaaS, integrating 263-265
cloud controller
  about 75
  database, consolidating 80
  deploying 83-85
  Horizon decision 80
  image management 79
  message queue, planning for 80

  network outfit 79
  nova-conductor 76
  nova-scheduler 77
  services 76
  X-api 78
cloud controller clustering 81-83
Cloud service brokerage 21
Cloud service provider 21
cloud storage 4
clustering
  about 74
  asymmetric clustering 75
  symmetric clustering 75
CMI (Clariion Message Interface) 123
components, Logstash
  Broker 310
  Elasticsearch 310
  Kibana 310
  Logstash Indexer 310
  Logstash shipper 309
components, Neutron architecture
  Neutron agents 11
  Neutron plugins 11
  Neutron-server 11
  queue 11
components, Nova
  nova-api 7
  nova-compute 8
  nova-network 8
  nova-scheduler 9
  nova-volume 8
compressed provisioning 126
compute node
  about 86
  deploying 97-99
  hypervisor, deciding 89-91
  overcommitment considerations 87
  storing instances alternatives 96
concepts, Neutron
  floating IPs 11
  networks 10
  ports 10
  private IPs 11
  routers 10
conceptual model design 22, 23
container server, Swift 106
continuous integration (CI) 48

Coordinated Universal Time (UTC) 337
copy-on-write cloning feature 129
CPU allocation ratio 88
crudini
　URL 193
CRUSH maps 129

D

database
　about 9
　consolidating 80
database performance, OpenStack
　caching 334, 335
　improving 332, 333
　memcached 336
　resources-wise 334
dd tool 296
deduplicated provisioning 126
deployment, example setup architecture
　about 21
　conceptual model design 22, 23
　logical model design 23, 24
　physical model design 31
Destination NAT (DNAT) 144
DevOps
　about 40
　cloud project 41, 42
Distributed Resource Scheduler (DRS) 77
Django web caching 340
Dnsmasq 18
Dynamic Resource Scheduler (DRS) 93

E

EGit
　URL 51
Elasticsearch 310, 311
ELK stack 310
EMC Storage Management Initiative
　　Specification (SMI-S) server 122
Environment as a Service (EaaS) 25
ephemeral storage 104
example setup architecture
　about 21
　deployment 21
external shared file storage
　about 96

advantages 96
drawbacks 96
Extreme Cluster/Cloud Administration
　　(xCAT) 210

F

File Descriptors 341
filesystem ID (fsid) 134
filtering 321
Firewall as a Service (FWaaS)
　about 152, 153
　firewall, coupling with Neutron 154-156
　Neutron plugin 157
　VPN as a Service (VPNaaS) 160
flat network 141
floating IP 143
front-cluster network, Swift 114

G

Galera
　URL 185
Git 47
Glance 5
glossary, Ceilometer
　agent 277
　alarms 277
　meter 277
　pipelines 277
　resource 277
　samples 277
　statistics 277
grok filter
　about 322
　match option 322
　patterns_dir option 322

H

HA
　about 172, 178, 181
　database 182-185
　failover 173
　fallback 173
　implementing, on MySQL 187-193
　implementing, on network nodes 203-205

implementing, on OpenStack cloud
    controllers 197-203
implementing, on RabbitMQ 194-196
measuring 175, 176
RabbitMQ 186, 187
stateful service 177
stateless service 177
strict service-level agreement 174, 175
switchover 173
HA levels
L2 173
L3 173
L4 173
HAProxy
about 178
Leastconn 179
load balancer failure 180, 181
Load balancing layer 4 178
Load balancing layer 7 178
Round robin 179
service failure 180
Source 179
URI 179
heat
about 287
heat-api 287
heat-api-cfn 287
heat-api-cloudwatch 287
Heat CLI tools 287
Heat Engine 287
installing 267, 268
using 268-272
Heat Orchestration Template (HOT)
about 265, 292
extending, for alarming 291-297
High Availability Proxy. *See* **HAProxy**
high performance clustering 173
Horizon
about 12
used, for managing security groups 145
Horizon decision 80
horizontal scaling 74
HTTP request, Swift API
DELETE 107
GET 107
HEAD 107

POST 107
PUT 107
hypervisor
color, changing 92-95
deciding 89-91
integration 92

I

image management 79
Infrastructure as a Service (IaaS) 2, 41
infrastructure code environment
preparing 49-52
init script, Kibana
URL 315
installation
Ceilometer 281-285
internal nonshared file storage
about 96
advantages 96
disadvantages 96
internal VM traffic
features 30
Internet Key Exchange (IKE) policy
creating 165
IPSec policy
creating 166, 167
IPSec site connection
creating 168, 169
iptables
about 144
chains 144
reference 145
target 144
target values 144
iptables, working on Linux
reference 143

J

Java 311
Java 8
download link 312
Jenkins 47
Juno 89
Just a Bunch of Disks (JBOD) 109

K

Keystone 4
Kibana 310, 311
Komodo
  URL 50

L

Lightweight Directory Access
        Protocol (LDAP) 4
Linux Bridge plugin 248-251
Linux Virtual Server (LVS) pool state 181
live migration 174
Load Balancer as a Service (LBaaS)
  about 246, 261
  integrating, in cloud 263-265
  working 262
load balancing 173
logging
  tackling 306
logical architecture, OpenStack
  about 3
  Cinder 6, 7
  database 9
  Glance 5
  Horizon 12
  Keystone 4
  Neutron 10
  Nova 7
  queue 9
  Swift 4
logical model design 23, 24
logical networking design 27, 28
logs
  adjusting, in OpenStack 308
  demystifying, in OpenStack 306
  location 307
Logstash
  about 309-311
  components 309, 310
  configuring 316
  installing 312-315
  placing 311
  requisites 312
  URL 322
  workflow 310

Logstash configuration
  about 316
  logs, shipping to central monitoring
        server 317-320
  OpenStack logs, filtering 321-324
  OpenStack logs, visualizing 326-328
Logstash configuration file
  filters section 310
  input section 310
  output section 310
Logstash Indexer 310
Logstash shipper 309

M

management network
  features 29
Master Initiator Node (MIN) 210
Mean Time To Repair (MTTR) 31
memcached
  about 334-336
  integrating 337-341
  running 335
message queue
  planning 80
metadata server (MDS) 129
MIN installation 216-225
monitor daemon server (MON) 129
multiline options
  negate 324
  pattern 324
  stream_identity 324
  what 324
multinode setup
  confirming 208
  OpenStack Initiator, preparing 210, 211
  OpenStack node provisioning 208
  OpenStack node role assignment 208
  physical nodes, assigning 208
multiple conditions (matches) 144
multiport-integrated solution 1
murano 348
MySQL
  architectures 183-185
  HA, implementing 187-193
MySQL architectures
  Block-level replication 184

Master/slave replication 182
MMM replication 182
MySQL Galera multimaster replication 184
MySQL shared storage 183, 184

N

nano flavor 350
network 142
Network Address Translation (NAT) 204
Network as a Service (NaaS) 10
Network File System (NFS) 174
networking
  about 27
  logical networking design 27, 28
network layout
  about 28
  external network 28
  internal VM traffic 30
  management network 29
  public network 28
  storage network 29
network nodes
  HA, implementing 203-205
network outfit 79
network switches
  limitations 19, 20
network topology
  about 211
  OpenStack network mode 212
  physical network topology 212-216
Neutron
  about 10, 246
  characteristics 10
  concepts 10
  plugins 247
  URL 247
  virtual switching infrastructure 247
  components 11
Neutron CLI
  used, for managing security
    groups 146, 147
neutron floatingip-associate 297
Neutron plugin
  about 157
  multiplugins, using simultaneously 158
  traffic isolation, empowering 158, 159

Ngnix 311
NIC bonding setup
  URL 249
Nova 7
nova add-floating-ip 297
nova-api component 7
nova-api service 78
Nova CLI
  used, for managing security
    groups 147-149
nova-compute 8
nova-conductor 76
Nova evacuate 174
nova-network 8
nova-scheduler 9, 77
nova-volume 8

O

object server, Swift 106
Object Storage Devices (OSDs) 128
one-to-many mapping 29
OpenStack
  about 2, 3, 43
  benchmarking, at scale 344
  database performance, improving 332, 333
  deploying 39, 44
  DevOps, using 43
  flow, provisioning 16, 17
  HA 181
  logical architecture 3
  logs, demystifying 306
  monitoring 301, 302
  reference link, for success stories
    of companies 3
  stack 265
  URL 174
  working 13-16
OpenStack cloud controllers
  HA, implementing 197-202
OpenStack deployment
  about 216
  adapting 234-237
  arming 232, 233
  Chef server preinstallation 226
  continuous integration 47-49
  cooking time 228-230

HA, implementing 233
HAProxy nodes 233
in toolchain 47
MIN installation 216-225
nodes, discovering 227, 228
tenant, running 238-242
testing 231, 232
OpenStack deployment, with Chef
about 58
cookbooks uploading, Berkshelf used 62, 63
cooking environment 69-71
environment, configuring 66
OpenStack cookbooks 59
OpenStack cookbooks' dependencies,
    resolving 60, 61
playground environment 66
roles, defining 63-65
vagrant file 67
OpenStack infrastructure
maintaining 45, 46
OpenStack monitoring
arming 297
Zabbix, used 297
OpenStack networks 212
OpenStack SLA 345, 346
Open vSwitch plugin
about 251-261
Open vSwitch daemon (ovs-vswitchd) 252
Open vSwitch database (ovsdb-server) 252
OVS Kernel Module 252
versus Linux Bridge plugin 252
Oracle VirtualBox
URL 48
overcommitment considerations,
    compute node
about 87
CPU allocation ratio 88
RAM allocation ratio 88, 89

P

panels 12
paravirtualization 90
persistent storage
about 104
object storage 104

physical design considerations, Swift
about 108
region 108
rings 110-112
storage criteria 109
storage device 109
storage nodes 109
zone 108
physical model design
about 31
best practices 36
CPU calculations 32, 33
hardware capabilities, estimating 31, 32
memory calculations 34
network calculations 34
storage calculations 35
physical network topology 212-216
PID 343
Placement groups (PGs) 129
Platform as a Service (PaaS) 2, 41
Pluggable Authentication
        Module (PAM) 4
pool, Ceph 129
port 143
Preboot Execution Environment (PXE) 211
preliminary calculations, Ceilometer
avg 277
count 278
max 278
min 278
sum 277
provider networks 158
ps command line 343
public network
features 28
publisher types
file 280
notifier 280
rpc 280
udp 280

Q

Quantum network service 10
queue 9
Quick EMUlator (QEMU) 89

R

RabbitMQ
  about 186
  clustering 186
  defining 341-343
  HA, implementing 194-196
  mirrored queues 186
RADOS Block Device (RBD) 128
Rally
  about 344, 345
  installing 346, 347
  scenarios 350-361
  using 348, 349
RAM allocation ratio 88, 89
recovery steps 101, 102
Redis 311
Reliable Autonomic Distributed Object
    Store (RADOS) 128
replication network, Swift 114
request per second 356
Resource Agents (RAs)
  URL 198
rings 110-112
router 143
rsyslog server 308
RubyMine
  URL 50
Ruby plugin
  URL 50
Ruby Version Manager (rvm)
  about 61
  URL 61
runners 348

S

sahara 348
scaleup policy 296
scaling down 74
scaling up 74
ScenarioClass.scenario_method 348
scheduling, in OpenStack
  about 353
  reference 353
scheduling state 342

security groups
  about 143
  managing, Horizon used 145
  managing, Neutron CLI used 146, 147
  managing, Nova CLI used 147-149
self cloud service 21
service-level agreement (SLA) 175, 332
service uptime 345
session persistence 262
shared values 40
Single Point Of Failure (SPOF) 4, 105, 171
sla section
  failure rate$ max 358
  max_avg_duration 358
  max_seconds_per_iteration 358
SMTA (System Management
    Tool Artifact) 47
snapshot management 6
Socket Descriptors 341
Software as a Service (SaaS) 2, 41
Software Defined Networking
    (SDN) 157, 251
Software Defined Storage (SDS) 105
Solid State Devices (SSDs) 334
Source NAT (SNAT) 144
stack
  about 265
  heat, installing 267, 268
  Heat Orchestration Template
    (HOT) 265, 266
  heat, using 268-272
stateful service, HA 177
stateless service, HA 177
storage
  CAP under scope 121
  selecting 120
  stirring up 122
storage cluster network, Swift 114
storage network
  features 29
storage types
  about 104
  ephemeral storage 104
  persistent storage 104

storing instances alternatives, compute node
  about 96
  external shared file storage 96
  internal nonshared file storage 96
strict service-level agreement, HA 174, 175
Sublime text editor
  URL 50
subnet 142
Swift
  about 4, 105
  API access 107
  architecture 105, 106
  benefits 105
  cooking 115-118
  data, indexing 107
  elasticity 105
  fire and forget 107
  hardware 112, 113
  hierarchy 109
  on-demand storage 105
  physical design considerations 108
  scalability 105
Swift API
  HTTP request 107
Swift network
  about 114
  front-cluster network 114
  replication network 114
  storage cluster network 114
Swift proxy server 106
symmetric clustering 75
system management tools
  Chef environment 52
  infrastructure code environment 49
  selecting 49

T

tagged port 213
tap interface 248
target values, iptables
  ACCEPT 144
  DNAT 145
  DROP 144
  RETURN 145
  SNAT 145

telemetry module 276
Tempest 344
tenant networks 158
thick provisioning 126
thin provisioning 126
traffic isolation, Neutron plugin
  empowering 158, 159
transactional 185
transformer types
  accumulator 279
  aggregator 279
  arithmetic 279
  rate of change 279
  unit conversion 279

U

unicast network
  URL 198
untagged port 213
User Mode Linux (UML) 89

V

Vagrant
  about 59
  URL 66
  using 59
VCS (Version Control System) 47
vertical scaling 74
virtual IP (VIP) 179
Virtual Link Trunking (VLT) 35
virtual machine monitor (VMM) 89
Virtual Router Redundancy Protocol
    (VRRP) 181
virtual switching infrastructure
  virtual network bridging 248
  virtual network interfacing 248
VLAN network 141
vMotion 93
vmstat 355
volume management 6
VPN as a Service (VPNaaS)
  about 160
  general settings 160-163

VPN as a Service (VPNaaS) configuration
  about 164
  Internet Key Exchange (IKE) policy,
    creating 165
  IPSec policy, creating 166, 167
  IPSec site connection, creating 168, 169
  VPN service, creating 167, 168
VPN service
  creating 167, 168

W

web server DMZ
  example 150-152
wordpress database 289
Write-Set Replication (wsrep) API 185

X

X-api 78
xCAT
  about 211
  reference 216, 217
  tasks 210

Z

Zabbix
  about 297
  installing 298, 299
  placing 298
Zabbix agent
  active agent 300
  configuring, on OpenStack nodes 300
  passive agent 300

Thank you for buying
Mastering OpenStack

About Packt Publishing

Packt, pronounced 'packed', published its first book, *Mastering phpMyAdmin for Effective MySQL Management*, in April 2004, and subsequently continued to specialize in publishing highly focused books on specific technologies and solutions.

Our books and publications share the experiences of your fellow IT professionals in adapting and customizing today's systems, applications, and frameworks. Our solution-based books give you the knowledge and power to customize the software and technologies you're using to get the job done. Packt books are more specific and less general than the IT books you have seen in the past. Our unique business model allows us to bring you more focused information, giving you more of what you need to know, and less of what you don't.

Packt is a modern yet unique publishing company that focuses on producing quality, cutting-edge books for communities of developers, administrators, and newbies alike. For more information, please visit our website at www.packtpub.com.

About Packt Open Source

In 2010, Packt launched two new brands, Packt Open Source and Packt Enterprise, in order to continue its focus on specialization. This book is part of the Packt Open Source brand, home to books published on software built around open source licenses, and offering information to anybody from advanced developers to budding web designers. The Open Source brand also runs Packt's Open Source Royalty Scheme, by which Packt gives a royalty to each open source project about whose software a book is sold.

Writing for Packt

We welcome all inquiries from people who are interested in authoring. Book proposals should be sent to author@packtpub.com. If your book idea is still at an early stage and you would like to discuss it first before writing a formal book proposal, then please contact us; one of our commissioning editors will get in touch with you.

We're not just looking for published authors; if you have strong technical skills but no writing experience, our experienced editors can help you develop a writing career, or simply get some additional reward for your expertise.

OpenStack Cloud Computing Cookbook

Second Edition

ISBN: 978-1-78216-758-7   Paperback: 396 pages

Over 100 recipes to successfully set up and manage your OpenStack cloud environments with complete coverage of Nova, Swift, Keystone, Glance, Horizon, Neutorn, and Cinder

1. Chapter 1 is available for free.

2. Updated for OpenStack Grizzly.

3. Learn how to install, configure, and manage all of the OpenStack core projects including new topics like block storage and software defined networking.

Learning OpenStack Networking (Neutron)

ISBN: 978-1-78398-330-8   Paperback: 300 pages

Architect and build a network infrastructure for your cloud using OpenStack Neutron networking

1. Build a virtual switching infrastructure for virtual machines using the Open vSwitch or Linux Bridge plugins.

2. Create networks and software routers that connect virtual machines to the Internet using built-in Linux networking features.

3. Scale your application using Neutron's load-balancing-as-a-service feature using the haproxy plugin.

Please check **www.PacktPub.com** for information on our titles

Implementing Cloud Storage with OpenStack Swift

ISBN: 978-1-78216-805-8   Paperback: 140 pages

Design, implement, and successfully manage your own cloud storage cluster using the popular OpenStack Swift software

1. Learn about the fundamentals of cloud storage using OpenStack Swift.

2. Explore how to install and manage OpenStack Swift along with various hardware and tuning options.

3. Perform data transfer and management using REST APIs.

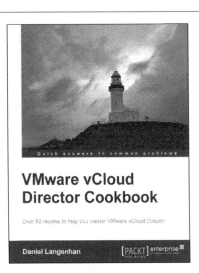

VMware vCloud Director Cookbook

ISBN: 978-1-78217-766-1   Paperback: 364 pages

Over 80 recipes to help you master VMware vCloud Director

1. Learn how to work with the vCloud API.

2. Covers the recently launched VMware vCloud Suite 5.5.

3. Step-by-step instructions to simplify infrastructure provisioning.

46506828R00222

Made in the USA
Lexington, KY
05 November 2015